FAITH IN THE PUBLIC REALM

Controversies, policies and practices

Edited by Adam Dinham, Robert Furbey and Vivien Lowndes

This edition published in Great Britain in 2009 by

The Policy Press
University of Bristol
Fourth Floor
Beacon House
Queen's Road
Bristol BS8 1QU
UK

Library University of Texas at San Antonio

Tel +44 (0)117 331 4054
Fax +44 (0)117 331 4093
e-mail tpp-info@bristol.ac.uk
www.policypress.org.uk

North American office:
The Policy Press
c/o International Specialized Books Services (ISBS)
920 NE 58th Avenue, Suite 300
Portland, OR 97213-3786, USA
Tel +1 503 287 3093
Fax +1 503 280 8832
e-mail info@isbs.com

British Library Cataloguing in Publication Data
A catalogue record for this book is available from the British Library.

Library of Congress Cataloging-in-Publication Data
A catalog record for this book has been requested.

ISBN 978 1 84742 029 9 paperback
ISBN 978 1 84742 030 5 hardcover

The right of Adam Dinham, Robert Furbey and Vivien Lowndes to be
identified as editors of this work has been asserted by them in accordance with
the 1988 Copyright, Designs and Patents Act.

Cover design by Qube Design Associates, Bristol.
Front cover: image kindly supplied by Dora Pete
[www.flickr.com/photos/porah/]
Printed and bound in Great Britain by Hobbs the Printers Ltd, Southampton.

Contents

List of tables and figures

Tables

Figures

Foreword

Professor Bhikhu Parekh

The traditionalist's fear or the rationalist's hope that modernity will see off religion as a legitimate form of thought has paradoxically both come true and been proved false. It has come true because religion today is no longer what it was in premodern times. It is self-conscious, argumentative, seeks rational justification, and is not a matter of a basic ontological trust, an unargued faith, or a taken-for-granted fact of life. The hope or the fear has been proved false because religion matters a great deal to a large number of people, in some respects even more than it did in premodern times, and continues to survive as a culture or a civilisation shaping the deepest thoughts of even those claiming to be free of it. The old question of how religion should be related to the state and what kind and degree of public recognition it should enjoy therefore remains as relevant as before, although of course it needs to be formulated and answered in terms suited to our times.

We can readily agree on two things. First, religion and state represent different human institutions. One is primarily concerned with the other-worldly destiny of the human soul, the other with the affairs of this world. One is a matter of belief and cannot be coerced, the other deals with matters requiring conformity and has coercion built into its structure. One talks in terms of largely non-negotiable absolutes, the other aims at a carefully assembled and inherently tentative consensus. Since the two are so different in their orientation, a close alliance between them is the surest way to corrupt and undermine both.

Second, although religion and the state differ radically in their approaches to human life, their spheres of activity overlap. Religious beliefs and practices have social consequences, and the state has a legitimate interest in the latter. This is why even liberal states rightly regulate religious activities on grounds of public order, public health, morality and social harmony, and criminalise or at least discourage religious beliefs that incite rebellion against it or hatred and violence against outsiders. Even as the state cannot remain indifferent to religion, the latter cannot remain indifferent to the state. Religious persons anchor their lives in certain fundamental moral and spiritual commitments. Since the latter relate, among other things, to the quality of social relations and the underlying structure of power, religious persons have a profound interest in the role of the state in maintaining these relations. This is why conservative religious groups have historically endorsed and blessed the prevailing political order, whereas radicals have challenged it, as in the case of anti-colonial, anti-slavery, anti-capitalist, anti-communist, anti-apartheid and other movements.

Since religion and the state can neither be identified nor kept totally separate, we need to establish some kind of working relationship between them, such that they can cooperate and complement each other while maintaining their independence and distance. This involves asking what unique contribution religion makes to public life and where and why its presence deserves respect and support.

At the most basic level, religion provides a valuable counterweight to the state, and nurtures sensibilities and values the latter ignores or suppresses. The state has traditionally claimed to monopolise morality, presenting its interest as of the highest importance and deserving of the greatest sacrifices. This attitude needs constant questioning, and religion is ideally equipped to do so. It stresses an alternative source of morality and fundamental human unity, and reminds us that the human being is more than a citizen. This is not to deny that religion has often supported aggressive nationalism and horrendous wars, but rather to say that it also has a universalist and humanitarian dimension, which can be used to criticise, contain and combat narrowly nationalist propensities.

Religion makes an important contribution at the practical level as well. Many of the problems facing modern societies are too complex and intractable to be tackled by the state alone, and require subtler approaches that religious organisations are well equipped to provide. Many of them have a long historical experience of running schools, hospitals and other charities and providing welfare services. Since religion matters deeply to many people, religious groups also have a great motivational power. They are able to inspire their followers to give generously of their time and energy for valuable social causes, to provide customised services in a non-patronising manner, take calculated risks and to be innovative in their approaches, and are often highly economical to run. At their best, they also have the capacity to build trusting relations between and with their clients, to reconcile individuals and communities, to heal wounds, to nurture self-esteem and to put together broken and despondent selves. These strengths make them particularly helpful in fostering self-discipline and dealing with such matters as premarital pregnancy, juvenile delinquency, gang warfare and the rehabilitation of prisoners and drug addicts, in all of which state bureaucracy is generally too blunt to be effective. One should not, of course, generalise from these experiences and ignore some of the problems they create. However, they show that religious communities can play a valuable part in tackling the pathological aspects of modern society and consolidating community cohesion.

While there is much to be said for state–religion partnership and giving religion a respectable but critically monitored presence in public life, it is not without its difficulties. Not all religions are equally central to the identity of the state. Take Britain. Over 80% of its citizens claim to be Christians. Christianity has played a profound role in shaping it, and its legacy is inscribed in all its major institutions. The British state cannot therefore grant *equal* recognition to Islam, Hinduism, Judaism and other minority religions. If it tried to do so, it would need to unscramble its cultural structure and render it culturally neutral and bland, and that is politically impossible, morally dubious, and likely to provoke strong hostility to the minorities in whose name this is done. At the same time, the British state must find ways of giving them *adequate* recognition if they are not to feel deeply alienated from, or unwanted in, Britain. This calls for generosity on the part of the state and self-limiting claims on the part of the minority religions, especially some radical Muslims who seem content with nothing short of a full equality of recognition.

There is also the question of who represents a religious community in the public realm and what they represent. No one can be said to speak for their community unless they are authorised by the rest, and that requires the community to be democratically constituted. This is, however, not enough. Not all sharing a faith are formal members of the community, and even the democratically elected representatives cannot be said to speak for them. This is also the case with those who belong to a religious community or tradition but are not believers. Gender inequality in some communities and the virtual disenfranchisement of women further complicates the situation. Any mechanism of public consultation with religious bodies needs to insist on their democratisation and allow for a diversity of voices, and that is not easy.

Faith schools are another contentious issue. Since they take several forms, we should not make the mistake of homogenising them. Some are schools first and religious second, and are secular for all practical purposes. Some have a strong religious ethos, but that neither affects the education they provide nor compromises their secular curriculum and aims. Some others are little different from seminaries, insist on the rote learning of scriptures, and discourage critical thought and liberal values. While we are right to discourage and even disallow the last kind of schools, we cannot raise the same objection to the first two. Whatever we may think of religious schools in general, they do matter a great deal to a large number of people. Over a third of primary, and a fifth of secondary, schoolchildren go to these schools in Britain. If they were to be abolished, determined parents would use their right to set up private religious schools or send their children to those run by religious organisations after normal school hours, and neither is open to public scrutiny. We need to find a sensible way out of this difficult situation.

These and related questions form the subject matter of this volume. The essays included in it are judicious and balanced in their approach, carefully argued, and sensitive to the complexity and political context of the relevant issues. They represent a variety of views and offer well-thought-out policy recommendations. Although they are primarily directed at the British experience, their value is not limited to Britain. The volume makes a most valuable contribution to the current debate and is to be warmly welcomed.

Professor Bhikhu Parekh
House of Lords
May 2008

Acknowledgements

The original inspiration for this book came from two research projects in which the editors were involved: on faiths and social capital (funded by the Joseph Rowntree Foundation) and on faiths and civil renewal (funded by the Home Office). We would like to thank our collaborators in those projects, and particularly the following who have offered continued intellectual and practical support: Rachael Chapman (De Montfort University), Richard Farnell (Coventry University), Doreen Finneron (Faith Based Regeneration Network) and Dilwar Hussain (Islamic Foundation).

The book is a key output from the ESRC-funded seminar series (2007-08), 'Faiths and Civil Society'. Convened by Adam Dinham and Vivien Lowndes, the series brought together academics from a range of different disciplines and institutions, and practitioners from faith communities and voluntary and statutory organisations. Many of the chapters in this book started life as seminar papers in the series. We would like to thank all those who participated in the seminars and offered their comments, criticisms and suggestions. These have contributed significantly to the quality of the final product.

Finally, we are grateful to the editorial and production team at The Policy Press for their support and patience, and to the manuscript reviewer for many helpful suggestions. We would also like to thank Di Mitchell (Goldsmiths, University of London) and Suzanne Walker (De Montfort University) for their assistance with running the ESRC seminars and producing the manuscript. Their contribution has been marked not just by efficiency but also by tremendous thoughtfulness, both in welcoming a diverse range of participants to the seminars and looking after the editors!

Notes on contributors

Maqsood Ahmed OBE is Senior Adviser on Muslim Communities in the Preventing Extremism Unit at the Department of Communities and Local Government, UK.
Maqsood.ahmed@communities.gsi.gov.uk

Christopher Baker is Director of Research at the William Temple Foundation based in Manchester, UK, and also Part-Time Lecturer in Urban Theology at the University of Manchester, UK.
www.wtf.org.uk

Ted Cantle CBE is Professor at the Institute of Community Cohesion, UK, which is supported by four Midlands universities in the UK. He is also Associate Director at the Improvement and Development Agency (IDeA).
www.idea.gov.uk/idk/core/page.do?pageId=1600021

Rachael Chapman is a Senior Research Fellow at the Local Governance Research Unit, De Montfort University, Leicester, UK.
www.dmu.ac.uk/lgru

David Cheesman is Visiting Professor of Society and Development in the Centre for Regional Economic and Social Research at Sheffield Hallam University, UK, and Joint Director of Equality in Diversity, a community-based management, research and training consultancy.
www.equalityindiversity.com

Adam Dinham is Reader and Director, Faiths and Civil Society Unit, Goldsmiths, University of London, UK.
www.gold.ac.uk
www.faithsunit.org

Richard Farnell is Professor of Neighbourhood Regeneration at Coventry University, UK, working with the Applied Research Centre in Sustainable Regeneration (Surge) and the Institute of Community Cohesion (ICoCo). He is Canon Theologian of Coventry Cathedral and an adviser on faith and cohesion to the Joseph Rowntree Foundation.
www.coventry.ac.uk/researchnet/d/184/a/602

John Flint is Professor of Housing and Urban Governance in the Centre for Regional Economic and Social Research at Sheffield Hallam University, UK.
www.shu.ac.uk/cresr/sp_john_flint.html

Robert Furbey is Principal Lecturer in Urban Sociology in the Urban and Regional Studies Subject Group at Sheffield Hallam University, UK.
www.shu.ac.uk/planning/regeneration/staff/furbey.html

Richard Gale is a Postdoctoral Fellow in Sociology at the University of Birmingham, UK.
www.sociology.bham.ac.uk/staff/gale.shtml

Dilwar Hussain is Head of Policy Research at the Islamic Foundation, Leicestershire, UK, and an Associate Lecturer at the Open University, tutoring on 'Islam and the West'. He is a Fellow of the Royal Foundation of St Katharine's Contextual Theology Centre, London, and the Citizen Organising Foundation.
www.islamic-foundation.org.uk/contactUs.htm

Nazia Khanum OBE is founder and Joint Director of Equality in Diversity, a community-based management, research and training consultancy and Chair of Luton Multi-Cultural Women's Coalition, UK.
www.equalityindiversity.com

Vivien Lowndes is Pro Vice Chancellor (Research) and a member of the Local Government Research Unit at De Montfort University, Leicester, UK.
www.dmu.ac.uk/lgru

Brenda O'Neill is Associate Professor in the Department of Political Science at the University of Calgary, Canada, and a Fellow of the Faiths and Civil Society Unit at Goldsmiths, University of London, UK.
www.poli.ucalgary.ca/Oneill.htm

Therese O'Toole is Lecturer in the Department of Sociology, Centre for Ethnicity and Citizenship, University of Bristol, UK
Therese.OToole@bristol.ac.uk

Paul Weller is Head of Research and Commercial Development, Senior Research Fellow, and Professor of Inter-Religious Relations at the University of Derby, UK.
www.derby.ac.uk/staff-search/professor-paul-weller

ONE

Faith and the public realm

Adam Dinham and Vivien Lowndes

Introduction

Academics, policy makers and practitioners are grappling with the emphatic return of faith to the public table, and seeking to make sense of its implications. Many have observed a surprising 'political revitalization of religion at the heart of Western society' (Habermas, 2007, p 2) and some have expressed concern about the renewed 'turn to faith'. This book is an attempt to unpack at least some of the 'grappling', and to surface the many questions, challenges and controversies it raises.

Such a project must occur at several levels, encompassing a wide range of debates. The place of faith in the public realm has been strongly contested over a long period, involving conflicts that resonate across the spectra of public feeling and thought. Some of these are embodied in the public imagination in events or periods such as the Crusades, the Reformation and the Inquisition, which remain alive for many in a somewhat distant, generalised way as examples of atrocities carried out in the name of religion. Others have far more immediate resonance because of their political and social implications for our own lives, or the lives of those we know. Northern Ireland, Kashmir, Israel–Palestine and Iraq are obvious examples. The so-called 'war on terror' (prompted, indeed, by real acts of religiously inspired terrorism) is another conflict that manages to encompass us all, constructing the beginning of a new 'global history' in terms of a struggle between Islamic fundamentalism and Western democracy. Like politics, faith is not generally considered a suitable subject for dinner-party conversation. That faith in the public realm is about both religion *and* politics makes this highly charged territory.

Debates arise also in part because the idea of the public realm is itself contested in Britain, as elsewhere. The UK's particular constitutional arrangements make for especial complexity. In one sense, faith has a very high public profile, with the Monarch as both Head of State and Head of the established Church. Church of England bishops sit in the upper House of Parliament as 'Lords Spiritual', a role rooted more in the historical fact of the landed wealth of bishops in the Middle Ages rather than in the direct privileging of one faith group over any other, although it is often argued that the effects are the same.

These arrangements of state set the conditions for a curious sort of 'playing out' of faith in the public realm, in which faith contributes to the 'decorative' element in British life. From the inauguration of a new university chancellor to a memorial service for a public figure, both local and national ceremonial events are mediated through religious services conducted by the Church of England, notably the Coronation service, which is both a state and a religious event. In this sense, faith remains being very visible in the public realm.

At the same time, it has been argued that public faith is an increasingly irrelevant and anachronistic anomaly of contemporary times, which should be tightly controlled, if not abolished. From these perspectives, public talk of faith is seen as an inappropriate sort of sentimentality (insanity, even) that politicians and other public figures acknowledge at their peril. Tony Blair has made a recent public profession of faith and even established a new 'Faith Foundation', but as former Prime Minister his Press Secretary, Alistair Campbell, insisted that 'Tony does not do God'.

Yet despite all this, there have been continuing high levels of self-reported religious affiliation across the country (and the world). In terms of self-affiliation, Christianity is the main religion in Britain (72%); 5% of the population belong to a non-Christian denomination (half of whom are Muslims); and people with 'no religion' make up 15% of the population (ONS, 2004). The religious make-up of some British cities varies considerably from the national profile. Focusing on Leicester, for instance, 45% of people identified themselves as Christian, 15% as Hindu, 11% as Muslim and 17% as having no religion (Leicester City Council, 2002).

Are secularists wrong, therefore, when they assert the end of religion? The idea of secularisation has always been more complex than it first appears. First, 'secularisation' in its early usages referred to 'the freeing of [certain] areas of life from their theological origins or basis' (Alexander, 2001, p 48), expressing the Latin concept of '*saeculum*' ('age') and the contrast between the immanency and time-boundedness of the world with the atemporality and eternal nature of the heavenly. In this sense 'secularisation' certainly includes that process whereby religious thinking, practice and institutions lose social significance (Wilson, 1966) but it by no means expels faith altogether from the public realm.

Second, it has been suggested that another aspect of this diminishing significance is the transfer to the state of certain specialised functions and institutions relating to the delivery of education, health and social care. Prochaska (2006) traces just such a handover in the early stages of the British welfare state, although he attributes this to government conviction that the establishment of welfare equality is a task too important to rest with actors other than the state. However, faith-based social action has maintained a long and unbroken tradition, despite years of centralised provision in which it was somewhat sidelined (Dinham and Finneron, 2002).

A third proposition in the secularisation thesis is that faiths lost much of their social significance under the dual pressures of urbanisation and technological innovation. As populations migrated to cities, communities broke down and the social control of religious leaders diminished. At the same time, technology promised ways round 'God-given' constraints, particularly obstructions associated with medical interventions and telecommunications: live longer; defy disease; fly across continents and oceans; and talk to anyone, anywhere, anytime! Nature knows no bounds.

Yet the data show these ideas to be highly Eurocentric, located in the urban lives and technological trends of Western Europeans, but far less in the developing world. Outside urbanised technological countries, religion's significance has not diminished. Neither has it done so uniformly within them. Alexander (2001) cites two contrasting statements by the sociologist of religion, Peter Berger. In 1968 the latter asserted that '[by] the 21st century, religious believers are likely to be found only in small sects, huddled together to resist a worldwide secular culture' (Berger, 1968; see Berger, 1969, for an extended exploration). More recently, however, Berger has observed that 'the world today, with some exceptions … is as furiously religious as it ever was' (Berger, 1996, p 3).

Indeed, the data show patterns that contradict those predicted by the secularisation thesis. Although church attendance has been in decline in the UK, reported levels of religious affiliation remain at about three quarters of the population (ONS, 2004). This reflects what has been described as the phenomenon of 'believing without belonging' (Davie, 1994) and expresses a turn to more 'spiritual' forms of faith outside of, but aligned with, the organised religions. This leads Cheesman and Khanum to note that even behind the 15.6% of Census respondents stating 'no religion' there lies 'a wider hinterland of agnosticism and doubt' (see Chapter Three, p 54). 'Believing without belonging' is sometimes understood in terms of the 'privatisation of religion', although it is also acknowledged that 'private religious beliefs can have social consequences' and from the perspective of voluntary social practices, 'churchgoing is currently the most popular British leisure past-time' (Alexander, 2001, pp 54, 60).

While only 10% of British people go to church regularly, attendance is more common among women and middle-class people, and is growing in some urban areas, particularly among Black-led and Pentecostal churches (CULF, 2006). And in relation to the US, it has been observed that:

> the country that is currently the world leader in terms of its contribution to the scientific enterprise, possessing a culture which is most 'modern' in terms of its production and use of technology, also has one of the highest levels of (voluntary) religious commitment of any country in the world. (Alexander, 2001, p 52)

This observation is a reminder, too, that the emerging economies of India and China have their own very distinctive religious cultures, which present a markedly different mix for the secular theorists – the one steeped in a combination of the Eastern traditions of Buddhism, Hinduism, Jainism and Sikhism alongside Islam; the other, a communist state that denies the possibility of God as a matter of political conviction and ideology. The future of faith in the public realm at the global level is set to be interesting.

There are many reasons why debates about the place of faith in the public realm are not as clear cut as might first appear. In engaging with these debates, we have observed the many positive ways in which faiths add to the public realm. But the book is not an apologia for faith. Rather, it seeks to highlight the debates raised in a context where faith has re-emerged as a significant social and political category. Our intention is not to 'take sides' on whether faiths are a good or a bad thing in public life. Instead, we seek positively to problematise the issues and to explore them through a range of lenses.

However, we have not included any wholly dissenting chapters. This is not because of a failure to recognise that faith can have its dark sides but because others, such as Richard Dawkins, (2006) Sam Harris (2006) and Christopher Hitchens (2007), have written extensively about these. Strong secularist arguments are reviewed by Furbey in Chapter Two. We do not see faith as a panacea in delivering the aspirations of governments through the mobilisation of their buildings, staff, members, networks and other resources across the country. Indeed, subsequent chapters demonstrate the dangers for faiths themselves in becoming 'captured' by government agendas and distracted from their own missions. But we are interested in the issues associated with the re-emergence of faiths in the public realm, not only with what shadows they might cast.

These shadows are not, of course, ignored. They are apparent throughout the book. We note their darkest and most compelling manifestation in the religious extremism embodied in the catastrophic events of 9/11 and 7/7. Several of our chapters refer to the threat of extremism, its impact on particular communities and its more general influence on contemporary perceptions of faith in the public realm. Accepting this context, however, we also focus on the role that faiths *can* play in the public realm, not the role that they shouldn't.

As in any book, we do not 'start from nowhere' (see Furbey, Chapter Two). In a book about religious faith it would perhaps be odd not to say something about our starting points, if only to anticipate the possible concern that an agenda lurks behind. All the contributors come with various backgrounds in, and commitments to, the social sciences. While some of the authors would describe themselves as people of faith and others not, our common starting point is an interest in faith as it is expressed in the public realm. Our ontological perspectives, theological views, beliefs and values vary. The book is offered as a contribution to social science and to wider public debate, exploring, in sequence, the controversies, policies and practices that attend the place of faith in the public realm.

Faiths, governance and civil society

A government minister recently observed that: 'The role of faith-based groups in ensuring people have access to welfare services will be of growing importance over the coming years ... [and] faith-based groups offer an invaluable link into communities' (Murphy, 2007). We observe that faiths are being welcomed to the public table in at least three important ways.

First, faiths are increasingly seen as repositories of resources – buildings, staff and networks – in a mixed economy of welfare (Home Office, 2004). Since the mid-1990s, and from 1997 in particular, governments have identified the potential for building on the traditional service role of faith bodies (for instance in education, housing, fostering and adoption) and extending this into new areas (including urban and rural regeneration, community safety, childcare and health promotion). Such developments are associated particularly with developing more responsive local services, and with diversifying provision to suit the needs of different communities.

Second, faiths are recognised by government as having a potentially important role to play in building 'community cohesion'. Faith bodies, and particularly inter-faith networks, are identified as important brokers in building better relationships between different communities and social groups, whether on the basis of ethnicity, generation or social class. Since the disturbances or 'riots' in Northern England in 2001, policy makers have sought to mobilise faiths in bridging the distance between 'parallel lives', whether through an intercultural leadership school for young people in Bradford; an annual cricket match between imams and clergy in Leicester; or an orientation for new migrants in rural Lincolnshire. In short, faiths are regarded as arenas for the formation and mobilisation of bonding, bridging and linking social capital (Furbey et al, 2006).

Third, government is interested in the engagement of faiths in extended forms of participative governance, for example through representation on Local Strategic Partnerships (LSPs), regional assemblies and neighbourhood management boards (Lowndes and Chapman, 2005; Dinham and Lowndes, 2008). Faith involvement is seen as helping to diversify community representation (getting beyond the 'usual suspects'), particularly in localities with high concentrations of minority faiths. More specialist roles are played by faith representatives on policy-specific consultation forums, with the police, health authorities and social care agencies. At the national level, the Faith Communities Consultative Council has been established to advise ministers on a cross-government basis.

An enhanced role for faiths in public life is not without its critics. Many challenge the instrumentalism of policy and its focus on the 'usefulness' of faiths, or on faith as a means of 'classification'. Respect for the values and traditions of faiths themselves may be absent. Indeed, it is paradoxical that, while it is suggested that religion is practised in private, if at all, in Britain, this new instrumentalism brings religion out of the private realm and into the public. These authors ask whether there is a 'contradiction between maintaining that faith is private and then adopting policies that encourage people to publicise their convictions'. These are questions that are also raised by Gale and O'Toole in their account of a college accused of 'Islamophobia' in a debate about providing a college prayer room. Here, the public space of the college becomes a symbol of the clash with the private space of faith (see Chapter Eight, pp 152ff). Flint also considers this point in his treatment of faith schools, which he regards as 'one site of a wider contestation between secular and religious authorities' (Chapter Nine, p 166). Is conflict between private and public expressions of faith inevitable or, as Weller notes, might the contemporary paradox be symptomatic of evolutionary change towards a new 'socio-religious' contract (Chapter Four, p 79)?

Such a renegotiation involves a reconsideration of the nature of religious plurality in relation to citizenship in Britain. It has been suggested that faith in the public realm is a feature of the 'unsettling' of the multicultural settlement, manifested in the street violence in Northern England in 2001 and in the more dramatic and deadly events of 9/11 and 7/7. Multiculturalism is facing new questions about identities and the relationships between them. How should faiths be valued, engaged and addressed? What account can we take of their differing capacities, motivations and aspirations and, indeed, of the relationships between their adherents? What role should faith play in our citizenship? In considering this, the practitioners involved in our policy conversation in Chapter Five emphasise 'commonalities rather than divisions' between faith traditions, while also recognising that faith can be 'a reflection of … global identities' (p 90). This is a reminder that local experience is increasingly linked with the global-political and that people often identify both with their own neighbourhoods and with the 'imaginaries' they construct of their faiths through news and images from other parts of the world. The increasing political significance of faith provides a compelling illustration of the 'glocalisation' phenomenon, as illustrated by Gale and O'Toole in Chapter Eight.

It is unclear how the relationship between ethnicity, identity and faith will play out in the public realm but, in Dilwar Hussain's view, we are at 'a moment of transition' (Chapter Five, p 93). He hints at a resolution in the concept of 'community cohesion', in which the idea of difference might be 'something for everyone', not just for minorities (Chapter Five, p 94). Weller also notes that we live in a landscape of 'religious plurality', in which race and ethnicity have been joined by a new focus on faith. He is concerned that government is seeking to 'incorporate' and 'neutralise' faith identities, particularly in the context of anxieties about religious extremism (Chapter Four, p 75). Here, once again, we are on fragile ground. Indeed, Cantle (2007) has asked whether 'faithism' might become the new racism. Certainly, there is concern that 'Muslims have a visibility out of proportion to their numbers' (Cheesman and Khanum, Chapter Three, p 41). The risks of discrimination and rising inter-communal tensions are high.

Nevertheless, this 'moment of transition' seems a positive one from many perspectives, not least because of a cultural embeddedness of many strands of Islam, as of other traditions. Nowhere is this better expressed, perhaps, than in the prevalence of Bangladeshi curry houses across Britain. Indeed, Cheesman and Khanum suggest that 'To say Muslims are outside the mainstream of British life is to ignore Britain's taste-buds' (Chapter Three, p 45). Likewise, in his view of schools as 'crucibles for the forging of the relationship between (future) citizens and the state' (Chapter Nine, p 166), Flint gives us a glimpse of a public realm renegotiated through education, in which faith can be a positive source of respect and cohesion.

However, one of the main concerns of secularist critics is that faiths are associated with 'conversation-stopping circularity' (see Furbey, Chapter Two, p 37). From this perspective, the question is whether faiths are well suited to the deliberative forms of democratic engagement with which liberal democracy is concerned and on which new forms of pluralistic culture might best be based. Cheesman and Khanum, in Chapter Three, observe in relation to Islam in Britain that democratic structures are fragile. They argue that this does not mean that Muslim citizens cannot, or will not, think democratically. But it does point to the challenges faced by government in attempts to engage 'Muslim communities' in democratic forums. It is also true that faiths can be places of certainty as much as of searching for meaning. When this translates into political influence, as many worry, what might be the implications for the freedoms of thought, speech and action that Britain enjoys? With regard to faith, should we be thinking about 'democracy' or worrying about 'despotism'?

While formal democratic structures are not necessarily associated with faiths (of any type), there is an association between faith communities and social capital, in the form of social networks, associational activity and active citizenship (volunteering, charitable giving, civic engagement) (Lowndes and Chapman, 2005; Furbey et al, 2006; Dinham and Lowndes, 2008). As suggested in Chapter Five, faiths often embody and express a 'spirit of community'. Inter-faith and multi-faith structures have much potential in terms of 'bridging' social capital, relationships of trust and reciprocity that connect those from different social backgrounds (see Weller's discussion in Chapter Four). Faith is not only an instrumental category in the mind of government but also part of the daily lived experience of people in communities.

The challenges of 'public faith'

The extension of the public table to include faiths presents faith communities themselves with a range of new issues, as well as many difficult dilemmas. There are, for instance, marked differences among faiths in their capacity to respond to these new opportunities. Faiths traditional to Britain are well placed to engage because of their organisational structures and networks. But those that are newer may not be organised so as to make this possible, or at least straightforward. Minority faiths generally have more limited capacity on the one hand and less power and influence on the other. None have the weight of the diocesan structures of the Church of England, with its national reach through the Archbishops' Council at Lambeth Palace and General Synod, the support of large diocesan regions (although these do not overlap neatly with government regions) *and* a local presence through the parish structure in every part of the country.

Weller argues that it is only the Christian churches 'that have the geographical spread, population, physical presence and current extra-local infrastructure that approximates to the areas in which regional governance operates', there being an asymmetry between the Christian churches and other religious communities (Chapter Four, p 74). This disparity has wider implications due to the association (with significant exceptions) between minority faiths and minority ethnicities. Limited power within minority *faith* communities can thereby reflect limited power within minority *ethnic* communities. This poses the danger that the weakness of one consolidates the relative powerlessness of the other. The manner in which minority faiths are engaged at the public table will help determine whether disadvantage is consolidated or otherwise.

Within faith traditions, there are also differences in power between participants. Women, for instance, may be assigned to roles that are highly differentiated from those of their male counterparts, who tend to enjoy higher status. Dilwar Hussain observes that in 'the Muslim community but also other faith communities – women seem to be remarkably absent and young people as well' (Chapter Five, p 95). Ted Cantle agrees that we tend to 'think about faith as a male institution', arguing that 'many of the faith bodies discriminate against women' (Chapter Five, p 98). These are factors that may sit uncomfortably with trends in wider society, although sexism is prevalent elsewhere. At the extreme, faith groups encounter serious challenges in this regard, for example in their approach to equalities legislation and frameworks. This may also apply to their attitudes and practices in relation to disability, age and sexual orientation. One notable example is the controversy in which Catholic adoption societies did not wish to place children with practising gay parents.

However, it is also the case that women are particularly active in faith-related volunteering, associational life and civic engagement (Furbey et al, 2006). O'Neill argues that 'Where men are more likely to be found in professional associations and sports clubs, women are more likely to be found in religious and charitable organisations'. Women seem 'able to benefit and find individual agency within the most patriarchal religious institutions' (Chapter Seven, p 123). At the same time, many women who are not active in organised religion find motivation for community activity and political participation in a broader 'spirituality'. But involvement is not the same as influence. In her Canadian study, O'Neill observes the 'dominance of women at the grassroots level' but their relative 'absence at higher decision-making levels' (Chapter Seven, p 126).

Young people also have distinctive perspectives when it comes to faith and the public realm, related to their relative lack of power and capacity vis-à-vis adults more generally. This is a particular issue for Muslim communities given that 75% of Muslims are aged under 35 and 52% are aged under 25 (Weller, 2007, p 32). Gale and O'Toole note a 'disengagement of young Muslims from mainstream political and civic life' (Chapter Eight, p 144). But, like Modood (2007), they observe a growing sense of Muslim political agency, even if this takes non-conventional forms. Gale and O'Toole argue that 'new technologies [have] facilitated the emergence of new global and virtual publics ... that [have] found particular expression within global Islamic movements' (Chapter Eight, p 146). The young people in their study were engaged in 'deliberation over matters of Islamic tradition and belonging' in the context of a 'globalised Muslim experience'. But a new emphasis on personal piety among young Muslims may express itself in forms of social, religious and political engagement that are both disconnected from, and challenging to, the influence and networks of older Muslims and their community leaders.

Power differentials are reflected, too, in the ways in which faiths engage in partnerships with others, whether for the delivery of specific public services or the purposes of more participative local governance. In an anthropological vein, Chris Baker argues that faith representatives must make sure 'to eat well ... or ... be eaten' (Chapter Six, p 106). Partnership can be threatening to all concerned. In his chapter, Farnell observes that 'Many professionals at the local level ... view faith organisations with a degree of suspicion' (Chapter Ten, p 183). In an attempt to neutralise the 'troubling presence' (Newman, 2007) of faith actors, the government prefers 'to relate to a defined "faith sector" rather than religious groups, organisations and communities in all their diversity' (Farnell, Chapter Ten, p 189). This resonates with debates throughout the book about the instrumentalism of many attitudes to faith in the public realm.

Chapman, however, suggests that this instrumentalism is a general fact of life when civil society organisations encounter government. She notes that 'Faith-based and secular VCS [voluntary and community sector] organisations ... experience similar partnership-related tensions and challenges ... [including] securing policy influence ... and maintaining their independence' (Chapter Eleven, p 215). Mistrust and scepticism are not, of course, the prerogative of public agencies. In this book we inevitably focus on those faith actors who *are* engaging in the public realm. But there exist faith leaders and organisations who see such involvement as having the potential to 'corrupt' people of faith (particularly where grants and contracts are at stake, and where there is access to political power), distracting them from more fundamental goals. Some faith groups may not regard public service delivery and civic engagement as within their 'calling'. Research on the contribution of the Diocese of Birmingham to urban regeneration commented on tensions encountered at the parish level between 'business decisions and Jesus decisions' (Cairns et al, 2005, p 50).

Some of these tensions concern the difficulties of communicating across different values and organisational cultures. Thus, Baker refers to the 'blurred encounters' between faiths and others as they attempt to work together in a situation where there is only a limited conception of each other's values (Chapter Six). In his study of regeneration partnerships, Farnell observes 'a lack of religious literacy' and 'understanding of the diversity and characteristics of faith communities' (Chapter Ten, p 193). The motivations of faith actors and those from government and public agencies may be very different, even while sitting at the same table. If these different narratives are consciously articulated and debated, there is the possibility of building a new 'discursive coalition' around faith engagement in public life (Dinham and Lowndes, 2008). But while these differences are unacknowledged, partners are 'destined to work in parallel languages' (Baker, Chapter Six, p 111).

Where faiths respond positively to invitations to participate at the public table, they require mediators. As Weller notes, 'The state cannot have dialogue with a "community"', but only with bodies that claim to be its representatives (Chapter Four, p 76). How such representatives are chosen, and the means by which they give 'voice' to communities, are important questions. We have noted already Cheesman and Khanum's concern for the limited extent of democratic structures in Muslim faith communities in Britain (Chapter Three). Lowndes and Chapman (2008) report disquiet among Hindu and Sikh communities that Church of England clergy act as 'representatives' when they are in fact involved as salaried staff. A contrast is drawn with representatives from elected temple or mosque committees, but the debate clearly reflects different traditions regarding the role of 'priests' and their relationships with (differently organised) worshipping communities.

Weller identifies potential means of progress through inter-faith and multi-faith bodies (Chapter Four). However, while such bodies may seek to be inclusive, they do not always achieve broad representation (particularly of women and younger people) across all faiths. As Weller argues, questions arise not only about 'who is in and who is out', but also about the relationship between 'representatives' and the constituencies from which they come (Chapter Four). A recent survey of faith representatives on Local Strategic Partnerships (LSPs) found that around 50% were concerned about issues of accountability and contact with their 'constituencies' (CUF, 2006).

Faith communities are not neatly organised settings with a distinct and linear continuity between the various parts. Worshippers, clergy, community projects, staff and volunteers may all 'belong' to the same faith setting but this does not necessarily mean that they will have involvement everywhere or at all times. In some cases people working in different parts of the same faith community may remain unknown to one another. When one or two people from such a setting are 'called forth' as its representatives, their task is daunting. The challenge is increased by official pressure for the formalisation of a 'faith sector' with which non-faith partners can engage. As Farnell asks, 'Should there be a faith sector representative ... how many would be appropriate ... should they be elected or nominated ... who should nominate them ... to whom should they be accountable...?' (Chapter Ten, p 187). Others have questioned the notion of a 'faith sector', fearing the conversion of diverse and creative networks into an instrument of public policy delivery. What is also clear is that, often, 'Leaders of faith groups aspire to a recognised role ... but are liable to resist uncritical co-option into government agendas' (Farnell, Chapter Ten, p 183).

The government's 'Citizenship Survey' shows that many people of faith operate already in the public realm and may bring to bear values and concerns motivated by their faiths and expressed in their everyday work (Home Office. 2005). Whether this is legitimate in the public realm is, of course, contested and likely to provoke strong feelings. Weller points to the distinction between *faith representatives* and religious people who are representative – for example, councillors who individually are believers (Chapter Four, pp 70–1). A study of faith representation on public partnerships drew a contrast between LSPs that 'endorsed the concept of "faith representatives" being there to represent the constituency of local faith communities' and primary care trusts where some non-executive directors were identified as faith representatives, but actually saw themselves as 'people of faith' rather than spokespeople for a specific constituency (CUF, 2006, p 3). The relationship between individual faith and public roles is vexed and may contribute to the anxieties of those who feel strongly about the separation of private belief and the public realm.

The chapters

The early chapters of the book focus on concepts and ideas. Chapters Six to Eight move on to a consideration of cross-cutting themes. Finally, Chapters Nine to Twelve explore specific policies and practices.

In Chapter Two, Rob Furbey considers the case for a presence for faith in the public realm and its possible consequences. He suggests that the meeting of religious fundamentalisms and widely read secularists such as Sam Harris, A.C. Grayling and Christopher Hitchens is a case of 'bad religion' meeting 'bad science'. Furbey argues that rationality, freed from the strictures of logical positivism, is pervasive in major religious traditions. At the same time, the simple assertion of a 'religious cause' to political conflicts risks neglecting complex patterns of causation and, indeed, empirical evidence. We should be sceptical of polarised arguments that deny the possibility of a 'civilised conversation' in a more inclusive public realm.

In Chapter Three, David Cheesman and Nazia Khanum consider the disproportionately high profile that Muslims have in the public realm in the wake of the events of 9/11 and 7/7. They see this in part as a sort of recasting of the medieval English 'othering' of Catholics. Cheesman and Khanum criticise a focus on the minority of radical voices at the expense of the quiet majority of rational and moderate Muslims, whose public 'quietness' is accounted for, in part, by family-centric social lives. They suggest that both these aspects contribute to a 'soft segregation', of hearts and minds rather than streets and houses, which is both the cause and the result of a suspicion of Islam. At the same time, the chapter shows how Muslims are in many ways at the centre of British life.

In Chapter Four, Paul Weller maps the diversity of faiths in Britain and shows how they are working together through inter-faith and multi-faith structures. Weller outlines the evolution of this approach, which started with British colonialism and the exposure of Christians to other faiths. He traces a 'coming home' of these nascent relationships during the mid-20th century, with the end of the Empire and large-scale migration from the former colonies. A growing politics of identity and difference, in relation to faith as well as ethnicity, has led to a 'mainstreaming' of inter-faith and multi-faith work. The simultaneous extension of forms of participatory governance, particularly at the local and neighbourhood level, has given extra impetus to the inclusion of faith actors. Weller links these interactions to the working out of a new 'socio-religious contract'.

In Chapter Five, in a 'policy conversation', three leading practitioners explore the relationship between faith, multiculturalism and community cohesion. Maqsood Ahmed, Ted Cantle and Dilwar Hussain debate whether the growing recognition of faith identities is displacing multiculturalism's focus on race and ethnicity, or even challenging the underlying paradigm of multiculturalism. While there have been important changes, the contributors agree that this is not so much the end of multiculturalism but 'a moment of transition', whose direction and outcome remains unclear. Faith actors are seen as central to policies of 'community cohesion', which seek to bridge the 'parallel lives' that Cantle (2005) originally observed in his report on the 2001 disturbances. The cohesion agenda seeks to emphasise commonalities as well as differences.

Chapters Six, Seven and Eight consider cross-cutting themes. In Chapter Six, Chris Baker talks about 'blurred encounters' between faith actors and other partners in the public realm. Asking 'are we destined to work in parallel languages?', Baker seeks to clarify the contribution of faiths by adapting the more familiar language of social capital. He identifies 'religious capital' as 'the practical contribution to local and national life made by faith groups', which is distinct from the 'spiritual capital' that motivates this contribution. Spiritual capital 'energises by providing a theological identity [and] value system'. More productive relationships are possible when partners move beyond a 'functionalist level of discourse' (focusing on what faiths can contribute) to one that also engages with underlying values.

In Chapter Seven, Brenda O'Neill looks at how religion shapes women's political and civic engagement through nurturing values that encourage community involvement, providing opportunities for participation, and encouraging the development of relevant skills.

O'Neill distinguishes 'spirituality' from 'religiosity' and how these different types are associated with different degrees and expressions of political participation. She argues that religion and spirituality, combined, offer important untapped avenues for encouraging women's participation in the public realm. If governments encourage participatory democratic practices that involve religious organisations, they are likely to see a direct increase in women's representation and also indirect effects, such as greater numbers of women standing for public office, and ultimately a political system that is more responsive to women's values.

In Chapter Eight, Richard Gale and Therese O'Toole extend this gender focus to consider faith activism among young Muslim men. Gale and O'Toole argue that 'the presumed withdrawal of young people from the mainstream public sphere' (p 159), far from evidencing a waning of the political, in fact 'overlooks the range of public domains within which young people may seek to express and realise their political concerns and goals' (p 159). Much of this, they suggest, is finding expression through a combination of internet websites and local community activities, which elide what they see as 'unresponsive mainstream institutions'. At the same time, they see these 'new repertoires of social action' as located within a 're-imagining of the relationship between faith identity, on the one hand, and ethnic and cultural identities on the other' (p 160).

The remaining chapters consider some of the specific policies and practices in which faith touches the public realm. Looking at faith schools, John Flint asks in Chapter Nine whether they contribute to 'parallel lives'. He considers the twin issues of a possible cultural impact of divergent curricula and a sociospatial segregation. He concludes that the evidence for curricula-based segregation is weak, although he cites arguments that 'it is the lack of inter-faith interaction, rather than the particular teaching ethos or practices of faith schools, which inhibit more positive attitudes to other religious and non-religious groups' (p 168). In terms of sociospatial segregation, the evidence is also weak, but suggests that students in integrated schools are more positive about other traditions. Flint concludes that 'the drift towards mono-ethnic or mono-cultural establishments' (p 167) is not confined to faith schools, but relates to a complex mix of social and economic factors.

Considering the role of faith in the practices of urban regeneration, Richard Farnell in Chapter Ten identifies three contrasting discourses: 'instrumentalist' (policy makers want something), 'sceptical' (partners doubt the efficacy of a faith contribution) and 'critical' (faiths desist from engagement due to the risk of becoming delivery agents for government). To these he adds an 'aspirational' discourse in which faith engagement 'is rooted in a desire to make a more significant contribution to community renewal' (p 187). Farnell argues that 'faith contributions will only happen if some of the assumptions outlined within the instrumentalist approach are challenged' (p 199). The sceptical strand is to be welcomed where it is based on evidence and not prejudice, and can be a basis for constructive improvement. Farnell observes that aspirational discourses are likely to 'reveal inadequacies as well as quality' (p 199). Releasing the full potential of opportunities for faiths to engage in regeneration requires a recognition and negotiation of these diverse discourses.

In Chapter Eleven, Rachael Chapman considers the distinctiveness of faiths as contributors to civil society. Taking the ideas of 'life views', 'resources' and 'representation', she considers what faiths have in common with the wider voluntary and community sector and what features mark them as distinctive. Chapman identifies many commonalities, in terms of values, resource distribution and types of activities undertaken. She also finds important distinctions, not least in terms of the motivation that underpins faith-based work, but also in the capacity that faiths have to provide access to specific and often hard-to-reach groups. This distinctiveness, Chapman suggests, is both cause and effect of the lack of understanding, even suspicion, that faiths encounter when they engage in the public realm. Chapman concludes that differences between faith actors and the wider community and voluntary sector are likely to be context specific and dependent on particular circumstances.

It is this 'situated-ness' of faith that seems to offer most to the public realm and also to present the most risks. Being situated means having knowledge, networks and confidence and these are of great value to the public realm (Bevir and Rhodes, 2006). Yet the mining of this asset might leave scars on the landscape if it is not undertaken with care. The chapters that follow seek to bring to the surface the most important controversies, policies and practices associated with the role of faith in the public realm.

Chapter Twelve draws on the preceding contributions to identify some key themes. 'Strong secularists' argue for the exclusion of religion from public life, identifying religion as a dwindling and destructive 'other'. However, even in Western Europe, public expression of religious faith remains both pervasive and diverse. Expressions of faith include 'fundamentalisms' which certainly present themselves as disturbing and 'other' in secular societies. However, a wider assessment of 'public faith' discourages the drawing of a fixed binary divide and the mutual 'othering' of faith and secular. Sharp and ongoing controversies notwithstanding, science and rationalism do not confront faith in necessary philosophical opposition. In terms of practical action, while there can be important differences in the assumptions and 'language' of faith and secular organisations in the public realm, there is much common sentiment and practice in approaches to both caring and radical campaigning, and shared tensions experienced by organisations in their relationship with the state. Both the secular and the religious can engage in constructive deliberation and both can deal in arguments marked by unhelpful circularity. Some public interventions by faith communities and organisations can be divisive; others are defined by their attempts to build dialogue and trust and to foster the negotiation of difference. All are operating in an increasingly diverse and changing public realm which is not straightforwardly 'neutral' and which challenges both the liberalism of classical liberals and the capacity of faiths to address the tensions between tradition and reform.

References

Alexander, A. (2001) *Rebuilding the matrix: Science and faith in the 21st century*, Oxford: Lion.

Berger, P. (1968) 'A bleak outlook seen for religion', *New York Times*, 25 January.

Berger, P. (1969) *The social reality of religion*, London: Faber and Faber.

Berger, P. (1996) 'Secularism in retreat', *National Interest*, no 46, Winter, pp 3-12.

Bevir, M. and Rhodes, R. (2006) *Governance stories*, Abingdon: Routledge.

Cairns, B., Harris, M. and Hutchinson, R. (2005) *Faithful regeneration: The role and contribution of local parishes in local communities in the Diocese of Birmingham*, Birmingham: Centre of Voluntary Action Research, Aston Business School.

Cantle, T. (2005) *Community cohesion: A new framework for race and diversity*, Basingstoke: Palgrave Macmillan.

Cantle, T. (2007) 'If faith is the new "race", is faithism the new racism?', Paper presented to the ESRC 'Faith and Civil Society' seminar, Anglia Ruskin University, Cambridge, January.

CUF (Church Urban Fund) (2006) *Faithful representation: Faith representatives on local public partnerships*, London: CUF.

CULF (Commission on Urban Life and Faith) (2006) *Faithful cities, a call for celebration, vision and justice*, London: Methodist Publishing House and Church House Publishing.

Davie, G. (1994) *Religion in Britain since 1945*, Oxford: Blackwell.

Dawkins, R. (2006) *The God delusion*, London: Bantam.

Dinham, A. and Finneron, D. (2002) *Building on faith: Faith buildings in urban renewal*, London: CUF.

Dinham, A. and Lowndes, V. (2008) 'Religion, resources and representation: three narratives of faith engagement in British urban governance', *Urban Affairs Review*, vol 43, no 6, pp 817-45.

Furbey, R., Dinham, A., Farnell, T., Finneron, D. and Wilkinson, G. with Howarth, C., Hussain, D. and Palmer, S. (2006) *Faith as social capital? Connecting or dividing?*, Bristol: The Policy Press.

Habermas, J. (2007) 'Religion in the public sphere', Unpublished lecture, www.sandiego.edu/pdf/pdf_library/habermaslecture031105_c939cceb2ab087bdfc6df291ec0fc3fa.pdf

Harris, S. (2006) *The end of faith: Terror and the future of reason*, London: The Free Press.

Hitchens, C. (2007) *God is not great*, London: Atlantic Books.

Home Office (2004) *Working together: Co-operation between government and faith communities*, London: Home Office.

Home Office (2005) *Citizenship survey*, London: Home Office.

Leicester City Council (2002) 'Area profile for the City of Leicester: demographic and cultural data', www.leicester.gov.uk/index.asp?pgid=1009#Rel

Lowndes, V. (2004) 'Getting on or getting by? Women, social capital and political participation', *British Journal of Politics and International Relations*, vol 6, no 1, pp 47-66.

Lowndes, V. and Chapman, R. (2005) *Faith hope and clarity: Developing a model of faith group involvement in civil renewal*, Leicester: Local Governance Research Unit, De Montfort University.

Lowndes, V. and Chapman, R. (2008) 'Faith in governance? The potential and pitfalls of involving faith groups in urban governance', *Planning Practice and Research*, vol 23, no 1, pp 57-75.

Modood, T. (2007) *Multiculturalism: A civic idea*, Cambridge: Polity Press.

Murphy, J. (2007) 'A greater role for faith based groups in UK welfare, Speech at the Alpha Building and Engineering Services Ltd offices, East London, 11 January.

Newman, J. (2007) 'Rethinking "the public" in troubled times', *Public Policy and Administration*, vol 22, no 1, pp 27-46.

ONS (Office for National Statistics) (2004) *Focus on religion*, London: ONS.

Prochaska, F. (2006) *Christianity and social service in modern Britain: The disinherited spirit*, Oxford: Oxford University Press.

Weller, P. (2007) *Religions in the UK: Directory 2007–10*, Multi-Faith Centre: Derby.

Wilson, B. (1966) *Religion in a secular society*, London: Watts.

TWO

Controversies of 'public faith'

Robert Furbey

Introduction

This chapter explores some fundamental philosophical, scientific, socio-political and theological controversies that underlie the place of faith in the public realm. The quality of these debates has been variable and often inflamed.

The two guiding questions of the chapter combine the normative and the empirical:

- Should religious faith have an organised presence in the public realm?
- What are, and what might be, the consequences of a faith presence?

Specifically, the chapter addresses a strong secularist critique of 'public religion' in the UK in which the following objections are prominent:

- Religion is irrational and essentially at odds with science and evidence-based debate.
- Religion is a source of division and conflict.
- Religion is oppressive, an obstacle to free speech, personal liberty and political democracy, and a threat to a neutral public secular space.

Nobody, including the present author, comes 'from nowhere' in these debates. Within the constraints of a short chapter, therefore, the following discussion aims, not only to present these secularist objections, but also to explore critiques. Nevertheless, the overall purpose is to prompt the reader's own assessment, informed further by the later chapters of this book.

Faith, rationality and 'civilised dialogue'

Are we required to choose between scientific rationality and religious irrationality? Or can the encounter between science and religion contribute to an enriching and plural 'civilised dialogue' (Parekh, 2005)? Debates on the relationship between religion, science and reason have been especially intense in recent years. Central to this controversy is the view that religion is irrational and a matter of 'blind faith'. This argument has been pressed by particular scientists, philosophers and cultural commentators in widely read books (for example, Grayling, 2004; Dawkins, 2006; Dennett, 2006; Harris, 2006; Hitchens, 2007).

Sam Harris (2006, p 25) argues that religion involves such a misuse of our minds that it constitutes 'a vanishing point beyond which rational discourse proves impossible'. He argues that this 'singularity' of religion, with which we have grown up and been asked to respect, should be challenged in the light of the 'hammer blows of modernity'. Exploring the nature of 'belief', Harris notes that there is not a single meaning and that beliefs exert overwhelming power in our lives. However, 'Certain beliefs place their adherents beyond the reach of every peaceful means of persuasion … there is, in fact, no talking to some people' (Harris, 2006, p 53). Religious beliefs fail the test of propositional truth because they float free of evidence and reason, taking refuge in an internal coherence that is immune to falsification by new knowledge and events. Science, on the other hand, represents 'our most committed effort to verify that our statements about the world are true (or at least not false)' (Harris, 2006, pp 75-6) through theoretically informed experiment and observation. 'Faith' rests on unreliable and contradictory religious texts, visionary experiences, reports of miracles and claims to tradition and infallibility, not observable events or historical facts. Religion may console but it fails the tests of *truth* and demands an unwarranted leap of faith.

Harris accepts that not all religious believers are fully locked into this conservative, self-confirming world. But, to the extent that religious liberals may be more questioning and open, their moderation and tolerance reflect the development of secular knowledge and modern awareness of human rights and the value of democracy, not static religious 'knowledge'. Moreover, moderate religion has been a fragile bulwark against extremism. The fundamentalists know their scriptures better than do the moderates; liberals, as liberals, have to respect the conservatives' freedom of belief, steadily giving ground to increasingly powerful religious obscurantism. Thus:

> We must find our way to a time when faith without evidence
> disgraces anyone who would claim it.... It is imperative
> that we begin speaking plainly about the absurdity of most
> of our religious beliefs ... while religious people are not
> generally mad, their core beliefs absolutely are ... the danger
> of religious faith is that it allows otherwise normal human
> beings to reap the fruits of madness and consider them *holy*.
> (Harris, 2006, pp 48-9, emphasis in original)

Such strong critiques of religion have been addressed by scientists
and philosophers with various religious, and indeed non-religious,
commitments. From varying perspectives, these writers reject the view
that the relationship between religion, rationality and science amounts
to a 'clash of civilisations'.

There is a perennial difficulty in defining 'religion' and there are
as many different religions as there are human cultures (see, for
example, Armstrong, 1999). Religion changes and develops, through
both experience and the impact of scientific discovery on human
understanding. Thus, Ward and Polkinghorne (respectively, distinguished
philosopher and scientist) celebrate the practice and discoveries of
science in transforming our image of God (Ward, 2006a) and yielding
accumulating evidence regarding the beginning and development of
the universe (Polkinghorne, 1983).

Most religions are in conflict with reductive materialism, not with
science. Polkinghorne (1994) sees the advance of science as having
been achieved through principled and self-imposed limitations. Science
addresses aspects of reality that can be controlled experimentally, publicly
observed, interrogated and measured. It brackets out consciousness,
personal experience, value, purpose, significance and any purely spiritual
reality such as God (Ward, 2006a). However, the claim that the methods
of empirical science alone can define reason is self-refuting. 'It is not
itself confirmable by observation and experiment. So, according to
its own criterion of reasonableness, it cannot be reasonable' (Ward,
2006b, p 85). Indeed, we 'know', not only when we are presented with
publicly observable evidence, but also, crucially, through experience.
This suggests a more capacious definition of rationality than that of
scientific evidentialism.

Experience is often not publicly accessible, repeatable, readily or fully
describable, predictable, objective, amenable to experimental control
and measurement, or capable of expression in the form of general
laws. So experiential data, including religious experience, may fail the
empirical evidential test. Yet, we nevertheless reflect on our experiences

and those communicated to us by others, interpreting and acting on them, informed by our personal understandings within a wider cultural context. Thus, in the important matters of life we can act rationally even in the absence of testable evidence. Kant, for example, saw faith as not a leap in the dark, but the application of reason in situations beyond empirical verification (Ward, 2006b, p 93). Midgley (2004, p 9) also presses for a less antiseptic understanding of reason because 'all reasoning is powered by feeling and all serious feeling has some reasoning as its skeleton'.

'Strong' secularist argument would regard 'rational religion' as an oxymoron. Ward, however, appeals to the historical association between rationality and religion in the West, arguing that figures such as Anselm, Aquinas, Kant, Kierkegaard, Hegel and Descartes define what we call reasonableness. Such a list, he argues, signals the continuing Christian, indeed Abrahamic, belief of the universe as the work of a rational creator, intelligible to rational and free creatures, making science possible and promising a fruitful association with theology. Sardar's (2007) lecture at The Royal Society confirms the historical association of other world faiths with science, in this case Islam. Ward (2006b, p 97) offers the following criteria for rational worldviews, religious and non-religious:

- clarity and precision in the component beliefs (organised, ideally, in order of logical dependence);
- readiness to explore alternative beliefs;
- coherence with other knowledge;
- integration of data into a convincing overall interpretation, yielding diverse interpretations; and
- 'creative power, generating new insights' (Ward, 2006b, p 97).

Many apologists of religion recognise the frequent suppression of rationality and freedom by religious institutions and hierarchies. But they also underline the regular challenge of new theologies and practices to established orthodoxies, both secular and religious. The most often cited example is the Protestant Reformation in Western Europe. The legacy of Protestantism has been deeply ambiguous. The displacement of the authority of the Catholic Church by the final authority of scripture, now translated into the vernacular, was a powerful source of democracy and civil liberties. Protestantism, therefore, with its emphasis on the 'word' and the text, the right to dissent and human equality in the form of a practiced participatory 'priesthood of all believers', can be seen as a major contribution to the quest for a secular 'public realm'.

Yet the reformers' commitment to critical reasoning and freedom of inquiry and belief also produced an unwitting challenge to scriptural revelation and religious belief, contributing to radical doubt and modern secularism. Moreover, from the Puritans onwards, scripture has been interpreted to sustain various authoritarian theocracies.

For all its contradictions, however, the development of Protestantism does serve to question a general 'conflict thesis' (Alexander, 2001) regarding science, rationality, religion and indeed liberalism. Ward (2006a, p 151) offers the following assessment of the part of Protestantism in the subsequent European 'Age of Reason':

> I am not pretending that religious beliefs alone gave rise to Enlightenment beliefs in liberty, equality and fraternity. But I am proposing that the basic religious beliefs of the Protestant revolution helped to set in train and motivate the whole complex movement we call the Enlightenment, and the growth of liberal attitudes in religion and politics. Liberalism was not a secular movement that forced religion reluctantly to follow. It was a movement rooted in religious thought, and it is traceable back to the foundational beliefs of the New Testament, which present Jesus as a religious dissident, executed by the establishment for his radical religious views.

A 21st-century assessment of Protestantism must accord greater weight to its contribution to the 'disenchantment' and 'desacralisation' of nature and the 'objectification' of the human subject (see McGrath, 2004 for a critical assessment from a present Protestant Christian perspective). Yet Protestants and other religious traditions also confront a narrow instrumental rationality, defending human personhood and respect for the environment (Ward, 2006b, p 152).

The preceding discussion has focused on the critique and defence of *religion*. What of the practice of *science*? Midgley (2004, p 3) is sharply critical of the reduction of science to the accumulation of facts, devoid of 'the grander and more interesting and imaginative structure of ideas by which scientists strive to connect, understand and interpret these facts'. In this task of scientific interpretation, she argues, myths play a central part, just as they do in religion:

> Myths are not lies. Nor are they detached stories. They are imaginative patterns, networks of powerful symbols that suggest particular ways of interpreting the world. They shape

its meaning.… Such ideas are not just a distraction from real thought, as positivists have suggested. Nor are they a disease. (Midgley, 2004, pp 1 and 4)

Myths can be illuminating but also limiting and distorting. For example, machine-metaphor myths of science in the 17th and 18th centuries first permitted discovery and understanding. Subsequently, however, they have proved naïve, simplistic and limiting, subordinating wider holistic thinking that draws on experience, imagination, intuition and feeling. Midgley is especially critical of the applications of particular myths and metaphors from the physical sciences to human life and relations, particularly through what she regards as the simplifying distortion of Darwin's ideas by some biological and genetic scientists. The rationality characteristic of much physical science is not omni-competent. There are different kinds of understanding, not least the exploration of motives and meanings by the arts, humanities and social sciences. We need therefore to embrace scientific pluralism. Great scientists have always recognised the need to engage with other ideas in their culture and beyond.

Midgley devotes as much attention to science *as* religion as to the relationship between science *and* religion. She is at her most provocative in identifying the specific myth of progress, which involves the exaltation of science as a route to material, spiritual and moral development:

> We must surely wonder now why so many people expected this wisdom to appear. That expectation set up a kind of cargo-cult which is only now giving way to blank disappointment.… What they [the 'scientistic prophets'] promoted as scientific thinking was actually a series of uncriticised ideologies, which gradually diverged from mainstream Enlightenment in various alarming directions. (Midgley, 2004, p 17)

Scientism, therefore, is identified with worldview, myth, faith and power, resembling past and present religious institutions and with similarly ambivalent consequences.

As for 'science and religion' debates, Midgley regards their (that is, scientific and religious) functions as too different for justifying the assertion of inevitable conflict. Currently, she argues, we are encouraged to see tension as endemic because creationist religion is claiming scientific territory while secularist science is moving beyond the limits described earlier to present itself as a 'religious' worldview. Bad religion meets bad science.

Faith and conflict

The charge that religion is irrational is joined by the related objection that religion is a source of social division, bloody conflict and tyranny. This view of religion as 'problem' is reflected in UK government anti-terrorism strategies. Yet other policy strands identify 'faith' as 'solution', contributing significantly to voluntary action, civic partnership, the renewal of civil society and (although there is some ambivalence here) social cohesion policies.

Grayling takes a strong 'problem' view, arguing that apologists for religion present a 'perfumed smokescreen':

> The real perfume in the smokescreen lies in the claim that the contemporary Churches, with their charities and their aid for the suffering in the Third World, are models of goodness in action. They accordingly present themselves as institutions devoted to peace, kindness, brotherly love and charitable works. But this soft face is turned to the world only when the Church is on the back foot ... whenever religion is in the ascendant, with hands on the levers of secular power too, it shows a very different face – the face presented by the Inquisition, the Taliban, and the religious police in Saudi Arabia. (Grayling, 2004, p 81)

Hitchens (2007) develops a more extended essay, encompassing all the major world faiths and numerous episodes in history: from the Crusades, to the European religious wars of the 16th and 17th centuries, to the role of Christianity and other religions in slavery, to the relationship of the Vatican with 20th-century fascism, to the Rwandan genocide, al Qaeda and American televangelists. Hitchens identifies in Jewish and Islamic religious texts the invocation to violence and fear. In the Christian Bible he regards the New Testament as still more dreadful than the Old (Hitchens, 2007, pp 175-6).

Hitchens connects religion to the concept of 'totalitarianism' (Arendt, 1994), whereby people surrender their lives to a supreme leader willing their own subjection and delighting in the subjection of others. He notes George Orwell's association of totalitarianism with theocracy and argues that 'For most of human history, the idea of the total or absolute state was intimately bound up with religion' (Hitchens, 2007, p 231). If such a rigid and self-confirming mindset is constitutive of religion, religious faith can fairly be seen as divisive and inimical to a constructive role in the public realm.

Writers from various faith perspectives recognise this danger of absolutism in religion. Husain (2007) describes the closed world of certainty and the demands for total loyalty that he encountered as he participated in Hizb-ut Tahrir and other Islamist organisations. He describes his student activism as an attempt to secure a 'total Islamisation of public space' at his college: 'At the Hizb we considered democracy as idolatrous, since it did not allow for the One God to control mankind, but allowed human beings to choose their own destiny. (Husain, 2007, pp 63, 89)

The danger of this phenomenon is generalised by a former Anglican bishop:

> There is a particular danger in religion, one that is more fraught with evil than even nationalism. For all religions claim to mediate the absolute. It is easy to topple over the brink and identify that absolute with the final human structures through which that absolute is disclosed to human beings. (Harries, 2002, p 78)

Similarly, McTernan (2007), a Catholic priest with a long career in conflict resolution, is unwilling to reduce religion to an epiphenomenon in wars and atrocities around the world. He concludes that:

> Whatever the psychological, social and political factors that trigger violence in fringe and mainstream religious bodies, the religious mind-set is itself an important factor that needs to be acknowledged and understood if durable solutions are to be found for many current conflicts. (McTernan, 2003, p 40)

Religion becomes particularly dangerous when, at any spatial scale, it achieves 'uninterrogated' political privilege and power, the extreme case being the absolutist religious state. However, given the diversity and development of religion emphasised earlier in this chapter, is it legitimate to assert that '"religion" poisons everything'? (Hitchens, 2007, p 25). Moreover, to what extent does secularist criticism itself display circularity of argument and resistance to falsification? It can be argued that such a stance fails to capture the empirically observable diversity, complexity and mutability of the religious landscape.

The centrality of myth and metaphor to human understanding was identified above with reference to science. But human beings also invoke symbols and metaphors to convey the pervasive experience of the transcendent and the numinous, drawing on their personal and shared cultural resources. Thus, 'All the major religions ... would agree that it is impossible to describe this transcendence in normal conceptual language' (Armstrong, 1999, p 6). This recognition of the partial and provisional status of religious understanding and the recourse to myth, metaphor and parable underlines the complexity and dynamism of religion. It questions a view of religious understandings as necessarily closed, literalist, static and inflexible, harbingers of inevitable division and conflict.

However, some forms of religion, notably modern fundamentalism, *are* marked by claims to certainty, embodying commitments to textual literalism and beliefs in scriptural inerrancy (Ruthven, 2004). Ward (2006b, p 15) is reminded of the association of fundamentalism and literalism with modernity: 'It could be that the obsession with "literal truth" is itself a product of the scientific outlook, and of the belief that only literal truths are truths at all'. Similarly, Ruthven (2004, p 87) notes a propensity for Islamist activists to emerge from 'the ranks of graduates in modern faculties such as medicine and engineering, who combine a sophisticated knowledge of the technical products of modernity with two-dimensional understandings of their inherited faith tradition', using scripture as a straightforward 'manual for practical action'.

In an empirically grounded exploration of Christianity and various major conflicts, Martin (1997) identified religion, ethnicity and language as 'markers of identity'. He concludes, however, that the most powerful cause of war is a confused blurring of nationalistic principles, with religion often pressed into service by nationalist leaders who seek to justify violent atrocity. Each conflict is subtly different and history does not support the attribution of a generalised and prime role to religion, much less the presence of a 'virus' of religious certainty (Dawkins, 2006, p 167). The diminution or absence of a religious marker is not associated with decreased enmity.

Martin's data, therefore, question the identification of religion as a universal poison. Indeed, critics see the secularist association of faith with conflict as marked by immunity from falsification. Both Harris (2006) and Hitchens (2007) are in opposition to religionists (for example, McGrath, 2004) who point to the 'industrialisation' of violence and oppression by the 'atheistic' Nazi and Communist regimes in the 20th century. They argue that, actually, these regimes were expressions of a Christian religious inheritance. Similarly, individual opponents of violence, injustice and oppression are detached by Hitchens from what are commonly seen as their religious moorings. Hence, Dietrich Bonhoeffer 'mutated into admirable but nebulous humanism'. Martin Luther King was 'in no real, as opposed to nominal, sense ... a Christian' (Hitchens, 2007, pp 7, 176). When 'ordinary' religious believers have protested at violence, it is 'a compliment to humanism, not to religion' (Hitchens, 2007, p 27). Schulman (2007) expresses the essential criticism of this argument in the following terms: 'For Hitchens, in short, everything religion touches is bad, and everything bad is religious – including anti-religion'. The reasoning is unhelpfully circular.

Accepting that religion can be a source of conflict, McTernan (2003, p 148) also affirms its contribution to conciliation, finding 'important resemblances in belief that exist between the mainstream world religions', which correspond with secular declarations of human rights, so that:

> In each faith tradition we see an affirmation of life that extends beyond the physical boundaries of their own communities.... In each tradition ... there is clearly a seminal presence of the right of the individual both to seek truth and to dissent – principles right at the heart of the Universal Declaration of Human Rights. (McTernan, 2003, p 148)

In terms of the Abrahamic faiths, therefore, it is possible to trace a development in Judaic understanding of God as belonging to a particular people, sometimes with the attributes of a tribal deity, to an inclusive vision of a God who prompts concern for the oppressed and recognition of all people as bearers of the 'image of God' (Ward, 2004, pp 118-22). Central to Christianity is Christ's distillation of the law into love for God and love for neighbour, the latter extending beyond 'people like us' to the reviled Samaritan stranger 'over the wall'. Islam holds the 'oneness' of humanity as a central principle and an understanding of God as compassionate and merciful. People are free moral agents with obligations to work for peace and justice, notably through the paying of alms (*zakat*) to benefit the poor and *jihad*, the responsibility to submit to God in the care of creation. Certainly, a common distinction has been made between the *dar al-Islam* (abode of Islam) and the *dar al-harb* (abode of war) – the world of Islam and the world of others – and to the *umma*, a community of specifically Muslim faith. However, the Qur'an also refers to a wider community

– *qawmi* ('my people') – which involves fraternal relationship and boundary-crossing between Muslims and other people, regardless of their beliefs, and a wider respect for diversity endorsed by the Prophet (Hussain, 2004):

> O mankind! Behold. We have created you from a male and
> a female, and have made you nations and tribes, so that you
> might come to know one another. (Qur'an, 49, p 13)

A central tenet for Sikhs is the essential unity of humanity and the equality of all people before God. Sikhs are expected, collectively and individually, to develop in honesty, compassion, generosity, patience and humility, providing *kar-sewa*, selfless voluntary religious and social service. A daily prayer for Sikhs is: 'By Thy Grace may everybody be blessed in the world'.

The complexity of Hinduism renders generalisation particularly difficult. However, this broad tradition upholds 'the divine qualities of forgiveness, compassion, the absence of anger and malice, and peace and harmlessness'. The world is seen as having 'a common ancestry' (McTernan, 2003, pp 45-6, 133). Material selfishness is a barrier to ultimate reality and the teachings of *dharma* enjoin the value of all beings more than ourselves, particularly the cherishing of strangers.

This necessarily brief review indicates important common ground between faiths amidst the significant differences. Peace, justice, honesty, service, personal responsibility and forgiveness are beliefs and values that may contribute to conciliation and peace across faith divides and faith–secular divides. If such principles were enacted, faith in the public realm might reasonably be accepted as a very positive presence (see the essentially confirming empirical reviews by Dinham, 2007, and NCVO, 2007) although the relationship between faith, motivation and actual expression in, say, volunteering, may be complex (Locke, 2007).

A 'neutral' public space?

In its 'strong' form (summarised by Parekh, 2006) the secularist thesis argues that religion and politics must be seen as separate activities, the former being other-worldly and personal and the latter this-worldly, communal and public. Religion is a matter of faith and deals in unbending absolutes, while politics requires rational deliberation and debate. Religion has little to contribute to public life; rather, it threatens mayhem. Public politics should be secular, omitting religion. Rawls crystallises such liberal secularist concerns in the following question:

How is it possible for those affirming a religious doctrine
that is based on religious authority, for example the Church
or the Bible, also to hold a reasonable political conception
that supports a just democratic regime? ... How is it possible
for citizens of faith to be wholehearted members of a
democratic society? (Rawls, 1996, pp 39-40)

Given Rawls' definition of the problem, Shah (2000, p 133)
concludes that 'it is not surprising that he considers the containment
of presumptively unreasonable and illiberal religion – Christianity
always being his paradigm case – an essential component of liberalism'.
Grayling's (nd) conclusion is similar: 'Now therefore is the time to
place religion where it belongs – wholly in the private sphere along
with other superstitions and foibles, leaving the public domain as
neutral territory where all can meet without prejudice as humans and
equals'.

The remainder of this section explores some specific responses to
this strong secularist position.

The public realm is not static and, after the initial rise of the absolute
nation state in the West, it became defined increasingly by classical
liberalism. Parekh (2006, p 181) argues that the modern territorial state
'represents a historically unique mode of defining and relating to its
members'. It gave space for individual autonomy and religious freedom
but also homogenised citizens by abstracting away their particularity.
The sovereignty of the state in the 21st century, however, is diminished
by globalisaton and growing cultural pluralism. In addition to changes
in the state, 'the space occupied by civil society has evolved as part
of a dynamic process of adaptation and change and in the course of
evolution has altered its character and composition' (Deakin, 2001,
p 16). 'Religion', too, has changed. Religious faith remains important
but, Hirst (2000, p 106) argues, it is no longer 'the all-inclusive human
concern'. The great majority of churches now accept the legitimate
existence of other religions within the nation and all religions are
now sects, notwithstanding the formalities of Church of England
establishment. The public realm, therefore, has changed and is changing
so that 'Today the state cannot be an absolute sovereign, confronted as
it is by a complex organised civil society' (Hirst, 2000, p 111).

Historical change in the public realm is joined by geographical
variation. Modood makes a particular distinction between the state and
religion and the place of religion in civil society in England, the US and
France. He emphasises that each national public realm and, within it, the
place of religion, is shaped historically by dominant groups (Modood,

2007).This reference to the power to define public and private provokes questions regarding the concept of a '*neutral*' public space.

The necessity of a neutral state for a free and cooperating citizenry is common ground for two of the major liberal political theorists – Rawls (1971) and Kymlicka (1989).The latter, however, identified a disjuncture between liberal theory and the actual practices of states. Territorially bounded nation states will have histories shaped by dominant cultural, linguistic and religious groups, with minorities subordinated so that state neutrality is impossible (see the discussion by Modood, 2007, pp 23ff). Kymlicka supports the demands of cultural groups for political participation, public resources and institutional recognition. But he is content for religious groups to be restricted only to limited legal exemptions on the grounds that, unlike other statuses, religion is optional. Modood argues that this view of religion as simply a matter of personal choice is sociologically naïve and reflects a 'secularist bias'. We need to be able to recognise 'ethno-religious groups' (Modood, 2007, pp 23ff and 35).

The delineation of the public realm by liberal universalism is challenged by both the actuality of accelerating ethnic and religious pluralism in Western states and the philosophical debate that has been provoked. Parekh (2006, p 16) reviews the history and diversity of moral monism, 'the view that only one way of life is fully human, true or the best, and that all others are defective to the extent that they fall short of it'. He identifies strong monist strands in both Christianity and classical liberalism and, indeed, strong links between them and suggests that 'liberals continue to absolutise liberalism' (p 110). Thus, they have made a strong divide between their own liberalism and the illiberalism of others, speaking of toleration of other ways of life rather than respect or celebration.

Such an argument suggests a capacity for oppression in a secular liberal public realm. Shah identifies in both the foundational writings of Hugo Grotius in the early 17th century and the modern liberal contribution of John Rawls a similar resolution of the tension between liberalism and religious pluralism. Both, he argues, seek to 'make the world safe for liberalism' (Shah, 2000, p 122) by making it unsafe for religious pluralism. In the case of Rawls, the language is ominous, redolent of the Cold War in its reference to 'containment'. In his call for 'reasonableness' in the public realm, Rawls sets 'a remarkably high standard' (Shah, 2000, p 134). He excludes 'unreasonable and irrational, and even mad, comprehensive [religious] doctrines', meaning not only militant terrorist fundamentalisms, but also major world religions that continue to hold comprehensive doctrines that others in the public realm cannot accept. If religions cannot accept the 'burdens of judgement' and put aside their truth-claims they cannot take their place with 'wholehearted' and uniformly 'reasonable' individuals in a 'liberal' and homogenised public realm (Rawls, 1993, pp xviii-xix).

This argument suggests a 'narrowness' and stasis in secular liberalism. Keane asks whether the '19th century doctrine of secularism' embraced by many liberals seeking the removal of religion from public politics, is, in fact

> a conflict-producing ideology that threatens the free-thinking pluralism of democracy as we currently experience it.... Should we stop looking for universal principles, like secularism, through which to regard religion? Must we instead give priority to context-bound judgements that recognise that all morality – including all religious discourse and that of its secular opponents – arises in particular contexts?' (Keane, 2000, p 18)

Similarly, in the context of an exploration of democratic associational politics in an increasingly plural society, Hirst (2000, p 117) suggests that 'Secular liberals might well be the group who would find this community self-governance most difficult to accept'.

Liberal prescriptions for the public realm have been challenged by multiculturalism. Modood (2007) argues that this latter term refers not to a fully developed political philosophy, much less one that is in simple opposition to liberalism. For him,

> multiculturalism could not get off the ground if one totally repudiated liberalism; but neither could it do so if liberalism marked the limits of one's politics. Multiculturalism is a child of liberal egalitarianism but, like any child, it is not a faithful reproduction of its parents. (Modood, 2007, p 8)

Modood (2007, pp 7, 20) seeks to develop multiculturalism, not in relation to a general theory or epistemology, but as 'a more intellectually modest and non-totalistic political perspective' with a significant element of pragmatism in pursuing 'moderate secularism' rather than 'ideological secularism'. Central here is the view that the equality of individuals should be joined by recognition of group difference and identity. Parekh (2006, pp 8, 296) stresses that culture matters deeply to people and that their self-esteem depends on others' recognition and respect. People have *cultural* rights and should not be subject to mockery.

The universalising tendencies of the nation state and defenders of a 'narrow' liberal political realm, therefore, are sources of harm, injustice and oppression. This applies particularly in a religious context, where the 'sacred' is of explicit significance, a source of deep feelings.

Modood and Parekh regard liberal *'tolerance'* as insufficient for an encompassing and democratic public realm. Dominant groups can readily put up with minorities if the latter tow the line, but 'tolerant' dominance is still a profound source and expression of power and inequality. Commitment to *respect* gives promise of genuine equality. This 'relies on the sensitivity and responsibility of individuals and institutions to refrain from what is legal but unacceptable' (Modood, 2007, p 57) and commitment to active support for minorities in the face of hostility. Liberal secularists often reject such a call, arguing that respect for what they perceive as repugnant nonsense is an obstacle to the truth. Modood's response is to distinguish between public recognition and respect for identities and their moral evaluation, so that 'When we argue for recognition of difference we are not necessarily morally approving or disapproving of that difference' (Modood, 2007, p 67).

However, recognition does point to support for a more pervasive 'co-presence' in public life. Such a development would address the lack of institutional public spaces that Parekh identifies as hamstringing the development of political deliberation as advocated by liberals. Moreover, a more inclusive public realm may engender positive change in the nature of public discourse. Parekh (2006, p 309) argues that 'It is a rationalist mistake to equate reason with argument'. Liberal deliberation is often characterised by cerebral and adversarial argument and debate and, to the victor, the spoils. Critical debate must not be stifled but we cannot neglect rational *persuasion*, which is not just about arguments but, echoing Ward's identification of various strands of rationality, also appeals to emotions, self-understanding, moral values, sense of identity and interpersonal and institutional trust in particular cultural contexts. This brings the enrichment of mutual learning as new 'knowledges', including religious perspectives, are explored, used or sometimes rejected in the public realm. However, the realisation of such benefits depends on the disposition and actions of players in an expanded and more diverse public realm.

The discussion here returns to Modood's distinction between 'ideological secularism' and 'moderate secularism', which, he argues, is more characteristic of varying politics and practice in most democracies. Ideological secularism is a barrier to integration and equality. Moderate secularism involves the inclusion of religious identities and organisations in the public realm; the replacement of the notion of secular 'neutrality' and a strong public/private divide by evolutionary 'institutional adjustment and a pragmatic, case by case, negotiated approach to dealing with controversy and conflict' (Modood, 2007. p 79).

Such 'moderate' secularism makes demands on all sides, not least religious communities and organisations. Thus, Keane (2000, p 9) cites Rorty's complaint that religion's contribution to public reason often acts as an inflexible 'conversation-stopper', rooted in dogmatic reference to internal religious doctrines and producing silence and antagonism. However, religious contributions to public debate do not necessarily take this form. Arguing as an atheist and drawing on the work of Rawls, Baggini (2006) argues that religious players in public debate must find ways of expressing religious contributions in terms that have intelligibility and purchase with people beyond a particular faith. They may use 'reasonable comprehensive doctrines' but these must be supported by 'proper political reasons', not simply reasons that stem solely from the comprehensive doctrines. The test is to 'find a way of expressing [beliefs] in universalist and not particularist terms' (Baggini, 2006, p 208).

Responding from a Christian perspective, Spencer (2006) judges this to be a sound and fair argument. However, he also notes that questions remain concerning issues of public reason and neutrality:

> If we are to take seriously the arguments of Isaiah Berlin or Alasdair MacIntyre that core human values are generally plural or incommensurable – and not just because certain people deem certain texts to be revelatory and others don't – we are faced with a problem. Who decides a proper political reason? Who says what goes?' (Spencer, 2006, p 28)

This is not to invalidate the search for universal concepts of public reason or human rights or deny that there is much on which religious and non-religious people can agree. But it *is* to underline the need for a greater recognition of difference in a public realm marked by more willingness to adapt to a wider range of reasoning. In summary: 'Religious participation within the public square must accommodate itself to public reason, but public reason must be willing to accommodate to religious participation' (Spencer, 2006, p 29). Regarding the latter, secularist positions can also be dogmatic and oppressive 'conversation-stoppers' (Keane, 2000). The rise of multicultural societies presents challenges unique in history to both the religious and the non-religious.

A specific challenge to the religious status quo in England and, by extension, to the rest of the UK, concerns the establishment of the Church of England. Parekh (2006) rejects the 'strong' secularist thesis for the separation of *politics* and religion, which he sees as requiring religious people to suppress their full identity. However, he has more sympathy with the 'weak' secularist thesis, the separation of the *state* and religion, because close association is mutually corrupting. Hence, it is not only secularists who make this argument. Barrow (2006, p 1) also welcomes the 'cultural shift away from the West's "Christendom settlement"' and the possibility of disestablishment as giving faith communities new opportunities to act more radically within civil society, often working with secular groups, as alternative sources of challenging values and practices. Another possible development is to recognise the value of the Church of England establishment for the public inclusion of non-Christian faiths and for 'civic responsibility for religion', while broadening the public realm by 'pluralising Anglican privileges' (Modood, 2000).

Conclusions

The aim of this chapter has been to engage with longstanding and sometimes rancorous debates that cannot be finally resolved. Religious belief and atheism are both metaphysical positions. Polkinghorne (1983, p 2) concludes that 'we are in an area of discourse where no one, believer or unbeliever, has access to knockdown final demonstration'. The best we can achieve is to present to each other 'a coherent and rationally motivated view of the way the world is'.

Nevertheless, there seem to emerge from the preceding discussion both philosophical and practical lessons to inform and challenge the understandings, policies and practices encountered in later chapters. First, many expressions of religion can be highly problematic, sources of conflict and conversation-stopping circularity in democratic deliberation, notably when they achieve undue secular power. There are legitimate demands to be made of faith in the public realm. Yet the major world faith traditions all have central doctrines that inform practices that, accumulating evidence suggests, can make significant and positive contributions to public life and discourse. This underlines the complexity and diversity of religion and the dangers of generalisation.

Second, secular liberalism has also been challenged, particularly when allied to reductive materialism and to a narrow understanding of 'rationality'. Scientists, theologians and human beings throughout history have all utilised myth and metaphor to make (often enriching) sense of 'the data'. The history of science and religion has not been a tale of two separate stories. Similarly, there has been a strong intertwining of religion and philosophy, with religion being a source of secularism and a secular public realm, not simply an antagonist. Meanwhile, circularity in argument has not been the preserve of the religious. In these various ways, therefore, the religious and the secular may be less 'other' to each other than is commonly supposed.

Finally, the idea of a relatively fixed liberal 'neutral' public realm has been challenged. Rather, it is a terrain characterised by inequality of power and increasing social plurality. Historically, the public realm has been shaped by monism, both Christian and classical liberal. Multiculturalist 'moderate secularism' challenges monism and the narrowness of the rationality and the 'knowledges' of the present public realm. Opportunities for encounter, mutual understanding and trust presently are lost as underrepresented or excluded groups, including religious groups, are unable to enrich public life through their particular experience, knowledge and tradition.

Acknowledgements

The author is grateful for encouragement and helpful criticism from his fellow editors and authors and also from Dr Camila Bassi, Pauline Gordon, Professor Martyn Percy, Professor Bhikhu Parekh and Dr Richard White. Responsibility for the final text rests with the author.

References

Alexander, A. (2001) *Rebuilding the matrix: Science and faith in the 21st century*, Oxford: Lion.

Arendt, H. (1994) *The origins of totalitarianism*, New York: Harcourt.

Armstrong, K. (1999) *A history of God*, London: Vintage.

Baggini, J. (2006) 'The rise, fall and rise again of secularism', *Public Policy Review*, vol 12, no 14, pp 202–10.

Barrow, S. (2006) *Redeeming religion in the public square*, London: Ekklesia, www.ekklesia.co.uk/oldsite/content/article_060724redeeming.shtml

Dawkins, R. (2006) *The God delusion*, London: Bantam.

Deakin, N. (2001) *In search of civil society*, London: Palgrave Macmillan.

Dennett, D (2006) *Breaking the spell: Religion as a natural phenomenon*, New York: Viking Penguin.

Dinham, A. (2007) *Priceless, immeasurable: Faith and community development in 21st-century England*, London: Faith-Based Regeneration Network.

Grayling, A.C. (nd) *The secular and the sacred*, www.acgrayling.com/secular.html

Grayling, A.C. (2004) *What is good? The search for the best way to live*, London: Phoenix.

Harries, R. (2002) *God outside the box: Why spiritual people object to Christianity*, London: SPCK.

Harris, S. (2006) *The end of faith: Religion, terror and the future of reason*, London: The Free Press.

Hirst, P. (2000) 'J.N. Figgis, churches and the state', in D. Marquand and R.L. Nettler (eds) *Religion and democracy* (pp 104-20), Oxford: Blackwell.

Hitchens, C. (2007) *God is not great*, London: Atlantic Books.

Husain, E. (2007) *The Islamist*, London: Penguin.

Hussain, D. (2004) 'British Muslim identity', in M. Siddique Seddon, D. Hussain and N. Malik (eds) *British Muslims between assimilation and segregation*, Markfield: The Islamic Foundation, pp 82-118.

Keane, J. (2000) 'Secularism?', in D. Marquand and R.L. Nettler (eds) *Religion and democracy*, Oxford: Blackwell, pp 5-19.

Kymlicka, W. (1989) *Liberalism, community and culture*, Oxford: Oxford University Press.

Locke, M. (2007) 'Faith as a motivation for voluntary action', in Jochum, V., Pratten, B. and Wilding, K. (eds) *Faith and voluntary action: An overview of current evidence and debates*, London: National Council for Voluntary Organisations, pp 29-34.

Martin, D. (1997) *Does Christianity cause war?*, Oxford: Clarendon Press.

McGrath, A. (2004) *The twilight of atheism: The rise and fall of disbelief in the modern world*, London: Rider/Random House.

McTernan, O. (2003) *Violence in God's name: Religion in an age of conflict*, London: Darton, Longman and Todd.

Midgley, M. (2004) *The myths we live by*, London: Routledge.

Modood, T. (2000) 'Should the Church of England be disestablished?' – Tariq Modood in correspondence with Bishop Colin Buchanan, *The Guardian*, 15 April.

Modood, T. (2007) *Multiculturalism: A civic idea*, Cambridge: Polity Press.

NCVO (National Council of Voluntary Organisations) (2007) *Faith and voluntary action: An overview of current evidence and debates*, London: NCVO.

Parekh, B. (2005) 'Multiculturalism is a civilised dialogue', *The Guardian*, 21 January.

Parekh, B. (2006) *Rethinking multiculturalism: Cultural diversity and political theory* (2nd edn), Basingstoke: Palgrave Macmillan.

Polkinghorne, J. (1983) *The way the world is: The Christian perspective of a scientist*, London: Triangle SPCK.

Polkinghorne, J. (1994) *Science and Christian belief: Theological reflections of a bottom-up thinker*, London: SPCK.

Rawls, J. (1971) *A theory of justice*, Cambridge, MA: Belknap Press of Harvard University Press.

Rawls, J. (1993) *Political liberalism*, New York: Columbia University Press.

Rawls, J. (1996) *Political liberalism* (2nd edn), New York: Columbia University Press.

Ruthven, M. (2004) *Fundamentalism: The search for meaning*, Oxford: Oxford University Press.

Sardar, Z. (2007) 'Islam and science', Lecture to The Royal Society, www.royalsoc.ac.uk/page.asp?tip=1&id=5747

Schulman, S. (2007) Review of 'God is not great' by Christopher Hitchens, *Commentary Online*, June, www.commentarymagazine. com/viewarticle.cfm?id=10890&page=all

Shah, T.S. (2000) 'Making the Christian world safe for liberalism: from Grotius to Rawls', in D. Marquand and R.L. Nettler (eds) *Religion and democracy*, Oxford: Blackwell, pp 121-40.

Spencer, N. (2006) *'Doing God': A future for faith in the public square*, London: Theos, www.theosthinktank.co.uk/Files/MediaFiles/ TheosBookletfinal.pdf

Ward, K. (2004) *The case for religion*, Oxford: Oneworld.

Ward, K. (2006a) *Pascal's fire: Scientific faith and religious understanding*, Oxford: Oneworld.

Ward, K. (2006b) *Is religion dangerous?*, Oxford: Lion.

THREE

'Soft' segregation: Muslim identity, British secularism and inequality

David Cheesman and Nazia Khanum

Introduction

Current controversies about faith in the public realm have been stirred by historical and contemporary developments and events relating specifically to Islam and the perceptions of, and by, Muslim people in the UK and in the wider world. This chapter brings the perspectives of two Muslim authors to the exploration of Muslim experience in the cultural context of Britain where public expression of faith is often met with unease or even hostility.

Muslims are now the largest religious minority in the UK. Like other recently settled minorities, they stand out because most are not white, and their customs and beliefs are not implicit in British tradition. Muslims have a visibility out of proportion to their numbers. Nationally and internationally, Islam has gained a special status from both terrorism and the 'War on Terror'. There is a grim litany. On the one hand, there have been cruel terrorist atrocities from the US embassy bombs in Kenya and Tanzania through 9/11, Bali and Madrid to 7/7 in London, and hatred disseminated through speeches and the World Wide Web by small but vociferous groups campaigning in the name of Islam for the overthrow of the world order. On the other hand, there have been military campaigns in Afghanistan and Iraq; security clampdowns; and, underlying everything, the festering sore of Palestine, Israel and Lebanon. Consequently, significant numbers of Muslims are seen, and seem to see themselves, as engaged in a struggle against the rest of society, including, perhaps especially, other Muslims.

Unsurprisingly, there is worldwide concern about the trajectory of Muslim communities. In September 2005, Trevor Phillips, as Chair of the Commission for Racial Equality, responded to the London atrocities of 7 July 2005 with a speech entitled, 'After 7/7: sleepwalking to segregation', in which he explored 'the causes of 7/7, the legacy of multiculturalism, and the place of Muslim communities' (Phillips, 2005). Muslims, he believed, were turning their backs on their neighbours. Muslim segregation continues to be hotly debated. In January 2008, Michael Nazir-Ali, the Bishop of Rochester, argued that some Muslims have created 'no-go' areas for all who do not adhere to 'the ideology of Islamic extremism' (Nazir-Ali, 2008).

The concern here is with 'soft' segregation, the segregation of hearts and minds. American-style 'hard' segregation, the segregation of housing and streets, is rare in Britain. A comprehensive study of residential settlement, comparing the 1991 and 2001 Censuses, was conducted for the BBC (2004). While there was evidence of communities clustering in areas where they could access facilities such as places of work and familiar groceries, the streets and neighbourhoods remained mixed. Across space and time, poverty has been the main driver of segregation as the more affluent simply buy their way out. Muslims in Britain suffer high levels of deprivation, so tending to live in the cheapest housing. The BBC research suggested that, once they have the money, Muslims are as ready to flee to the suburbs as anyone else. This is confirmed by detailed spatial investigations into ethnic residential segregation in Bradford, focusing on the South Asians who form the largest minority and who are mainly Pakistani Muslims (Phillips et al, 2002; Simpson, 2004; Carling, 2008). The interpretation of the results has become enmeshed in conflicting statistical definitions of segregation (see Carling, 2008), but what stands out is the absence of any evidence of hard physical segregation. In line with the BBC's national findings, South Asians in Bradford have also moved to new districts as their wealth and confidence have increased. There are now more areas with a preponderance of South Asians but none are exclusively South Asian. However, cartography does not tell the full story as residential location may not have direct implications for social interaction.

This is the segregation that alarmed Trevor Phillips and Nazir-Ali, the emotional and spiritual segregation that goes beyond settlement patterns. In 2001, Sir Herman Ouseley (2001, p 6) found that attitudes in Bradford 'appear to be hardening and intolerance towards differences is growing'. Following Ouseley, Cantle (2001, p 9) consolidated the concept of 'parallel lives' in his influential report on community. The Cantle report continues to set the terms of the government's social policy, and the theme was underwritten in 2007 by the Commission on Integration and Cohesion with its report *Our shared future*, raising broader questions of social integration and the nature of Britishness (Commission on Integration and Cohesion, 2007).

This chapter explores soft segregation in relation to the Muslim communities. It argues that two features of contemporary British culture militate against the development of a society fully inclusive of Muslims: first, a suspicion of Islam and, second, a suspicion of public expressions of religious faith in general, both of which impede the development of mutual understanding. An initial context is set through a brief profile of Muslims in Britain. The chapter then explores Muslim identities. Finally, the discussion focuses on the secular consensus to which Muslims are attempting to adjust.

Muslims in Britain

While large-scale settlement of Muslims in Britain did not start until after the Second World War, Muslims have been visiting the country for centuries (Ansari, 2004). According to the 2001 Census, there are now around 1.6 million Muslims in the UK, representing 2.8% of the population. They live mostly in English towns, with smaller concentrations in Scotland and Wales, and 38% of all Muslims live in London (Office for National Statistics website: www.statistics.gov.uk). The community is diverse. About two thirds (67%) originate from the Indian subcontinent, mainly Pakistan and Bangladesh. Others include Arabs, Africans (especially from Somalia and Nigeria) and Europeans, mainly from Bosnia and Kosovo.

Collectively, Muslims are among Britain's most deprived communities, with the highest unemployment rates. At 14%, Muslim male unemployment was nearly three times the national average of 5% in 2004. Muslims also have the highest rate of economic inactivity. No less than 30% of Muslim men were economically inactive in 2004, compared with 16% of Christians and Hindus, and over two thirds of Muslim women (68%), more than double the rate for Christians (25%) and Hindus (33%) (ONS, 2004, p 14). Patricia Sellick (2004) illustrates the cumulative impact of Muslim deprivation by analysing Census data relating to children (see Table 3.1).

Such deprivation damages children's health and also their education. Overall, Muslims' educational attainments are below the national average. In 2003-04, Muslims were twice as likely as the rest of the working-age population to have no qualifications – 31% against 16% (ONS, 2004). Nevertheless, despite the difficulties, the examination results of Muslim schoolchildren are steadily improving and so the rising generation is developing a different educational profile from its parents (Cheesman, 2005a). Muslims under the age of 30 born in the

Table 3.1: Deprivation among Muslim children, 2001 (%)

Living in households with:	Muslim children	All children
No adults in employment	35	18
Overcrowded conditions	42	13
No central heating	13	6
No car or van	28	17

Source: Sellick (2004, pp 12, 13, 18)

UK are nearly twice as likely as those born overseas to have a degree or equivalent qualification – 18% against 10% (ONS, 2004).

Education is not a universal panacea. Racial discrimination inevitably holds Muslims back, whatever their qualifications. Black and minority ethnic people have to be better qualified than their white competitors to obtain the same jobs (Parekh, 2000). However, better qualifications do create opportunities. Education remains the best route out of poverty into higher career aspirations and higher incomes.

Although multiple deprivation restricts the options open to many Muslims, a national survey of housing association tenants in 2004 revealed a striking degree of optimism among the poorest households in the country. The Muslim respondents displayed remarkably high aspirations for home ownership. Whereas 70% of tenants overall said they aspired to remain in social housing in 10 years' time, this was the ambition of only 52% of Muslims. Nearly a third (29%) of Muslims wanted to own their own homes, compared to 13% of tenants overall. Tenants were asked to give reasons for their choices. Their preferences are ranked in Table 3.2.

The choices are significant because Islam stresses the importance of securing the future of the family. While other tenants put greater emphasis on the personal freedom and greater choice offered by

Table 3.2: Ranking of preferences for home ownership by tenants, 2004

Muslims	All tenants
1. Investment for the future	1. Greater freedom to choose location
2. Something to pass on to children	2. Investment for the future
3. Greater freedom to choose location	3. Something to pass on to children

Source: Cheesman (2005b)

home ownership, Muslims valued the family asset (Cheesman, 2005b). Although home ownership among Muslims nationally was, at 51% in 2001, far below the rate of 69% for the general population, banks are becoming alert to this emerging market, and have started offering Islamic finance products to target Muslims (Ainley et al, 2007). Banks follow demand. Muslim home ownership is likely to increase.

Meanwhile, Muslims account for 10% of the British restaurant trade. In the process they have restructured traditional British eating habits and South Asian cuisine has become a staple of the British diet. Almost all Britain's 9,500 'Indian' restaurants and take-aways are owned by Muslims, 85% by Bangladeshis. With an annual turnover of £3.2 billion, they directly employ 72,000 people along with 50,000 workers in supply and related industries (Cheesman, 2005a). To say that Muslims are outside the mainstream of British life is to ignore Britain's taste-buds and a significant part of its weekend culture. 'Indian' restaurants are found not only in cities but also in small towns and rural areas, alongside the pub and the church.

This is not the behaviour of a community sleepwalking into segregation. However, it may not lead to profound social interaction. Since Muslims do not drink alcohol, they do not participate in the British pub culture. The social focal point for men is often the mosque, where there are opportunities for discussion after prayers. Few women go to mosques, so they meet in each other's homes. The main forums for public mixing include the two religious Eid festivals, community events and the many weddings in a youthful community with a disproportionate number of young adults.

However, these events tend to be restricted to specific ethnic, linguistic or cultural groups: Pakistani, Bangladeshi, Nigerian, Somali and others. They do not usually extend to the wider Muslim community, still less non-Muslim society. Inter-marriage between Muslim communities is rare. Even many mosques cater primarily for specific communities, especially linguistic groups. Although standard prayers and recitations are always in Arabic, sermons, special prayers and public announcements use the *lingua franca* of the congregation: Urdu, Bengali, Gujarati, Somali and others. Muslims who do not speak the appropriate language may feel ill at ease. No statistics are maintained, but personal experience suggests that English-language mosques that cross community lines, welcoming white and African Caribbean converts, appear to be in the minority.

A dramatic manifestation of the lack of intra-Muslim cohesion in Britain comes during the holy month of Ramadan, when Muslims are obliged to fast from dawn to dusk. British Muslims cannot agree common dates for the start and finish of the month. Different communities take their lead from Pakistan, Bangladesh and Saudi Arabia. Inter-mosque attempts to set agreed dates have so far been shortlived. Each year, some Muslims are still fasting while others are celebrating the festival of *Eid-ul-Fitr.*

Like many other people in Britain, therefore, Muslims' primary social circles tend to lie within their ethnic or linguistic circles. Social interaction beyond these boundaries is limited, whether with Muslims or with non-Muslims. These communities of language, culture or ethnicity also form the basis for social and cultural conventions. Like Hindus and Sikhs from India and Christians from Africa, the building block of community life for most Muslims is the extended family, although this is adjusting to match British realities. Few now live in multi-generation households. Two thirds (65%) live in homes containing one family only, close to the national figure of 63% (Sellick, 2004). This reflects a desire for independence among younger Muslims. However, research among Bangladeshi and Pakistani families in Manchester found that, although they might not live as single households, the extended family structure was surviving. Instead of living all together in one overcrowded building, the family members bought or rented properties nearby, perhaps just a few houses away, so that they were close enough to provide mutual support and companionship (Karn et al, 1999), a pattern not made apparent through formal Census statistics.

Nevertheless the extended family is not universal. According to the 2001 Census, 12% of Muslim households are lone parents, slightly higher than the general figure of 10%. Most are women; widowed, separated or divorced, or refugees and asylum seekers who fled their countries alone. In 2003, no fewer than 53% of Somali households in Hackney were women bringing up children alone (Holman and Holman, 2003). Lone parents are an isolated and deprived section of Muslim society, which is often ignored because Muslim activists and policy makers alike focus on the extended family.

Another potential exception to the norm, which Muslims in general may not yet have confronted, is the likely future isolation of older people. This may seem surprising given the cultural and religious emphasis Muslims place on caring for older people. Respondents in Khanum et al's (2005) study of Birmingham expressed this through vehement opposition to sheltered housing. The attitude of a 25-year-old man was typical: 'I would not send my mother to a place like that. She looked after me for 25 years so it's only right I look after her. And Islamically it's not correct' (Khanum et al, 2005, p 36). This may be the ideal, but it can be difficult to maintain in a competitive society.

When they obtain work, children often have to move away from their parents.

Until now, Muslims have avoided this challenge. The Muslim community as a whole has the youngest age profile in Britain, with 34% of its members under 16 in 2001, compared with 20% of the wider population. The priority has been to support children and their parents and to educate young people. With only 3% of Muslims nationally aged 65 or over, compared with 16% of the general population, older Muslims are not prominent in official policy making. It is generally assumed that the families will provide but, as discussed above, this is not always so. Muslims, like other Britons, have problems and failings in supporting lone parents and ageing parents. None of this has anything to do with religion. These issues relate to the communities Muslims belong to, not their faith.

Nevertheless, there are experiences that transcend the divisions between Muslim communities, giving coherence and a sense of collective Muslim identity. The unemployment, overcrowding, and continuing discrimination faced by all minority ethnic communities are exacerbated by a British intellectual culture that often appears uncomfortable, first, with religious expression in general and nervous of Muslim religious expression in particular, and second, by an international Islamist intellectual culture that seeks to unite the disparate Muslim communities around a common political and religious agenda.

Islam, Christendom and identity

Religious minorities are sometimes awkwardly placed in a Europe whose cultural assumptions have been shaped by Christianity. The position of Muslims is complicated by centuries of mutual suspicion. A global attitudes survey (Pew Research Center, 2006) indicated a dispiriting worldwide consensus that relations between Muslims and Westerners were generally poor (see Figure 3.1).

The similarity of opinion between Muslims and the majority populations in Europe was striking. Nearly two thirds of respondents, across all countries, believed the situation was bad. The study found that, while non-Muslims believed that Muslims were, in order of frequency, fanatical, violent and arrogant, Muslims believed that Westerners were selfish, arrogant and violent – almost a mirror image. This reflects an ancient divide. As Hourami (1991, p 7) explained, 'From the time it first appeared, the religion of Islam was a problem for Christian Europe. Those who believed in it were the enemy on the frontier'.

Figure 3.1: Views on relations between 'the West' and Muslims, 2006 (%)

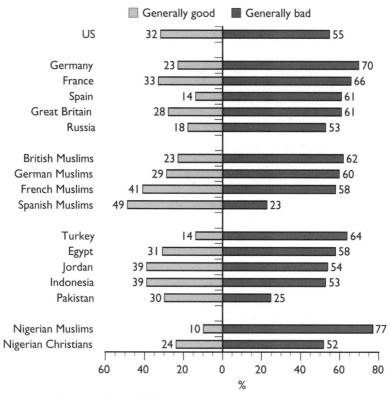

Source: Pew Research Center (2006)

Over the centuries, Muslims and European Christians have played the role of the 'external other' for each other, the aliens against whom they defined who they were not. Europe's identity has been constructed through myths of 'the clash of civilisations and the exclusion of the Other' (Micheau and Senlac, 2006). While large minorities of Christians and Jews remained in the Middle East after the arrival of Islam, in Europe geography and religion were almost contiguous: to the north and west, the natural barriers of the Arctic and the Atlantic; to the south and east, Muslims and trouble; in between, Europe itself ... and Christendom.

In a continent plagued by religious schism, war and persecution, antagonism towards non-Christians was often Europeans' sole point of agreement. Europe has for centuries been almost universally Christian. Small minorities of Jews and Muslims in Eastern Europe merely proved the point. This history still shapes current views. Between a quarter and a third of respondents to a survey in 2007 agreed that the European Union (EU) was a Christian club; from 23% in Britain to 35% in France and Germany (Harris Poll Global Omnibus Pan Euro, 2007). During 2002-04, several governments campaigned for a reference to Europe's 'Christian heritage' to be inserted into the European Constitution. The idea that Europe and Christendom are synonymous is not dead.

An ill-defined historical memory of Muslims as the enemy at the gates, updated by the fear of terrorism after 9/11 and the various terrorist atrocities and threats in Europe, provides the cultural template of 'the West' at odds with Islam, one that sustains contemporary tabloid perceptions of Muslims as fanatics and potential terrorists. In the past, they were safely on the other side of the map. Now, they are in the European heartland.

One other religion, of course, has a similarly uncomfortable special status in European consciousness – Judaism. While Muslims performed the role of the 'external other', Jews were Europe's 'internal other', the only significant non-Christian minority in most European countries until the mid-20th century. It is no coincidence that it was a Jewish group, its antennae sensitised by centuries of persecution, which first drew public attention to the importance of Islamophobia in Britain. Thus, a Commission established by the Runnymede Trust in 1994 to investigate anti-Semitism recommended a similar examination of Islamophobia. The report of the Commission on British Muslims and Islamophobia concluded that: 'The expression of anti-Muslim ideas and sentiments is becoming increasingly seen as respectable' (Runnymede Trust, 1997, p 10).

A later review of discrimination and Islamophobia across Europe by the European Monitoring Centre on Racism and Xenophobia (EUMC) came to the same conclusion. Islam was commonly perceived as 'primitive, backward and inferior', and 'the construction of a European identity that marginalised or rendered invisible the contribution of Islamic society and culture to world civilisation provided a powerful ideological underpinning to current expressions of Islamophobia' (Choudhury et al, 2006, p 43).

Much the same could be said about the position of black and minority ethnic communities in general across Europe, often finding themselves on the receiving end of a stubbornly persistent Eurocentric worldview that excludes them from 'civilisation'. As the EUMC indicated, Islamophobia can act as a surrogate for old-fashioned racism: 'Racism, xenophobia and Islamophobia become mutually reinforcing phenomena and hostility against Muslims should also be seen in the context of a more general climate of hostility towards migrants and minorities' (EUMC, 2006, p 19).

Islamophobia and racism are inextricably entwined. The proportion of white Muslims is negligible. Almost all are from Asia, the Middle East and Africa. Many are refugees and asylum seekers. There is a strong correlation between Islam and ethnicity across contemporary Europe. Since straightforward racism is presently much less publicly acceptable, some far-Right organisations focus on Muslims rather than other minority groups, while some liberals find in Islamophobia an outlet for repressed chauvinism. When in 2005 the *Jyllands-Posten* newspaper used freedom of speech to justify its publication of cartoons of the Prophet Muhammad, this could be seen as the white liberal establishment asserting its freedom over one of the most marginalised sections of Danish society. If the caricatures had been racist instead of Islamophobic, this excuse would not have been entertained. Europe's religious prejudices have yet to be confronted in the way that Eurocentric assumptions that fostered racism were challenged in the 1960s and 1970s.

Like racism, Islamophobia can be measured on the streets. The victims of racially motivated crimes are disproportionately Bangladeshis and Pakistanis (Clancy et al, 2001). When housing association tenants were surveyed in 2004, 8.9% of Muslims said that they had been physically assaulted, mugged or robbed, or suffered abuse or harassment over the previous year. If the impetus was purely racial, one would have expected other black and minority ethnic tenants to report similar experiences – but the figures were only 3.5% for Black Caribbeans and 1.5% for Hindus (Cheesman, 2005b).

However, Islamophobia does not express itself mainly through active violence but more subtly. Allen (2001) conducted a review of Islamophobia in the media in which he found that 'Islam is commonly interpreted … as being retrogressively backward and unidimensional; inherently separate and other to the West; the perpetual and inferior enemy to modernisation and Western values; and manipulative as an ideology solely to oppress and control'.

In 2007, a Harris omnibus poll asked respondents in five European countries whether there was any contradiction between being Muslim and a citizen of their country. Reassuringly, the majority felt there was not, but it was hardly a ringing endorsement. The lowest approval rate (59%) was in Britain, the highest (80%) in France. British acceptance of Muslims was especially grudging, with nearly one third (29%) of respondents prepared to state positively that being Muslim was incompatible with being British and a further 13% unsure. The lowest negative response came from France (14%, with 6% undecided) but even this suggests that over 10% of the population believe Muslims cannot truly be French citizens (Harris Poll Global Omnibus Pan Euro, 2007). In 2003, no less than 62% of French people said that Islamic values were not compatible with the values of the Republic. By contrast, 78% of French Muslims thought they were compatible (Ipsos-LCI-LePont, 2003). Such attitudes impede Muslims' sense of belonging to Europe.

Young Muslims interviewed in 2001 complained that 'they were constantly viewed as foreigners and had difficulties fitting in as they feel they are not accepted' (Anon, 2002, p 43). They felt that 'their status as British Muslims was not accepted by many non-Muslims' (p 47). Some turn instead to the *umma*, the worldwide Muslim community. A Policy Exchange study in 2007 (Mirza et al, 2007) found nearly a third of Muslims (31%) willing to agree that 'I feel more in common with Muslims in other countries than I do with non-Muslims in Britain'. The majority (59%) disagreed, but there was an important generational divide. Only 20% of Muslims aged 55+ said they did not have as much in common with non-Muslims as with Muslims but, for 16- to 24-year-olds, the proportion was 33%. In 2006, Muslims were asked whether they felt that Britain was 'my country or their country'. Only 55% of those aged 45+ answered 'my country,' and the response was even lower – 44% – among 18- to 24-year-olds (Mirza et al, 2007, pp 38-9).

As the younger generations born and brought up in Britain feel more distant from the heritage countries of their parents, they find that Islam 'can give them a sense of belonging, which neither Britain nor their parental homeland provides' (Mirza et al, 2007, p 32). They challenge both the received wisdom of their parents and the conventions of British society, turning away from a British society that they feel consigns them to unemployment, suspicion and poor housing. They see the ethnic divisions among Muslims, with segregated mosques and arguments over the dates of Ramadan, as a mark of degeneration and often put the blame specifically on their heritage cultures, which they feel have corrupted Islam. Many study Islam enthusiastically, trying to find a purer version of the religion that can overcome these divisions.

This quest for religious purity frequently leads to the portfolio of ideas that has come to be known as Islamism. This is not the place to discuss the range of Islamist thought, which Kepel (2004) describes as a corpus of doctrines, but also a set of attitudes and behaviour. The common thread is concern that corruption, superstition and intellectual confusion have contaminated Muslim beliefs and practices over the centuries, leaving societies weak, degenerate and prey to non-Muslim domination. The solution is a *jihad* (struggle) to recapture the straightforward piety of the *al-salaf al-salih*, the Companions of the Prophet, in the earliest days of Islam. The most influential group of *salafists* form the dominant theological voice in Saudi Arabia, inspired by the 18th-century Arab preacher, *Abd al-Wahhab*. As custodians of the holy cities of Makkah and Madina, they have a uniquely authoritative international status. El Fadl (2004) comments on the simplicity, decisiveness and incorruptibility of the religious thought of *Abd al-Wahhab*. These qualities appeal strongly to young people looking for straight answers in a complex world.

Salafist thinking gets a political edge from two 20th-century movements: the Society of Muslim Brothers, founded in Egypt in 1928; and the Jamaat-e-Islami, founded in Lahore (then British India, now Pakistan) in 1941. Established under European colonial rule, both highlighted the removal of colonialism and its local allies as the essential first step towards the creation of a just Islamic society. With the retreat of Empire, their critique has extended to the wider Western hegemony and the nationalist and secular Muslim governments on which it depends. Contemporary Islamist suspicion of 'the West' (however defined) forms part of a longstanding continuum of rejection of 'Western' interference in the Muslim world.

The most common way for young Muslims to mark adherence to the universal *umma* is the wearing of Arab-style dress, to assert independence both from their ethnic backgrounds and their Western upbringing. Young men wear robes and beards. Young women put on the *hijab* (headscarf). In 2004, a British schoolgirl demanded the right to wear a *jilbab* (an Arab robe) at school. She and her supporters saw it as a culturally neutral, Islamic garment. By contrast, the *shalwar kamiz* (tunic and trousers) of the school uniform reflected South Asian culture and was non-Islamic, favoured by Hindus and Sikhs as well as Muslims (Cheesman, 2005a). In insisting on the *jilbab*, she was not simply asserting her rights as a Muslim; she was also rejecting the traditions of her own community. This is an example of local action aimed at promoting Islamist standards among Muslims. Other *salafists* tackle poverty and injustice and many try to influence governments. These are all different forms of *jihad*.

For a small minority, *jihad* is interpreted exclusively as murderous campaigns to overthrow corrupt (in effect, all) Muslim governments, destroy Western power and influence, and re-establish a Caliphate to lead the Islamic world. It may just be a sinister handful, but its impact is disproportionate. The attitudes that motivated the British Muslim suicide bombers of 7 July 2005 present a challenge to both Muslims and society at large. Although their actions are often perceived by Muslims and non-Muslims alike as anti-Western, *salafism* is essentially about Islam. Events such as the assassination of Benazir Bhutto confirm that terrorism poses the most direct threat to political stability in the Muslim world. In Britain, the constitutional, as opposed to personal, dangers of violent terrorism are less immediate. It is community cohesion that is at risk, not the political system.

The British state has a perplexing record of sustaining the opponents of cohesion. Bright has argued that many British Muslims feel excluded by the government's preoccupation with Islamists (Bright, 2004). The failure to take action against demonstrators inciting the murder of Salman Rushdie in 1988 fostered the impression that extreme and even violent expressions of opinion were tolerated by the government and encouraged in the interests of sensationalism by the media. Mainstream Muslim concerns were confirmed in 1998, when the police refused to intervene in support of the Finsbury Park Mosque Committee after they were ejected from the premises by the extremist preacher, Abu Hamza, and his associates. The congregation who had founded the mosque were forced to pray elsewhere while he and his supporters proceeded to use it as a recruiting base (Thomas, 2003). It took the shock of the 7 July 2005 bombings to jolt the public authorities out of their complacency and the police at last closed down Abu Hamza's operation. Meanwhile, he had been a familiar figure on television and radio, popular with the media as a suitably ferocious 'representative' of Islam.

Wild-eyed chauvinists provide good copy and the Muslim community is deprived of a voice, shouted down by the raucous cries of those claiming to speak in its name. As Sami Yusuf, a British Muslim popular singer, expressed it, 'Abu Hamza, and Abu this and Abu that – they don't represent us. They can go back to wherever they came from, frankly…. I'm scared of the guy with the hook – I mean, who is he?' (Edemariam, 2007).

Nevertheless, it is from the small pool of extremists that the media customarily seeks Muslim spokespeople. Meanwhile, it is not yet clear whether the British government's lassitude in addressing intimidating extremist views has changed.

Secularism, ethnicity and religion

Those such as Abu Hamza reinforce the stereotype of the Muslim as fanatic. This in turn reinforces secular dislike of religious expression in general. The original hostility towards Islam in European culture may have been born from Christian antagonism. However, the strongest antagonism towards Islam does not necessarily come from Christians, who may find fellow-feeling with believers from other religions, but from those who identify themselves as secular. Thus, the main impulse was, and certainly has become, secular, stemming from wider issues of identity, not theology.

Europeans have a complex, often contradictory, attitude towards the public expression of religion. Most claim adherence to Christianity of some sort, but religion is kept out of the public space. Britain is constitutionally a theocracy, yet its public culture is so aggressively secular that Tony Blair as Prime Minister was not prepared to admit he had prayed with George Bush (Harris, 2003). Few European politicians invoke God during elections. This is a striking contrast to the rest of the world, including the US. In Europe, the public space tends to be dominated by the secular, the sceptical, even the anti-clerical.

However, this is largely a debate within the white majority in Europe. The cultural gap in Britain was illustrated by the 2001 Census. While Muslims may, at 2.7%, have been the largest religious minority, the largest minority faith group was formed by those with no religion (15.6%). They outnumbered all non-Christian minorities combined by a factor of nearly three. No more than 3.1 million people (5%) professed a religion other than Christianity, but 9.1 million people said they had no religion. Beyond this 'committed' non-religious group there is a wider hinterland of agnosticism and doubt.

The contrast with Britain's wider range of ethno-religious communities is striking. All minority communities delineated in the Census except the Chinese displayed a lower level of religious disbelief than the white British (see Table 3.3). The Chinese exception arises partly because many consider Confucianism to be a philosophy rather than a religion.

The scale of disbelief among the white British is perhaps less than one might have expected given the strength of secular public culture, but the contrast with the near unanimity of belief among Asians illustrates the relative importance the minority communities attach to religion as a public statement. A study of young Bangladeshi women in 2001 found that almost all 'defined themselves first and foremost in terms of their religion' (Khanum, 2002, p 35). In 2007, no fewer than

Table 3.3: Proportion of ethnic group with no religion, 2001 (%)

Ethnic group	%
Bangladeshi	0.4
Pakistani	0.5
Indian	1.7
Irish	6.3
African	8.1
Black Caribbean	11.2
White British	15.4
Chinese	52.5

Source: Office for National Statistics website: www.statistics.gov.uk

86% of Muslims agreed with the statement, 'My religion is the most important thing in my life', compared with only 11% of the general population of Britain (Mirza et al, 2007). When respondents to the Home Office's 2001 Citizenship Survey (O'Beirne, 2004) ranked factors that contributed towards their identity, all ethnic groups placed family first. Asians placed religion second and black people third. White people placed religion last, in tenth place. When the responses were analysed by religion, omitting those identifying as 'non-believers', Christians and Muslims again placed family first. However, whereas Muslims placed religion second, Christians placed it seventh. Since 92% of the Christians, but only 1% of the Muslims in the sample, were white British, this reflected differences in attitudes across the communities (O'Beirne, 2004). Religion comes lower down the scale of priorities even for white people who consider themselves Christian.

Steve Bruce (2002) argues that this represents indifference towards religious ideas. But it goes deeper than that. A 2006 Guardian/ICM poll (Glover and Topping, 2006) found that no fewer than 82% of British people considered religion to be 'a cause of division and tension'. This reflects mainstream European thinking. El Yazami (2005, p 88), analysing secularism in France, commented that:

> Believers or not, almost all Europeans are convinced that religion and politics should not … encroach upon their respective fields: to politics the public space, to religion the private space. Respecting these differences has brought long-lasting peace to relationships which in the past were often in conflict. (El Yazami, 2005, p 88)

Europe's history of religious persecution has been overcome through a secular consensus that confines religion to the privacy of the home and the church or chapel, where it can cause no offence and provoke no bloodshed. David Hume's condemnation in 1742 of 'the deluded fanatic' peddling 'religious enthusiasm' still stands (Hume, 1742). Preston updated Hume in 2007 when he highlighted British fears of 'the spectre of all this stuff turning too serious'. He explained: 'Benign agnosticism finds it hard to pick many fights. We 40 million or so in the muddling middle are a positive advertisement for just jogging along, not getting over-excited' (Preston, 2007).

Many members of Britain's minority ethnic groups are not included in this '40 million of us'. When people from the traditional societies of Africa and Asia meet someone with strong religious convictions, of whatever faith, they are inclined to see this person as one to be admired. Other Britons are inclined to see overexcitement and, potentially, Hume's 'deluded fanatic'.

The Rushdie affair of 1988 embroiled Muslims in a longrunning argument with secularists. Riots involving minority ethnic communities earlier in that decade caused a policeman's death, many injuries and extensive property damage. Yet these riots, which were not perceived as having religious causation, were widely recognised as expressing legitimate grievances, notably in the Scarman report of 1982 (Scarman, 1982). There was no comparable understanding of the grievances underlying the Rushdie agitation. Bloody secular protest provoked sympathy, whereas the language of violent religious protest provoked enmity. Modood (2000, p 52) identifies the beginning of an intellectual rift between Muslims and secularists: 'the Rushdie Affair very clearly demonstrated that the group in British society most politically opposed to (politicised) Muslims were neither Christians, nor even right-wing nationalists, but the secular, liberal intelligentsia'. This 'liberal intelligentsia' determines policy, edits newspapers, runs television channels, and sets the national agenda. It also matches the profile of non-religious respondents in the Home Office Citizenship Survey: 'Respondents without a religion tended to be white, aged 25-49, hold the highest qualifications and were employed in professional or managerial occupations' (O'Beirne, 2004, p 15).

Two surveys of housing association tenants and staff in 2004 corroborate this picture. Figure 3.2 shows the respondents who professed a religion or declined to answer in the two surveys and the 2001 Census. Religious belief is revealed as the faith that dare not speak its name. Nearly 80% of tenants and the general population professed a religion of some kind. Among housing association staff, by contrast,

Figure 3.2: Religious belief among housing association tenants and staff, 2004

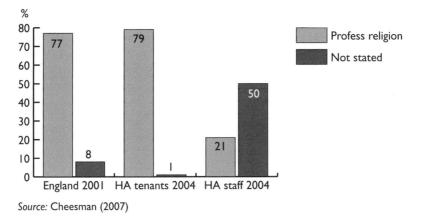

Source: Cheesman (2007)

only half were prepared to answer the question at all. Of these, less than half admitted to having a religion, so that even among respondents the rate of belief was low. With half the staff unwilling to answer and only a fifth professing any religion, it seems that housing associations operate within an uncompromisingly secular culture (Cheesman, 2007).

These findings raise uncomfortable questions about the capacity of secular policy makers and service providers to respond to and address the concerns of communities for whom religion is a fundamental feature of their lives. Modood (1999, p 265) argues that 'Most theorists of difference and multiculturism exhibit very little sympathy for religious groups ... and there is usually a presumption in favour of secularism'. His argument finds support in a review of faith communities conducted for the Office of the Deputy Prime Minister (ODPM) in 2006. This set out a formula for taking the faith out of religion:

> Over the past fifty years, the discourse in Britain about 'racialised minorities' has mutated from 'colour' in the 1950s and 1960s, to 'race' in the 1960s, 70s and 80s to 'ethnicity' in the 90s and to 'religion' in the present time. This focus on religion has been driven by international events which have highlighted the political demands associated with religious movements and by an increasing recognition by academics, policy-makers and service-providers of the importance of religion in defining identity, particularly among minority communities. (Beckford et al, 2006, p 11)

The ODPM review approached religion solely as a means of defining identity, although only for certain groups of recent settlers, since it confined itself to the Hindu, Muslim and Sikh religions, which it idiosyncratically describes as 'emerging faiths'. For the civil servants who commissioned the research and the academics who conducted it, religion was just a means of classification.

Paradoxically, this philosophy brings religion to the forefront for it sets the terms of grant aid from central and local government. Where public money leads, cash-strapped community organisations follow. They inevitably emphasise their religious commitment if it increases their chance of funding. Similarly, banks, government departments and local authorities reinforce stereotypes of religious identity in promotional material illustrating diversity: for example, women in *hijabs* representing Muslims. In this way, the most secular section of society – the white middle-class professional – undermines the secular consensus by encouraging the public affirmation of religious beliefs and promoting conformity to religious stereotypes. Those who dislike public displays of faith may respond with what one commentator has described as 'combative secularism' (Lorcerie, 2005). Secular-minded people who are at ease with Pakistanis or Bangladeshis can feel awkward when confronted by Muslims. The secular consensus may not provide a neutral public space for religions in Britain.

Conclusion

The Muslim communities are among the most deprived in Britain. The racial discrimination they encounter as black and Asian people is universally condemned, but there is sometimes ambiguity about the Islamophobia they encounter as Muslims. The development of a more cohesive society concerns community as well as religion. People divide themselves on ethnic, cultural, class and linguistic grounds and these can present more barriers than faith. However, the experience of the debates on race equality might offer pointers to the development of multi-faith discourse. During the 1970s recognition grew that racial prejudice was ingrained in British culture and demanded confrontation. Many white people recognised and addressed prejudice in themselves and others, creating the conditions for non-judgemental discussion. Perhaps understandably, the process was limited by its preoccupation with white racism, leaving prejudice unchallenged within other communities.

Applying these lessons to inter-faith dialogue implies recognition that Britain's heritage is Christian and largely Protestant, and that this shapes attitudes towards religion generally and other religions in particular. Most British people are rooted in Judaeo-Christian values and traditions, whether they are practising Christians or not. Unless this is recognised, other religions are stranded on the periphery. This is especially important, and probably especially difficult, for those non-religious people who believe themselves to be above the religious fray. At the same time, each religion or belief, including atheism and agnosticism, must recognise and come to terms with the intolerance, bigotry and persecution in its own tradition so that all can approach the other, with suitable humility, willing to work together to address past and present antagonisms and injustices. As the Archbishop of Canterbury reflected in his much misquoted speech at the Royal Courts of Justice on 7 February 2008: 'We need a fair amount of "deconstruction" of crude oppositions and mythologies' (Williams, 2008).

In developing a neutral public space for religious debate, government and public agencies should reconsider the wisdom of bringing personal faith into the public arena by treating it simply as a label for grant aid and specific policy development. Faith is more than a taxonomic 'identity'. It is not possible to tick the box and put the file back into a drawer. In any case, there is a contradiction between maintaining that faith is private, and then adopting policies that encourage people to assert their religious identities.

The development of an inclusive dialogue on faith would promote better relations between Muslims and the rest of society. Fortunately, despite many challenges, including Islamist terrorism, day-to-day inter-communal relations are generally good. Muslims are found in the mainstream of British society in an increasing range of roles and careers, encouraging promise for future community cohesion.

Finally, perhaps one of the signs frequently interpreted as an indication of Muslim separatism may be the opposite: the trend to 'look' Muslim, by wearing beards and 'Islamic' dress. This development may be read as a signal of increasing self-assurance whereas conformity to wide popular culture may be a sign of insecurity. Displaying individuality is a way of asserting that one belongs. Britain's long record of maintaining liberty and political stability in the face of social, economic and industrial upheavals has been achieved not by imposing uniformity, but by absorbing a multiplicity of ideas, values and outlooks.

References

Ainley, M., Mashayekhi, A., Hicks, R., Rahman, A. and Ravalia, A. (2007) *Islamic finance in the UK: Regulation and challenges*, London: Financial Services Authority.

Allen, C. (2001) 'Islamophobia in the media since September 11th', Paper presented to the conference 'Exploring Islamophobia', University of Westminster, 29 September.

Anon (2002) 'British Muslim youth survey', *New Impact*, vol 8, no 3, October/November, pp 42-5.

Ansari, H. (2004) *'The infidel within': Muslims in Britain since 1800*, London: Hurst.

BBC (2004) 'Born abroad: an immigration map of Britain', Research undertaken by the Institute of Public Policy Research and the University of Sheffield, http://news.bbc.co.uk/1/shared/spl/hi/uk/05/born_abroad/html/overview.stm

Beckford, J.A., Gale, R., Owen, D., Peach, C. and Weller, P. (2006) *Review of the evidence base on faith communities*, London: Office of the Deputy Prime Minister.

Bright, M. (2004) *When progressives treat with reactionaries: The British state's flirtation with radical Islam*, London: The Policy Exchange.

Bruce, S. (2002) *God is dead: Secularization in the West*, London: Blackwell.

Cantle, T. (2001) *Community cohesion: A report of the independent review team*, London: Home Office.

Carling, A. (2008) 'The curious case of the mis-claimed myth claims: ethnic segregation, polarisation and the future of Bradford, *Urban Studies*, vol 45, no 3, pp 553-89.

Cheesman, D. (2005a) 'British Muslims: migration, settlement and identity', *Journal of the Asiatic Society of Bangladesh*, vol 50, pp 552-53.

Cheesman, D. (2005b) *Muslim tenants in housing associations: Feedback and engagement*, London: The Housing Corporation.

Cheesman, D. (2007) 'The margins of public space – Muslims and social housing in England', *People, Place & Policy Online*, vol 1, no 1, pp 39-46.

Choudhury, T., Azis, M., Izzidien, D., Khreeji, I. and Hussain, D. (2006) *Perceptions of discrimination and Islamophobia*, Vienna: European Monitoring Centre on Racism and Xenophobia.

Clancy, A., Hough, M., Aust, R. and Kershaw, C. (2001) *Crime, policing and criminal justice: The experience of ethnic minorities – findings from the 2000 British Crime Survey*, London: Home Office.

Commission on Integration and Cohesion (2007) *Our shared future*, London: Commission on Integration and Cohesion.

Edemariam, A. (2007) 'Muslim superstar', *The Guardian*, 5 November.

El Fadl, K.A. (2004) 'The ugly modern and the modern ugly: reclaiming the beautiful in Islam', in O. Safi (ed) *Progressive Muslims*, Oxford: Oneworld, pp 33-77.

El Yazami, D. (2005) 'Une exception française à l'épreuve', in Commission Islam et Laïcité, *1905–2005: Les enjeux de la laïcité*, Paris: L'Harmattan.

EUMC (European Monitoring Centre on Racism and Xenophobia) (2006) *Muslims in the European Union: Discrimination and Islamophobia*, Vienna: EUMC.

Glover, J. and Topping, A. (2006) 'Religion does more harm than good - poll', *The Guardian*, 23 December.

Harris, P. (2003) 'Bush says God chose him to lead his nation', *The Observer*, 2 November.

Harris Poll Global Omnibus Pan Euro (2007), www.harrisinteractive.com

Holman, C. and Holman, N. (2003) *First steps in a new country: Baseline indicators for the Somali community in LB Hackney*, London: Sahil Housing Association.

Hourami, A. (1991) *Islam in European thought*, Cambridge: Cambridge University Press.

Hume, D. (1742) 'Of superstition and enthusiasm', in J. Fieser (ed) (1995) *The writings of David Hume*, Internet Release, www.sacredtexts.com

Ipsos-LCI-LePont (2003) 'Islam, intégration, immigration: l'opinion des français', www.ipsos.fr

Karn, V., Mian, S., Brown, M. and Dale, A. (1999) *Tradition, change and diversity: Understanding the housing needs of minority ethnic groups in Manchester*, London: The Housing Corporation.

Kepel, G. (2004) *The war for Muslim minds: Islam and the west*, Cambridge, MA, and London: Harvard University Press.

Khanum, N. (2002) *Resilient spirits: The needs and aspirations of young Bangladeshi women in Luton*, Luton: Equality in Diversity.

Khanum, N., Blackaby, B., Begum, S. and Miah, J. (2005) 'Aston Pride Bangladeshi Housing Study', Birmingham: Birmingham City Council, Unpublished.

Lorcerie, F. (2005) 'Islam, laïcité, integration: l'école sans boussole', in Commission Islam et Laïcité, *Islam de France, Islams d'Europe*, Paris: L'Harmattan, pp 15-34.

Micheau, F. and Senlac, P. (2006) 'La bataille de Poitiers, de la réalité au mythe', in M. Arkoun (ed) *Histoire d'Islam et des Musulmans en France*, Paris: Albin Michel.

Mirza, M., Senthilkumaran, A. and Ja'far, Z. (2007) *Living together apart: British Muslims and the paradox of multiculturalism*, London: The Policy Exchange.

Modood, T. (1999) *Ethnic diversity and public policy in Britain,* ESRC Award R000222124: End of Award Report, Bristol: University of Bristol.

Modood, T. (2000) 'La place des musulmans dans le multiculturalisme laïque en Grande-Bretagne', *Social Compass*, vol 47, no 1, p 52.

Nazir-Ali, M. (2008) 'Extremism flourished as UK lost Christianity', *The Daily Telegraph*, 11 January.

O'Beirne, M. (2004) *Religion in England and Wales: Findings from the 2001 Home Office Citizenship Survey*, London: Home Office.

ONS (Office for National Statistics) (2004) *Focus on religion*, London: ONS.

Ouseley, H. (2001) *Community pride not prejudice: Making diversity work in Bradford*, Bradford: Bradford Vision.

Parekh, B. (2000) *The future of multi-ethnic Britain*, London: Runnymede Trust.

Pew Research Center (2006) 'The great divide: how Westerners and Muslims view each other', http://pewglobal.org/reports

Phillips, D., Butt, F. and Davis, C. (2002) 'The racialisation of space in Bradford', *The Regional Review*, July, pp 9–10.

Phillips, T. (2005) 'After 7/7: sleepwalking to segregation', 22 September, http://83.137.212.42/sitearchive/cre

Preston, P. (2007) 'A lofty conversion', *The Guardian*, 24 December.

Runnymede Trust (1997) *Islamophobia: A challenge of us all*, London: Runnymede Trust.

Scarman, L.G. (1982) *The Brixton disorders, 10–12 April 1981: A report of an inquiry*, Cmnd 8427, London: HMSO.

Sellick, P (2004) *Muslim housing experiences*, London: The Housing Corporation.

Simpson, L. (2004) 'Statistics of racial segregation: measures, evidence and policy', *Urban Studies*, vol 41, no 3, pp 661–81.

Thomas, D. (2003) *Le Londonistan: La voix du djihad*, Paris: Michalon.

Williams, R. (2008) *Archbishop's lecture – civil and religious law in England: A religious perspective*, 7 February, www.archbishopofcanterbury.org/1575

How participation changes things: 'inter-faith', 'multi-faith' and a new public imaginary

Paul Weller

Widening circles of engagement: context, definitions and scope

In recent decades the 'religious landscape' of the UK has changed significantly, as has the approach of government to religions. Especially at local and regional levels, government and other public bodies have become engaged with inter-faith initiatives, organisations and structures that have the contribution of religions to public life and civic society as a central part of their rationale.

It was argued in *Time for a change: Reconfiguring religion, state and society* (Weller, 2005a p 73) that the UK's 'religious landscape' has become increasingly 'three-dimensional' and is now 'exhibiting contours that are Christian, secular and religiously plural'. Each of these dimensions is contextually important in achieving an appropriate and balanced public policy understanding of the religious situation in the UK, including the emergence and role of inter-faith and multi-faith initiatives.

These initiatives are known by a variety of names. Exploration of this terminology can assist an understanding of the 'inter-faith' and 'multi-faith' initiatives that are the focus of this chapter. Thus,

> When a society or an event or a project is described as 'multi-faith', it usually means that it includes a variety of religious groups. While the use of '*multi*-faith' highlights variety, use of the term '*inter*-faith' points more to the relationships *between* religions and the people who belong to them.... The term 'inter-religious' is occasionally used interchangeably with 'inter-faith' ... 'inter-religious' can sometimes be used in ways that denote the simple state of encounter between different religions in a religiously

plural context, whereas 'inter-faith' tends to be used in circumstances which involve 'dialogue' between the religions and the faiths. The unhyphenated term 'interfaith' is found but some prefer to avoid this for fear of giving the impression of a movement that blurs the distinctiveness of the religions involved. (Weller, 2001, p 80)

The names of these organised initiatives, such as the descriptors of 'group', 'council' or 'forum', often reflect how their participants understand their aims and objectives. Thus, 'group' in the title, as in the Derby Multi-Faith Group, can indicate a more informal style of organisation and individual basis of membership rather than an attempt to be a more 'representative' body. By contrast, 'council' in the title is generally indicative of something more 'organised', a project that attempts to achieve a 'balanced' representation between the principal religious traditions. Initiatives of this kind also often tend to direct a major part of their work to the interface with wider public life. This is also the case with regard to the increasing number of inter-religious initiatives at both local and regional levels that are known as 'forums' of faiths. Such forums have emerged in response to an attempt on the part of local, regional and national government to connect with religious organisations and communities as potential partners in service delivery and policy implementation.

Beyond this, there are what might be called more 'structural' initiatives, among which can be numbered the Faith Communities Consultative Council, formed in 2006, which acts as an interface between faith community representatives, government ministers and civil servants across a range of mutual concerns and issues.

The fourth edition of the Inter Faith Network for the UK's directory of inter-faith organisations in the UK recorded 25 inter-faith organisations operating at the national level within the UK (Inter Faith Network for the UK, 2007). Many of these organisations are, in principle, UK-wide in scope. But, following the devolution of governance in the UK, they also include the Scottish Inter Faith Council, the Inter Faith Council for Wales/Cyngor Rhyng-greyfyddol Cymru, and a Northern Ireland Inter-Faith Forum. In England, in all regions except the North East, regional faith fora have emerged to engage in relationships with the structures of regional assemblies, regional development agencies and other regional bodies, while there are also a number of other regional inter-faith initiatives.

The directory of inter-faith organisations in the UK also lists details of 207 local inter-faith group initiatives (excluding local groups linked to the Council of Christians and Jews or the Three Faiths Forum). These include 10 in Scotland, three in Wales and one in Northern Ireland. For England, there are details of 193 groups, including 38 in London, 30 in the North West, 30 in the South East, 22 in Yorkshire and Humberside, 19 in the West Midlands, 17 in the South West, 15 in the East of England, 15 in the East Midlands and seven in the North East. Ten other local groups are also listed as being 'under development'.

While some of these initiatives is that, while some had already been engaged at the interface between religion and public life without any official incentive, in other (and particularly more recent) cases, they have been 'called into existence' by public policy developments. This highlights critical questions concerning the relationship between the proper autonomy and self-organisation of religious (including inter-faith) groups involved with public bodies, and the policy imperatives of public funding.

Although diverse, inter-faith and multi-faith initiatives can be broadly seen in terms of individual or group-based inclusiveness in relation to people of diverse backgrounds, orientations and commitments on matters of religion and belief. Such initiatives can be 'one-off' gestures that seek to reach out and create a bridge of communication across divisions rooted in theology and history. Initiatives of this kind can have a 'symbolic effect' that has both influence and impact beyond the limited scope of the original action. But the focus of this chapter is on inter-faith and multi-faith initiatives that are more persistent in time and space, especially those that also contribute to the wider societal context of 'inter-religious relations', understood as broader in scope and effect than initiatives to do with inter-faith dialogue as more narrowly conceived.

On the periphery: early modern inter-faith initiatives

In order to achieve a better understanding of inter-faith initiatives, the contemporary pattern of such inter-faith initiatives must be set within the wider inheritance of inter-faith developments (see Braybrooke, 1980). Between the early 20th century and the opening years of the 21st organisations seeking to work across the religions have moved from a socially and religiously peripheral position to a more 'mainstream' one.

Modern organised inter-faith initiatives generally began at international rather than national or local levels. For example, the World Parliament of Religions (see Barrows, 1893) was held in Chicago in 1893, and the First International Assembly of the World Fellowship of

Faiths (see Weller, 1936) was held also in Chicago during its second World's Fair in 1933. One of the earliest initiatives in the UK was the Religions of the Empire Conference, organised by Sir Denison Ross and held in conjunction with the 1924 British Empire Exhibition (Hare, 1925). In 1936, Sir Francis Younghusband convened the World Congress of Faiths (see Millard, 1937), which then established itself as an ongoing inter-faith organisation that continues its work to the present day (see Inter Faith Network for the UK, 2007).

These early initiatives illustrate one of the unintended by-products of colonial and imperial projects: they became catalysts for a growth in consciousness about religious diversity and plurality and their related challenges. Thus, a significant number of colonial administrators, members of the imperial armed forces and Christian missionaries contributed to the dissemination in the UK of the texts, ideas and beliefs of a variety of religions. Several of these individuals also became leading personalities in one or more of the early inter-faith initiatives.

Although many of these initiatives were important and pioneering, they usually remained peripheral to government, the wider society and the 'mainstream' religious groups. This is because, until comparatively recently, the 'religious landscape' of the UK was much less religiously plural than today. Eventually, however, the Empire 'came home', with substantial migration to the UK of people of other-than-Christian religions from former colonies. The ensuing social diversity was initially seen in terms of the categories of 'race' and 'ethnicity' and comparatively little account was taken of the specificities of religious difference.

However, as these migrant groups developed into settled communities, the significance and challenge of increased diversity, initially in terms of 'culture' and ultimately in terms of 'religion', became increasingly evident. Eventually, recognition grew that 'Community relations problems cannot be fully understood unless the bodies concerned take account of the religious dimension insofar as its public manifestations are concerned' (Council of Europe, 1999, p 13).

In the earlier part of the 20th century, because of the lack of substantial religious communities other than Christian and Jewish, there had been a tendency for inter-faith organisations to be, or to be perceived as being, organisations only for 'inter-faith enthusiasts'; for those individuals who had, for doctrinal or moral reasons, become 'refugees' from the established religious traditions; or for those from more socially and religiously marginalised religious traditions (Weller, 1992).

These earliest initiatives tended to be multilateral, involving a range of different religions. In due course, initiatives developed that focused on relationships between two or three particular religions and, more specifically, between Christianity and one or two other religions. These bilateral initiatives generally secured a greater degree of endorsement from the leaderships of the 'mainstream' religious bodies of their sponsoring religions, as, for example, in the case of Christian–Jewish relations.

Other than Paganism and Christianity, Judaism is the religious tradition that has the longest settled community presence in the UK. Initiatives concerned with Christian–Jewish relations were among the earliest forms of organised inter-faith activity. These included the foundation in 1927 of the London Society for Jews and Christians, which originally emerged from an initiative of the Social Service Committee of the Liberal Jewish Synagogue. In 1942, partly as a response to the situation of Jews in Nazi-occupied Europe, a Council of Christians and Jews (CCJ) was formed (see Braybrooke, 1991). Like the London Society for Jews and Christians, it still exists today.

Becoming 'mainstream': inter-faith initiatives at the national level

The pioneering nature of these initiatives almost inevitably meant they remained somewhat tangential to the foci, concerns and organisational priorities of the majority religious groups, communities and organisations. As the population diversified, however, the challenge of living together in an increasingly plural society pressed 'mainstream' religious communities and groups to develop pragmatic ways of interacting and cooperating with one another. Meanwhile, the presence and claims of diverse religions posed profound philosophical and epistemological challenges for all religions and systems of beliefs and values.

For varying practical, theological and philosophical reasons, therefore, religious groups and organisations from within both majority and minority religious traditions in the UK began to give attention and structural form to relationships with people from religious traditions other than their own. Thus, Churches Together in Britain and Ireland (CTBI) developed a Churches' Commission for Inter-Faith Relations. Its predecessor body, the British Council of Churches' Committee for Relations with People of Other Faiths, was formed in 1978. The Board of Deputies of British Jews has an inter-faith officer, while the Muslim Council of Britain has an inter-faith relations committee.

One of the most significant national developments has been the emergence of the Inter Faith Network for the UK, founded in 1987 (see Weller, 1994). This has been a major catalyst in the transformation of inter-faith initiatives from relatively marginal initiatives into what is now a much more central feature of the UK's religious landscape. At the time of writing, the Network links over 110 affiliated organisations within four different categories of membership. These include representative bodies from within the historic world religious traditions with significant communities in the UK (Bahá'í, Buddhist, Christian, Muslim, Hindu, Jain, Jewish, Sikh and Zoroastrian); UK-wide, national, regional and other inter-faith organisations; local inter-faith groups and councils; and several educational and academic centres that are concerned with the study of religions, including the relationships between them.

The Network is primarily a framework for cooperation and communication rather than a special interest or campaigning body or council of faiths. It provides information and advice on religious community and inter-faith matters to organisations and individuals. It holds regular national and regional meetings; organises seminars and conferences; and publishes a range of material designed to encourage and resource inter-faith activity. Within its overall framework, a Faith Communities Forum has recently been developed to provide a mechanism for consultation between community representative bodies on matters of mutual concern, including issues that are on wider public and governmental agendas.

A range of other inter-faith organisations operate at the national level, including some, like the World Congress of Faiths, that have a longer history. Some focus on a particular bilateral or trilateral relationship. Examples here are the Three Faiths Forum (bringing together Jews, Christians and Muslims); Alif Aleph UK; the Joseph Interfaith Foundation (focusing on Jewish–Muslim relations); and a more recently established Christian–Muslim Forum. Many multilateral national bodies are also part of a wider international body, including the British Chapter of the International Association for Religious Freedom; the UK and Ireland body of the World Conference on Religion and Peace; and the United Religions Initiative (UK).

These national inter-faith bodies reflect different organisational logics and rationales. For example, while the Inter Faith Network is an umbrella organisation for the relationships between faith community and related groups, the Faith Communities' Consultative Council is specifically designed to facilitate the interface between religions and government across a range of national policy areas. The Faith-Based Regeneration Network (founded in 2002) gives expression to a more community development approach to engagement with public policy.

Accelerating developments: local inter-faith initiatives

Despite these national developments, the accelerating development of local inter-faith initiatives has been a particularly distinctive and recent feature of the UK's contemporary religious landscape (see Inter Faith Network for the UK, 2003. For many years, the network of local Councils of Christians and Jews provided a link between local, national and international dialogue among Jews and Christians. But, starting in the last quarter of the 20th century, one of the most significant developments was the emergence of multilateral local inter-faith initiatives and groups in towns and cities throughout the UK.

The majority of these groups are found in localities with a high degree of ethnic diversity and visible religious plurality, including groups like the Harrow Inter-Faith Council, the Leicester Council of Faiths and the Wolverhampton Inter Faith Council (see Inter Faith Network for the UK, 2007, for details of all these examples). But such groups can also be found in less visibly diverse areas: for example, the Beaminster One World Fellowship and the West Somerset Inter Faith Group (Inter Faith Network for the UK, 2007).

Many, but not all, local groups are affiliated to the Inter Faith Network, although those that are affiliated exist independently, in many cases having been founded before the Network emerged. However, through mechanisms such as the organisation of regular regional meetings for representatives of local inter-faith groups (including both those in membership with the Network and those not) the Network has encouraged the emergence and development of these groups. Thus, for example, the Network publishes *The local inter faith guide* (Inter Faith Network for the UK, 1999). This provides advice on the establishment and development of local inter-faith initiatives.

As local authorities have sought increasingly to engage with, and to facilitate, the contribution that religions can make to wider public life, a pattern of local inter-faith initiatives has emerged, the main rationale for which lies in the wish of religious groups to work together through mechanisms such as Local Strategic Partnerships (LSPs) and in relationship with local authorities, business and other community groups. The Inner Cities Religious Council (ICRC), established within the Department of the Environment in 1992, played an important early role in the development of such initiatives (Beales, 1994). It has changed its name subsequently, as government departments have restructured and changed their names, but in essential respects it has endured within the Department for the Environment, Transport and the Regions, the Office of the Deputy Prime Minister and, most recently, the Department of Communities and Local Government.

Although now replaced by the Faith Communities Consultative Council, the ICRC was set up under the Conservative government as part of a shared response between the Church of England and the government to the Church of England's critical *Faith in the city* report on disadvantaged areas and communities (ACUPA, 1985). This report underlined the economic and networking potential of places of worship and religious groups within the wider voluntary sector. That the ICRC was established rather than a Christian church body reflected the willingness of the Church of England to share some aspects of its privileged position. It also heralded a trend that has since accelerated whereby initiatives need to reflect the religious plurality of wider society to achieve legitimacy.

Governance, inter-faith and multi-faith initiatives

The changes in both the religious landscape and the approach of government to the engagement of religions in public life are associated with a now well-established policy imperative to support the creation of inter-faith and multi-faith initiatives, especially at the local and, more latterly, regional levels.

There is no devolved government in England of the kinds now existing in Scotland through the Scottish Parliament and Executive; the Northern Ireland Assembly and Executive; or even the Welsh Assembly with its more limited powers. However, there *is* a machinery of local government, based on an elected body with limited decision-making powers on aspects of local taxation and public spending, and which has responsibility for local provision and delivery of a range of statutory and other services.

In rural areas, forms of 'neighbourhood governance' have continued in which the intersection between religions and local governance has remained strong. This includes parish councils, which are historically rooted in the parochial system of the established Church of England. In the governance of towns, cities, districts and counties, however, religious groups were for a long time not generally 'represented' in a formal sense, although there have always been substantial numbers of individual religious believers and practitioners who have served as elected local councillors of various political parties, or as independents.

Moreover, despite their historic exclusion from election as members of the Westminster Parliament, there is a history of Church of England and Catholic priests becoming local councillors.

With the exception of the Local Agreed Syllabus Conferences and the Standing Advisory Councils on Religious Education (SACREs), dealing respectively with matters of religious education curriculum and collective worship in local authority schools, there has not been representation of a 'formal religious component' within local governance. In modern times, therefore, the main form of intersection between religion and local authorities has been primarily concerned with the 'ceremonial' functions of the local state; what the 19th-century constitutionalist Walter Bagehot called the 'dignified' part of the Constitution.

Such functions have recently been opened up to the involvement of other religious groups. Here, the Church of England has frequently acted as a kind of 'broker' of such expansion. However, some of the early local inter-faith initiatives have begun to connect with the 'dignified' aspects of local governance through liaison with the mayoral office (for example, the Wolverhampton Inter-Faith Group). More recently, cross-religious initiatives have developed that have engaged with the interface between the religions and the wider society, in relation to what Bagehot called the more 'efficient' parts of the Constitution. Thus, in contrast with the 1970s and much of the 1980s, when many religious organisations and groups often felt frozen out from participation in local authority-driven development, a situation has developed in which religious groups are being positively 'wooed' to join in partnership as part of a new approach to the development of local governance.

Beginning with the Conservative government's 1980s' project of 'rolling back the state', there has been a greater emphasis on the provision of services by community, voluntary and charitable groups. These trends have continued into the New Labour project of community 'partnerships', which has been based on a policy orientation that holds that the state cannot, and should not, directly provide for all social needs solely through public sector agencies. Coupled with this has been an argument that voluntary sector groups (including religious ones) might be better placed to provide more appropriate services and developments to their local communities.

Etymologically, 'governance' has a broader meaning than 'government'. While 'government' can be understood as the exercise of political authority over the actions and affairs of a political unit, 'governance' is more concerned with the action, manner or system of governing, including those diverse policies, structures and mechanisms through which the legislation, policies and practices of national and local governments are translated into the wider context of civil society. Thus, while 'government' will always include 'governance', it is possible to share in 'governance' without being in 'government'.

Guidance on the interface between local government and inter-faith initiatives, produced under the title of *Faith and community*, states that 'The value of more formal structures of this kind in multi-faith cities and towns is becoming increasingly apparent' (LGA, 2002, p 24, para 7.9). Or, as explained in *The local inter faith guide* (Inter Faith Network for the UK, 1999, pp 5-6), local inter-faith initiatives can often be

> ... places where members of the different faith communities come to know each other; learn more about their neighbours' deeply held beliefs; and develop relationships of trust which can underpin co-operative work on social issues, [acting as] a resource for local government, hospitals, police forces and other bodies which need information on particular faiths; or a reliable pattern of contacts for consultation and partnership; [being] of assistance to local authorities in allocating resources more efficiently and with appropriate attention to the particular needs of faith communities; for example in the areas of education and social services.

It is important here to note the significant role that the concept of 'social capital' has played (Weller, 2005b, pp 271-89). The idea was initially introduced into political theory by Coleman (1988, 1990). The concept's most influential exponent, however, has been the political scientist Robert Putman, who applied it to American society (Putman, 1995, 2000). Although his overall thesis of a decline of 'social capital' in the US has been critiqued with regard to both its data collection and interpretation, the concept has become firmly established in UK policy discourse through New Labour's 'communitarian' philosophy.

Stemming from this approach has been increasing recognition of the potential, and actual, social engagement of religious groups and organisations, coupled in social policy discourse with an increasing degree of reference to the 'faith sector'. Individual religious traditions and groups have been seen as producing 'bonding' social capital (on Jewish groups see, for example, Harris and Harris, 1997; Slesinger, 2003). However, these groups are also seen as having resources that can be deployed for the creation of 'bridging' social capital that can benefit the wider society.

Against this background, the role and strategic significance of existing local Inter Faith Councils that have engaged with public bodies has been enhanced. Where such initiatives did not previously exist, there is a new impetus towards their creation. Once the contribution of religious groups and organisations to the development of 'social capital' is recognised, inter-faith organisations and structures increasingly come to be seen as contributors to 'bridging' social capital. Thus, although there is a continuing role for more 'internal' dialogue at the theological and philosophical levels, in order to gain a wider public benefit it is important for public authorities to be involved (Furbey et al, 2006).

Under New Labour, the creation of LSPs has been a key catalyst here. Through the City Partnership approach, the original LSP model extended beyond its original 88 target areas of the most socially and economically deprived local authority areas. In City Partnerships, elected councillors and council officers engage with representatives of civil society from the private, public, and voluntary and community sectors to create a shared vision for the area and to help coordinate better services. City Partnerships are necessarily involved in local strategic planning, and bodies that participate in them can therefore have an impact on defining the strategies that inform the criteria by which funds are allocated, thus involving civil society groups in local governance.

Partly called into being in response to these developments, forums of faith have emerged to relate to City Partnerships or similar structures concerned with local governance. At the regional level, meanwhile, cross-religious bodies have been developed to relate to the assemblies and the development agencies, which constitute key structures in English regional governance.

Organic or artificial? Inter-faith and multi-faith initiatives at the regional level

Devolution within the UK and regionalisation in the European Union has been paralleled in England to some extent by the development of a range of regional bodies such as regional development agencies and the emergence of regional assemblies. This is not regional government in the sense that applies in federal states. The assemblies are not directly elected bodies, although they include political representatives as well as representatives from a wide range of other interests. They do not have any legislative powers, nor can they raise local taxation. Yet, they came during the late 1990s and early 2000s to play an increasingly significant part in the governance of regions, especially in terms of economic planning and the implementation of social policy. Shortly before the time of writing their future became uncertain when, following the appointment of Gordon Brown as Prime Minister in 2007, a review of them was announced. Nevertheless, a range of regional inter-faith bodies have now been developed.

These bodies include the London Boroughs Faiths Network; the Northwest Forum of Faiths; the South East of England Faith Forum; the West Midlands Faiths Forum; the Yorkshire and Humber Faiths Forum; and the Forum of Faiths for the East Midlands, which the author chaired until recently. In the East of England, the Churches' Network facilitated the formation of what is now the East of England Faiths Council. There is also an East of England Faiths Agency set up by invitation to representatives of the inter-faith groups in the region and a *faithneteast* under the joint auspices of the East of England Faiths Council and the Faiths and Civil Society Unit based at Goldsmiths, University of London. In the South West, there is a South West Council of Faiths and also a *faithnetsouthwest*.

There are important differences between these regional initiatives and those at more local levels. Locally, while many minority religious organisations have reasonably well-developed structures and networks, their regional-level profile and organisation are patchy. There are city-level bodies such as the Birmingham Council of Gurdwaras and also a few bodies operating at county level, such as the Federation of Muslim Organisations in Leicester, and the Lancashire Council of Mosques. But there are few that operate at the level of whole regions.

This relative lack of regional infrastructure means that a short-term way to develop effective regional contributions from minority religious groups could be through the facilitation of Christian churches and the latter's resources. This is because the Christian churches have a geographical spread of population, physical presence and extra-local infrastructure that approximates to the areas in which regional governance operates. Thus, many Anglican and Roman Catholic Dioceses, United Reformed Church Provinces, Methodist Districts, as well as numerous ecumenical 'Churches Together' bodies, map on to the footprints of regional governance in England. Several regional ecumenical Christian bodies have also been formed, such as the East Midlands Churches Forum and the Churches Regional Commission in the North East, supported through a national Churches Regional Network.

By contrast, together with the relative weakness of other-than-Christian religions at regional levels, there are varying degrees of fragility in regional inter-faith structures. Consequently, progress in inter-faith working at regional levels is likely to be a gradual process. As argued in a report for Engage East Midlands on infrastructure support for faith-based groups, '… for longer-term sustainability, the capacity of the "other than Christian" faith groups should be developed alongside a maximising of collaboration with what is already in place among the Christian Churches' (Weller and Beale, 2004, p 44).

Hence, if regional inter-faith organisations are to avoid the risk of being merely semi-detached mediating bodies (with all the attendant dangers for representation and accountability), then capacity-building resources are needed to enable an appropriate investment in regional 'foot-slogging' and relationship-building exercises with minority religious groups in the regions.

Who serves who on what basis? Inter-faith structures and the state

The state at local, regional and national levels is an important part of the social reality with which religious organisations have to deal. To function in contemporary society, religious organisations need to become legal entities. In so doing, they become accountable for their actions and activities within society's wider social and legal frameworks. These include: the legal framework for charitable recognition; financial accounting and auditing requirements; and compliance with health and safety and equal opportunities legislation.

The laws, rules and regulations that emanate from the state at all levels significantly shape and influence the development of religious organisational forms and what the historian of religion, Wilfred Cantwell Smith (1978), called the 'cumulative traditions' in and through which religious individuals express their personal faith. But the impact of the modern, liberal and bureaucratised state on the organisational forms of religion extends beyond issues of regulatory function. Rather, the state also seeks dialogue and consultation partners, which, according to one's political perspective, are needed either to enable the proper and inclusive functioning of the state's democratic ideals or to incorporate, and thus potentially neutralise, potential sources of alternative values and perspectives.

However, the state cannot have dialogue with a 'community', but only with bodies that present themselves, and/or that the state regards, as constituting organised representation of that community. As the institutions of the state set out to consult with specifically religious opinion and interests, they seek 'representative' partner organisations and structures. Sometimes, the partnership and representation is sought directly from the religions concerned. Thus, notwithstanding the existence of the Faith Communities Consultative Council, communication with individual religious organisations remains more normal at the national level.

However, the regional and local state *has* increasingly looked to inter-faith mediating bodies as partners in dialogue and consultation. This has often been for pragmatic reasons. Consultation with numerous and varied organisations within individual religions presents a complex and difficult challenge since public bodies rarely contain what might be called the 'religious literacy' necessary to make informed choices about which organisations to consult (Yorkshire and Humber Regional Assembly, 2002). At the point at which it recognises the need to engage with religions, therefore, the state can find inter-faith mediating bodies very attractive. Consequently, the state is acting here as a powerful developmental force that calls forth organisational expressions of 'cumulative tradition' that might not have developed on the basis of an internal rationale and impetus alone. Moreover, the involvement of public bodies in legitimising participating groups through recognition of inter-faith bodies has an effect on how the latter are constituted and on the criteria used for specifying the range of traditions that are welcomed into particular organised inter-faith initiatives.

This was a source of national debate in relation to the Inner Cities Religious Council. Questions were asked about its membership being limited to Christian, Hindu, Jewish, Muslim and Sikh involvement, excluding Bahá'í, Buddhist, Jain and Zoroastrian traditions. Such issues persist with regard to the Faith Communities' Consultative Council. Matters of this kind have also been pressed upon the Inter Faith Network for the UK where, at successive Annual General Meetings, the issue has been debated of Pagan Federation inclusion under the Network's category for affiliation of national faith community organisations.

Locally, there has been a much wider range of practice. The Lincoln Inter-Faith Forum (Inter Faith Network for the UK, 2007, p 69) lists Pagans among its member traditions. Other local bodies, such as the Leicester Council of Faiths, have not yet admitted Pagans to corporate membership. It is likely that this issue will become more pressing (for a discussion of these matters in connection with the development of a Forum of Faiths for Derby, see Weller and Wolfe, 2004; Weller, 2008). A pragmatic case is commonly used against the inclusion of such forms of religious life. It is argued that their participation would undermine the credibility of the inter-faith body as a dialogue and consultation partner with the state.

Those who press for inclusion invoke a principle of equity in relation to religion and belief. It is increasingly likely that there will be pressure to consider these issues, not only on the basis of an 'inter-faith pragmatism' (whether or not masking an underlying more theological or ideological position), but also in the light of legislative requirements relating to 'religion and belief' within an overall framework of equality and diversity policy and practice. Nevertheless, it is unlikely that the issues involved will be solved purely in this mode, but are likely rather to require active confidence-building measures between Pagans and others.

The question of 'who is in' and 'who is out' is also pertinent in connection with the wish of some Humanist individuals and Humanist bodies to become involved in inter-faith initiatives. For inter-faith groups composed primarily on an individual basis this question does not generally arise as a problematic issue, since individuals generally participate on the basis of their interest and commitment to the aims and objectives of the group rather than on the basis of the religious or other 'badge' that they might wear.

However, in the case of bodies formed by representative groups of various kinds – as, again, in the case of the Inter Faith Network for the UK – the question of Humanist organisational membership highlights complex issues of self-definition, other-definition and the relationship between the two expressed in terms of organisational boundaries. What is, nevertheless, clear is that increasingly in the 21st century, is that however inter-faith and multi-faith bodies define their boundaries, their work increasingly needs to take account not only of the relationships between people from the traditional world religions, but also of broader approaches to spirituality and values, whether understood in strictly Humanist terms or not.

The problem of 'representation', however, is not only one of 'who is in' and 'who is out'. Questions are also raised regarding the connection or otherwise between those in inter-faith and multi-faith bodies who act as 'representatives' of the constituencies from which they come. This aspect of representation is also linked with the important issue of the extent to which inter-faith bodies are connected with, or detached from, the broader faith communities that the more formalised 'councils' or 'fora' of faiths claim to represent.

In addition, where inter-faith bodies strongly reflect the formal leadership of the religions concerned, it is often the case that women, who generally form majorities in the active membership of religious groups, are not so prominent. At the same time, in the development especially of local inter-faith groups, individual women have often played leading and, indeed, pioneering roles, as, for example, in the case of Ivy Gutridge who was a key figure in the development of the Wolverhampton Inter-Faith Group.

Equally, there has been concern about the degree to which young people have been involved in either the past or present of inter-faith bodies. The question of 'generational change' is one that is often raised and about which there is often considerable concern, especially in the context of the attraction that more 'radicalised' forms of religion can present to some young people. Some established inter-faith bodies have made progress in this regard, a good example being the Yorkshire and Humber Faiths Forum, which has developed a Youth Council. But there remains a question about how far existing inter-faith bodies and structures are able adequately to engage with the concerns, perspectives and energies of young people.

Inter-faith initiatives as 'parallel worked alternatives'

The preceding discussion has identified some of the weaknesses and issues that mark inter-faith developments. More positively, it can be suggested that inter-faith and multi-faith initiatives may provide creative models in addressing wider questions of the relationship between religion(s), state and society. Such models would neither presuppose the dominance of one religious tradition or the exclusion of all, nor the full incorporation of religions into government, nor their complete detachment from it. This pattern of emerging inter-faith activity might contribute, albeit untidily, to the evolution of a new 'socio-religious contract' in the UK. In recent years the Church of England has often facilitated the inclusion of many contributions to the public realm by other-than-Christian religious groups. However, for reasons of equity, participation and representation, it may still be important for religious groups and the wider society collectively to evolve and negotiate religiously inclusive and religious–secular 'parallel worked alternatives'. Such a 'public imaginary' might ultimately replace the 'one-dimensional' Christendom model that characterises the present status and role of the Church of England (see Weller, 2005a, for a fuller discussion).

In comparison with the historical inheritance of the establishment of Anglican Christianity, the current range of inter-faith initiatives is, of course, untidy, fragile and ambiguous. Yet, this reality is in many ways more organically rooted and offers better prospects than would be the case for a more managerially constructed, top-down initiative such as the artificial construction of a national Council of Faiths, which has been proposed by some as an alternative approach. What this untidy proliferation and loose network of inter-faith and multi-faith initiatives does offer is a complementary, additional and parallel way for structuring the relationships between religion(s), state and society.

As the range and scope of such initiatives both broadens and deepens, their credentials could begin to be better established in terms of both legitimacy and utility. Gradually, but also fundamentally and structurally, they could bring about evolutionary and organic change. The construction of such multilayered structures would be consistent with the evolutionary tendency of constitutional change in the UK. Social and religious stakeholders would no longer be faced with a choice between a currently known and constitutionally entrenched religious establishment and a set of purely theoretical alternatives. Rather, on a practical level, some 'intermediate' and 'convergent' goals might be shared with the increasing numbers of those in the Church of England who work within a model of an 'extended establishment'.

Such developments might also help to ameliorate the dangers of a purely state-imposed, probably secularising, disestablishment of the kind feared by many. Meanwhile, the negotiated evolution of both 'emergent' and 'managerial' forms of multi-faith and religious–secular 'parallel worked' structures, functioning as *signposts* for the possibility of a new socio-religious settlement, can be helpful. While fragile and fraught with difficulties, both in their creation and their maintenance, inter-faith and multi-faith initiatives need to be positively encouraged and carefully nurtured, especially those that work at the interface of religions and secularity.

Such initiatives are particularly important in contexts where the transmutation of religious identities into the service of absolutist identity politics fuels communal conflict. Although the capacity and potential of inter-religious initiatives for combating conflict should not be overestimated, they do have potential for creating 'bridging' social capital by facilitating the development of a common stakeholding (religious and secular) in wider community life. They can also provide channels of communication to address the kind of destructive trends that undermine national and community cohesion. In summary, 'A combination of such initiatives, legitimated by the state and public bodies alongside the continued development of local inter-faith councils and inter-faith initiatives emerging from within a vigorous wider voluntary sector, offers the most constructive way forward' (Weller, 2005a, p 214)

References

ACUPA (Archbishop's Commission on Urban Priority Areas) (1985) *Faith in the city: A call for action by church and nation – The report of the Archbishop of Canterbury's Commission on Urban Priority Areas*, London: Church House Publishing.

Barrows, J. (ed) (1893) *The world's parliament of religions*, Chicago, IL: The Parliament Publishing Company.

Beales, C. (1994) 'Partnerships for a change: the Inner Cities Religious Council', *World Faiths Encounter*, no 8, pp 41-6.

Braybrooke, M. (1980) *Inter-faith organisations, 1893-1979: An historical directory*, Lampeter: Edwin Mellen Press.

Braybrooke, M. (1991) *Children of one God: A history of the Council of Christians and Jews*, London: Valentine Mitchell.

Braybrooke, M. (1992) *Pilgrimage of hope: One hundred years of global interfaith dialogue*, London: SCM Press.

Cantwell Smith, W. (1978) *The meaning and end of religion*, London: SPCK.

Coleman, J. (1988) 'Social capital in the creation of human capital', *American Journal of Sociology*, no 94, pp 95-120.

Coleman, J. (1990) *Foundations of social theory*, Cambridge: Cambridge University Press.

Council of Europe (1999) *Religion and the integration of migrants*, Strasbourg: Council of Europe Publishing.

Furbey, R., Dinham, A., Farnell, R., Finneron, D., Wilkinson, G., with Howarth, C., Hussain, D. and Palmer, S. (2006) *Faith as social capital: Connecting or dividing?*, Bristol: The Policy Press.

Hare, W. (ed) (1925) *Religions of the Empire: A conference of some living religions within the Empire*, London: Duckworth.

Harris, M. and Harris, R. (1997) *The Jewish voluntary sector in the United Kingdom: Its role and its future*, London: Institute of Jewish Policy Research.

Inter Faith Network for the UK (1999) *The local inter faith guide: Faith community cooperation in action*, London: Inter Faith Network for the UK in association with the Inner Cities Religious Council of the Department for the Environment, Transport and the Regions.

Inter Faith Network for the UK (2003) *Local inter faith activity in the UK: A survey*, London: Inter Faith Network for the UK.

Inter Faith Network for the UK (2007) *Inter faith organisations in the UK: A directory* (4th edn), London: Inter Faith Network for the UK.

LGA (Local Government Association) (2002) *Faith and community: A good practice guide*, London: Local Government Association Publications.

Millard, A. (ed) (1937) *Faiths and fellowship: The proceedings of the World Congress of Faiths*, held in London, 3-17 July 1936, London: J.M. Watkins.

Putnam, R. (1995) 'Bowling alone: America's declining social capital', *Journal of Democracy*, no 2, pp 65-78.

Putnam, R. (2000) *Bowling alone: The collapse and revival of American community*, New York: Simon and Schuster.

Slesinger, E. (2003) *Creating community and accumulating social capital: Jews associating with other Jews in Manchester*, London: Institute for Public Policy Research.

Weller, C. (ed) (1936) *World fellowship: Addresses and messages by leading spokesmen of all faiths, races and countries*, New York: Liveright Publishing Corporation.

Weller, P. (1992) 'Inter-faith roots and shoots', *World Faiths Encounter*, no 1, pp 48-57.

Weller, P. (1994) 'The Inter Faith Network for the United Kingdom', *Indo-British Review: A Journal of History*, vol 20, no 1, pp 20-6.

Weller, P. (ed) (2001) *Religions in the UK: Directory, 2001–03*, Derby and London: Multi-Faith Centre, University of Derby, and the Inter Faith Network for the UK.

Weller, P. (2005a) *Time for a change: Reconfiguring religion, state and society*, London: T & T Clark.

Weller, P. (2005b) 'Religions and social capital: theses on religion(s), state(s) and society(ies) with particular reference to the United Kingdom and the European Union', *Journal of International Migration and Integration*, vol 6, no 2, pp 271-89.

Weller, P. (2008) *Religious diversity in the UK: Contours and issues*, London: Continuum.

Weller, P. and Beale, D. (2004) *Multi-faith infrastructure support in the East Midlands: An investigation into activity and needs in the East Midlands*, Derby: University of Derby.

Weller, P. and Wolfe, M. (2004) *Involving religions: A project report on religious group participation, inter-faith infrastructure, and capacity-building in Derby*, Derby: School of Education, Health and Sciences, University of Derby.

Yorkshire and Humber Regional Assembly (2002) *Religious literacy: A practical guide to the region's faith communities*, Wakefield: Yorkshire and Humber Regional Assembly.

FIVE

Faith, multiculturalism and community cohesion: a policy conversation

Maqsood Ahmed, Ted Cantle and Dilwar Hussain.
Edited by Vivien Lowndes

Introduction

This chapter considers whether the rise of faith identities poses a challenge to multiculturalism as a settlement within the public realm. It also looks at the relationship between faith and the policy agenda for 'community cohesion', which has emerged from a critical engagement with multiculturalism. The chapter hosts a 'policy conversation' between three people who are currently active in civil society and governance, and have a long and varied experience in working on faith and diversity. The chapter captures the views of those who are actually shaping policy and practice on faith in the public realm. It is interactive and deliberative and finds new reflections and creative syntheses.

The contributors

Maqsood Ahmed OBE is Senior Adviser on Muslim Communities in the Preventing Extremism Unit at the Department of Communities and Local Government (DCLG). He is engaged in Muslim–Jewish inter-faith dialogue and in capacity-building for faith groups in the public realm. Ted Cantle CBE is Professor at the Institute of Community Cohesion, and Associate Director of the local government Improvement and Development Agency. He was appointed in August 2001 by the Home Secretary to lead the review of the causes of the urban disturbances that year in Northern England. The 'Cantle Report' was responsible for the initial development of the 'community cohesion' policy agenda (Cantle, 2001). Dilwar Hussain is Head of Policy Research at the Islamic Foundation, Leicestershire. He was a Commissioner at the Commission for Racial Equality (CRE) (2006-07) and was active in the Preventing Extremism Together working groups set up by the Home Office after the London bombings of 7 July 2005. He also served on the Archbishop of Canterbury's Commission on Urban Life and Faith (2005-06) (CULF, 2006).

The issues

Tariq Modood (2007, p 2) defines multiculturalism as 'the recognition of group difference within the public sphere of laws, policies, democratic discourses and the terms of citizenship and national identity'. It is not about difference per se, but refers specifically to culturally derived, or culturally embedded, differences (Parekh, 2006, p 3). Although these differences are not necessarily ethnic or 'racial' in character, multiculturalism in Britain has become associated with issues of racial equality. Indeed, as Modood (2007, p 5) puts it, multiculturalism has come to represent 'the political accommodation of minorities formed by immigration'. While 'multicultural' refers to the fact of cultural diversity, 'multiculturalism' denotes a 'normative response to that fact' (Parekh, 2006, p 6). Britain is undoubtedly a multicultural society, but the role of multiculturalism in the public life is more contested.

One element of this contestation is the rise of faith identities in political and social life. There are 'top-down' pressures on the multiculturalist settlement as governments seek to engage with 'faith communities' instead of, or at least in addition to, ethnically based interests and associations. Pressures also come from the growing critique of public and social policies (in housing, education, social care and community development), which, in acknowledging and celebrating diversity, are seen to have reinforced cultural difference and separation. The former director of CRE, Trevor Phillips, has gone as far as to say that the perverse effects of multiculturalism have found Britain 'sleepwalking to segregation' (Casciani, 2005). Emphasising commonalities rather than differences, policies of 'community cohesion' have sought to bridge the 'parallel lives' observed among different communities in some towns (Cantle, 2008). In this context, faith actors are identified as potentially important brokers in fostering dialogue and interaction between different communities within and across ethnic lines.

There are 'bottom-up' pressures on multiculturalism too, with the rise of faith-based identities in politics and civil society. These pressures relate to the fracturing of monolithic ethnic identities in a context of hyperpluralism, and a growing awareness of the complex and 'transversal' nature of difference (the identity of a 'black' person may also be related to gender, sexuality, age, social class and other factors). The relationships between faith and ethnicity are particularly complicated: for instance, in one British city, the 'Asian' community has Hindu, Jain, Muslim and Sikh elements, while the 'Muslim' community includes citizens originally from countries in Africa, Asia and Central and Eastern Europe.

The 'emergence of Muslim agency', as Modood puts it, has produced a rapid growth in civil society activity of all sorts as well as forms of 'corporatist' engagement with government – and, of course, the political radicalisation and criminalisation of small numbers of extremists. Other faiths, partly reacting to this, and partly building on their own long traditions of social action and public service, are asserting themselves as political and civic actors in their own right. Citizens are increasingly laying claim to faith identities in a hotly contested politics of difference that links forms of 'group classification' with access to resources and visibility in the public domain. Recent research found that white working-class youths in a Northern town identified themselves as 'Christian', while adding that they did not believe in God (Woodhead and Heelas, 2005). Cutting across all these trends is an increasing demand for legally protected *individual* human rights.

While Modood (2007, p 78) argues for 'the extension of a politics of difference to include appropriate religious identities and organisations', others link the rise of faith identities to both the causes and the effects of a demise of multiculturalism. Does 'community cohesion' as a new policy paradigm challenge, or expand, the multiculturalist settlement? The Commission on Integration and Cohesion (established after the 7/7 bombings in 2005) argues that the goal should be to 'create supportive communities', 'where everyone feels at home' and 'sticks together regardless of pressures such as economic inequalities, or ethnic, racial, faith, political or other differences' (CIC, 2007, p 12). Attempting to combine a celebration of diversity with the consolidation of common bonds, a 'cohesive community' is described in policy guidance as one where:

- there is a common vision and a sense of belonging for all communities;
- the diversity of people's different backgrounds and circumstances are appreciated and positively valued;
- those from different backgrounds have similar life opportunities; and
- strong and positive relationships are being developed between people from different backgrounds and circumstances in the workplace, in schools and within neighbourhoods (LGA, 2002).

Does the promotion of shared values and cross-cultural contact represent a challenge to, or a rebalancing of, the multiculturalist settlement? Anthony Giddens (2008) argues for a 'sophisticated multiculturalism', which 'emphasizes the importance of national identity, and national laws, but also the fostering of connections between different social and ethnic groups'. As Giddens goes on to point out, this form of multiculturalism 'is all about social solidarity – not separateness'. The prospects for such a sophisticated multiculturalism are debated in the following conversation, which engages not just with multiculturalism and community cohesion but also with wider issues of faith, civil society and democracy.

The conversation

Ed: Does the growing policy concern with faith imply a critique of multiculturalism?

TC: I think there's no doubt that the whole discourse has changed. From the 1960s, multiculturalism was built around cultural pluralism. It was about ethnicity – a white society coming to terms with new ethnic identities. And in so far as there was a sort of politics of identity, it was conditioned by the whole notion of a Black identity – black as a political term encompassing different ethnicities. This has moved over the last 40 years to where we're now talking in terms of faith as the major fault line in multiculturalism – or perhaps a mixture of faith and ethnic divisions which are mutually reinforcing. So I think discourse has changed, the whole language has changed.

DH: Yes, I would agree it has changed. I think it's been Muslim identity politics that has been the driver of some of that change but you also have a growing Christian consciousness as well. We saw the impact that *Faith in the city* had in the 1980s and there is an ongoing attempt to see how values are relevant to evolving contexts.[1] And as those contexts change, faith interpretations are also shaped. What we're seeing in the Muslim community is a struggle to somehow assert an identity – to exhibit a sense of attachment to a faith and spiritual tradition in what was initially an alien environment, to indigenise it to a new social and political reality. And I know that, from my experiences in Leicester with the Hindu community and the Sikh community, that has reverberations on other communities in terms of questioning whether we should now begin to assert ourselves in faith terms or not.

MA: I think there is much more consciousness that multiculturalism needs to be coupled with faith, but I don't think we should just depart from multiculturalism itself. I think it is important that faith identity is much more visible now than it ever was before. But I certainly still feel that the strength of our society – and of cohesion in the UK – lies in multiculturalism. I think the values of our society are that we recognise the differences but look for the commonalities which unite different cultures. Post 9/11 there may have been some more emphasis on one particular religion, because obviously Islam and Muslims are under the spotlight, but issues relating to the cohesive society have to be linked and related to the multiculturalism.

Ed: Is the increasing importance of faith identities a good thing?

DH: I'll put my cards on the table. Ten years ago I would have said that what was happening was a positive thing – a growing Muslim assertiveness. We saw organisations like the Muslim Council just coming into being. And we'd just come out of the Rushdie affair and there was the lobbying around having a question in the 2001 census on religion. All of that I felt initially was a positive thing. Post 9/11, I'm not sure how positive it was because I think maybe what we did was to overshoot that sense of assertiveness. What I now see is an entrenchment, almost a sense of victimhood in Muslim communities. Now there's a sense of introspection as to whether the change was good or bad.

TC: We've seen an organisation of communities according to finer divisions – again based on ethnicity and faith – for example, the way that the black identity broke down to produce an Asian identity and then further into Sikh and Hindu and other identities. And, of course, from a cohesion point of view, I constantly want to emphasise commonalities, rather than more and more divisions.

DH: Is there a trend in society that is leading to an increasing sense of questioning around faith? This may be a reaction to what is perceived to be a growing secularisation of society. Is it a sort of anxiety of modernity – a search for the self or for new identities in light of modern values and ideas? Are all these things playing together to create an environment of 'Balkanisation', where individual identities are far easier to assert than collective identities?

Ed: Are stronger faith identities associated with segregation and 'parallel lives'?

MA: I think that the Muslim community needs to be brought into mainstream funding streams. If you start funding one particular faith you are going to antagonise the others who are equally in need of funds and support. In a nutshell, I would strongly reject any notion of singling out any community. It has to be multi-faith funding from local authorities and government. There is a lot more which unites different faiths, and there is a commonality in faith and non-faith communities as well. I call it common values or shared values. And I think we need to highlight those shared values about humanity.

DH: But I was listening to our annual Radio Ramadan programme in Leicester and heard somebody quite prominent in the Muslim community say, well, *is* segregation a bad thing? Why shouldn't we challenge that assumption? Now, for me it is a bad thing – from the way I look at life from my faith tradition, but also from the way I have experienced life. And there's enough data out there, from people like Ted, showing that segregation and separation is potentially harmful for a city.

TC: But we don't, well I don't want, a sort of flat homogenising society. We want some way of people being able to express different cultural, religious, other identities without it tipping over into parallel lives. I like the idea of some sort of clustering and supportive arrangements for different communities, upon which people can draw but still feel connected to the wider community. So there's a sort of balance there. You can actually have it both ways but there's got to be a strong sense of commonalities. And that's where we get to the question of whether faith should be in the public realm because faith can often reinforce separatism rather than commonalities.

Ed: Did policies of multiculturalism encourage a splintering of identities?

DH: In the 1980s and '90s it was clear that faith groups were not getting funding but that you would get funding for being an ethnic minority group. So funding would be available to your Pakistani mother-tongue teaching class or Pakistani Cultural Association or Bangladeshi Boys Football Club. But then there was a growing consciousness and desire for a Muslim identity that looked beyond those ethnic barriers. It was a noble motive to try and transcend some of those national barriers of migration – to say, 'hold on, can we not imagine new identities for the second and third generations?' It's a motive that we may today categorise as a move towards integration. There was almost a sense of giving up on the first generation – that they were not really able to make that sort of cultural shift. But for people growing up here, who were born here and going to schools together and playing on the same streets, this was a possibility. So that was one thing. The other, I think, much more adventurous project was to say, if we can redefine Islamic practice in a more nuanced British voice, then actually we can transcend the cultural baggage altogether and say, we're British! We can jump over all that stuff and create a new vision of living Islam in a British context. So that was the positive vision.

MA: Yes, people are starting to move away from Pakistani or Bangladeshi identities into thinking of a British life and about Muslims in Britain. In the past, Muslim communities failed the young British Muslim, which is part of the reason some young people moved away from mainstream Islam into the extremists' hands.

TC: Well, just reflecting on the report that I did on the riots in 2001, bearing in mind that this was before 9/11, most of the stuff on the streets was nothing to do with anti-Muslim sentiment, it was very much anti-Asian sentiment. It wasn't until after 9/11 that the BNP [British National Party] and others started to characterise this as anti-Muslim. But people like Tariq Modood were already pointing out that the whole notion of a black community had broken down – some minority communities were doing very well, some parts of the African Caribbean and Irish communities, for example. And we knew that Chinese and Indian youngsters were excelling at school. So I think what we've found in the last 40 years is that, you know, we can't just characterise minority communities in one dimension as we used to and that they're actually pushing for different approaches as well. So it's not just top-down, it's a very much to do with a bottom-up shift in identities.

DH: Right from the Rushdie affair, there was a questioning of whether this project, this liberal plural project of accommodating minorities, was actually working. And there was, I think, perhaps an unrealistic assumption of where multiculturalism would eventually go. There was an assumption that people who were migrating would sort of eventually disappear, go under the radar – they would not cause trouble, they wouldn't cause a fuss. The Rushdie affair was a primary signal that this model wasn't working with the Muslim communities but that later became crystallised post 9/11, when all of this became entangled with security concerns.

Ed: How do you explain the turn to faith in public policy?

TC: In the 1990s the focus was still very much on ethnicity. There was some mention of faith but I took that to be really a response to a sort of moral case agenda – *Faith in the city*. It wasn't so much an identity issue, more a sort of social justice approach – the need to invigorate the whole moral agenda. It was not until 2002/03 really that it began. There was no real funding of faith groups, and inter-faith networks were very lightweight. It was always understood that you couldn't fund faith groups because of the assumption that you'll be adding to the proselytising of each faith. But now some funding is available to support some of the infrastructure. Faith has simply become more salient in public policy terms, probably as a reflection of the global identities it can represent through diaspora communities. These were much more difficult to sustain, say 20 years ago, but the ease and low cost of modern communications has changed all of that.

DH: The Muslim community was growing in consciousness – there was a sense of the positive impact that faith can have on society. Why could we not get funding for that? That coincided with a policy shift post 9/11 to recognise capacity-building projects that faith communities can carry out as quite distinct from faith activities like prayer and worship and proselytisation. Separating these out allowed for the former to be funded and the latter not to be funded. But the issue of extremism has, ironically, created a great deal of momentum for faith discourse to appear in policy circles (and vice versa). That's where we are currently with pots of money that target the Muslim community, like the government's Pathfinder Fund on Preventing Violent Extremism.[2]

MA: I have a very strong feel that nobody else has more access to the normal citizen than people of the faith. Traditionally, local authorities would say this is a faith-based group and we can't talk to them. Now it is normal for local authorities and regional assemblies to get the views of the faiths and faith-based organisations in the communities. Central government has moved from non-communication with faith groups to talking and working together. There are capacity-building funds for faith communities for the first time in our history. The new inter-faith strategy is important too.[3] I don't want every government office to have a Muslim adviser and a Christian adviser and a Hindu adviser. But I do feel that there is a need for the mainstream civil servant to know about these perspectives. There is benefit for the government as well as for the community to have that faith element, interlinked with mainstream services at national, regional and local authority levels.

Ed: How does this turn to faith relate to other aspects of British politics?

DH: It goes hand in hand with a 'third way' approach to politics introduced by the Blair government. I think that's really opened up space. If 9/11 had happened under a more right-wing government, you'd probably have seen further clamping down. But Blair created some genuine space – funding for Muslim schools, representation in the House of Lords, engagement with the Muslim Council and other organisations.

TC: *Faith in the city* was a critique of the Thatcher government. You could argue that, following the fall of the Berlin Wall, the only serious critique of capitalism now is the ideology represented by the international Muslim community and, indeed, that of some other faiths.

DH: I think that breaks down if you look at actual Muslim behaviour across the world because it is remarkably capitalist. I mean you only need to go to places like Dubai and Saudi Arabia. If you look at debates within Christianity, you know, you'll have those who prop up capitalism and those who critique capitalism. So I think this goes beyond a singular faith group. But I think one of the things that Muslims have done is to say, we don't care what anybody thinks of how we say these things – you know, just throw caution to the wind. It could be seen as a very foolish thing, being brave to the point of being foolhardy. I think it's the way in which Muslims have articulated their demands that means that it's their voice that gets heard. And many Muslims look at it and sort of cringe and say, well this is not the way to do politics in this country and this age.

Ed: How do faith groups relate to a democratic political system?

DH: Repeatedly, surveys show how Muslims, when asked about democracy, actually like democracies. So I think there is a misunderstanding of how the notion of religious authority plays in faith communities. I think people are fairly pragmatic about these things. They separate these things into ideals and into realities. But in the current surge of identity politics in the Muslim community, the bulk of that is about political assertion. There is a small sector that would totally denounce democratic politics and secular politics, but their influence is wider than their numbers. On the other hand, the vast majority of people have always seen the importance of strategic lobbying and engagement. But there isn't enough of a spirit of deliberation or a schooling of this. At least it's not developed well enough yet – the structures aren't there. So this groundswelling of political interest and activism ends up being quite naïve and probably too idealistic. And a lot of grassroots politics is still quite clan based, if you look at places like Birmingham and Bradford, and the councillors that come from Muslim communities.

MA: After 9/11 the Muslim community felt under siege, just didn't know what to do. But 7/7 was a homecoming. This is not a US problem, this is a UK problem – British Muslims are involved, some of them are convicted, some of them killed themselves. So I think there was a change from 9/11 to 7/7. We haven't shifted to where we need to be, but I think that provoked a debate within the Muslim community that we need to do something. I am very pleased our British Muslim communities are far ahead of other EU [European Union] partners when it comes to partnership working with other faiths and with the government. But the first and second generation of British Muslims still feel that this is interference in the faith. But the third generation are thinking that we need to have our own kind of stake, if I can put it that strongly, within the government. So there is definitely movement, but I think it would be wrong for me to say that there is clarity in the Muslim community mind. One of the major reasons is the diversity in the community and diversity of leadership – the different Muslim councils and Muslim forums. They are all angling for change but there is little consensus about the final goal. We also have 300 Muslim councillors in local authorities. Traditionally they were picked on a tribal basis, but now you see the young councillors coming from the different political parties.

Four MPs [Members of Parliament] and up to a dozen Muslim members of the House of Lords are taking part in the democratic process and raising the issues faced by Muslim communities. Muslim communities want to get somewhere politically but I don't think there is clarity about the destination at this stage. I would say that there is no conflict between democratic values and religion.

Ed: Is multiculturalism being replaced with a new policy model?

DH: My instinct is that we're in a moment of transition. We're moving on from a system but we're not quite sure where it is we're actually going – we don't have a clear vision of where to go beyond this. We know certain things that we would like to achieve and certain things that we don't want to happen. I think there is more or less a consensus on segregation – we know that we want a more cohesive and more unified, as opposed to a fragmented, society. We're not quite sure what the social model will be that will deliver that, as opposed to multiculturalism which was there in the '60s or '70s. And part of my anxiety about the criticism of multiculturalism has been that we shouldn't ditch it until we've constructed an alternative. That anxiety is all the more acute because minorities are disproportionately affected by these sorts of policy shifts. They have a huge stake in the social model, whether we're talking about assimilation or multiculturalism or something else.

TC: It's interesting to look at this from the viewpoint of the majority population rather than the minorities. I think the majority population have always felt unrepresented by the notion of multiculturalism. So if you ask white people, for example, if they have an ethnicity, they don't seem to appreciate that they have. They see ethnicity as something which only applies to minorities. They also see 'diversity' as something that is only relevant to minorities. Similarly, most people see faith as another dimension which doesn't include them – the British tradition has been built upon the submerging of faith differences in the public sphere. Asked about faith schools, for example, most people say they don't want them. They don't like the idea of extending them; they don't like the idea of extending faith in the public realm. All the time we're looking at this through the eyes of minority communities in ethnicity, faith and cultural terms. We also have to look at it through the eyes of the majority population, which generally feels uncomfortable – but perhaps the bringing together of age, gender, disability, sexual orientation with race, under the EHRC [Equality and Human Rights Commission[4]]will mean that, at last, 'difference' really will become something for everyone.

DH: What is the new model? This is where Ted has made a huge contribution, to his credit.[5] At the moment it's a discourse around cohesion, around integration, around a society that is much more intertwined than it was 20 years ago or 30 years ago. But I think that vision still has to evolve and crystallise into a model as such. It is confusing for people at the grassroots who have to implement these policies because they're not quite sure exactly where it is we're going. They know where we've come from and they're used to certain methods of working, which I think sometimes they have carried forward with them. And there is a genuine issue with trying to find representation for faith communities. How do you find democratic representatives in the Muslim community, where there are no internal democratic structures to percolate those sorts of representatives?

TC: I'm not somebody who says, multiculturalism is dead. I actually think it is about a new model of multiculturalism. I don't think we should attempt to bury multiculturalism. I think we've got to formulate it so we are clearer about the commonalities and assert them. The Commission for Integration and Cohesion[6] has been doing that – like the English language and dimensions of citizenship. So I think that's a key debate and I agree with Dilwar that the debate has moved on quite a bit. It's surprising how many people now accept the promotion of Britishness, for example, that everybody should have English language skills. It was very difficult even five or ten years ago to say that. So I think this model is going to evolve from the emphasis on separate identities to much more on trying to build up the commonalities and be clearer about what they are.

DH: I welcome that very much. I think we see remarkably eye to eye on these issues. I think also, as Ted mentioned earlier, it's very important that there is engagement with these issues in the wider public, the wider British society. There is a sense that these issues are for ethnic minorities only. That's not healthy, I think, even for those people in those minority boxes. I think breaking down the sort of otherness of those groups is a very crucial part of the whole integration process. And that needs a psychological shift where, you know, that net is cast out so it includes everybody.

Ed: How do you see the contribution of inter-faith work to community cohesion?

MA: I strongly believe that if you start funding one particular faith you are going to antagonise the others who are equally in need of funds and support. Look at the infrastructures within the Salvation Army, within the Church of England and the Free churches which have helped society come together. I would advocate that we need to strengthen those institutions, which could in turn help the minority faiths – rather than just singling out Muslims for funding. We need a partnership with the established church and the minority faiths. St Philip's Centre in Leicester, for example, is doing a marvellous job when it comes to the training of Muslim institutions and developing partnership working.[7]

TC: Inter-faith networks have burgeoned enormously – there's much more of an attempt now at a local level to reach across different faith boundaries. What I don't get much feeling for is whether that percolates down beyond the faith leaders into the communities. There's a number of programmes, which are pretty crude, like getting 200 Muslims to go to the local church and 200 Christians to go to the local Mosque in Burnley. These are the sort of one-off programmes. I guess they have some impact but it seems to me that the burden of cohesion is still very much in the leadership area. Actually, often they're really only talking to each other in times of crisis, rather than actually how do you make inter-faith knowledge and understanding a reality to people on the ground. So I think there's a long way to go with this.

DH: Well, it's something that everybody seems to agree on – there seems to be a consensus on this issue. While I think inter-faith forums do a tremendous amount of good, often – especially with the Muslim community but also other faith communities – women seem to be remarkably absent and young people as well. It's very much about talking and discussing – literally dialoguing. There's very little, I think, about social impact, although I think that this is an emerging aspect of inter-faith work. I think it's beginning to happen in some places. So you've got your, I don't know, Imams and clergy playing cricket together but you've also got youth leadership programmes.

Ed: What about the contribution of faith to civil society more generally?

TC: I'm not sure how much support there is to civil society really – to those sorts of institutions that the government talks about wanting to encourage. You don't actually see anything on the ground that supports them, in fact just the opposite. Government trends seem to undermine civil society and the value of local democratic frameworks. I don't think there's real clarity about what they're expecting from civil society, particularly at a local level, and how we build it and make it meaningful, a place where people want to be. Why would people actually get involved in those sorts of civil society things if they're constantly denigrated and there's no real power to them? In terms of non-governmental civil society, it seems to me at a low level. We've had various reviews but actually I find it very hard to believe that social capital is meaningful in the UK at the moment. There's no real will from employers to support it, you know, the amount of work that they do with getting their employees involved in civil society. Yes, there's some good examples but it's not anything which is pervasive. We still have problems with anybody volunteering for anything from the Brown Owl in a Brownie pack to any other role. So I just think there's a huge gap there.

DH: I agree. I suppose it's interesting that the major funders now of civil society initiatives are Quakers and religious foundations – Joseph Rowntree and other such groups. Unless there is that groundswell of vibrancy in civil society, you could argue that citizenship itself would only ever be about politics and voting. But there is the London Citizens[8] sort of model of organising that very consciously targets trade unions and faith groups – faith organisations and congregations because it feels that these are the networks that can actually pull people in. The model very much relies on you bringing a particular number of people to assemblies to show that you have democratic capital. Faith networks have that community spirit. We've said a lot of negative things about faith groups, but this is one of those things that is an enduring positive aspect of faith communities. They still provide that sense of community and shared identity and a sense of sharing and belonging at a very local, very real level. And I think that's why they will remain relevant in policy terms for a long time to come.

MA: There are tools within every faith which could help society – these need to come out of the pulpit. The pulpit leader needs to be spelling out those things – these are our values, this is how we can conduct ourselves, this is how we can contribute to society. Look at faith charities raising money for any calamity that takes place anywhere in the world. Faith is always at the forefront. I think if that comes from the pulpit – in all faiths – it will show how we enhance the life of all British citizens regardless of their faith and race. We need to move away from the negative view that faith divides people. Leadership from all faiths, and in particular I am emphasising Muslim leadership, needs to move out and have an open dialogue with wider communities. Places of worship should not only be places of worship, they need to be community centres and focal points for the community, where people can go with ease and seek help to participate in the wider society. An open door policy for all faiths is in the interest of our country.

Ed: Critics argue that multiculturalism offered undue respect to certain 'negative' aspects of minority cultures. Do you agree?

DH: Multiculturalism could be seen as relativising everything and therefore creating an absolute plurality – so that everything was above criticism. And I think this is one of the aspects of multiculturalism that definitely needed to be changed. So I welcome this debate, I think it's an important way in which we can critique the status quo. Within Muslim circles, there have been the usual community reactions of not washing dirty linen in public and so on, but I also think that 9/11 has been an important breaker of that taboo. 9/11 forced people to come out and – on the issue of extremism – be quite critical about extremist tendencies and individuals. It's really only after 9/11 that you see a very public criticism of individuals by other Muslims. And so you get groups like the Muslim Parliament[9] quite clearly talking about forced marriages and issues like that. I presume this will increase with time. I think there is a sense of confidence that people are now able to discuss these issues more publicly and want to be more vocal about them. But I wouldn't pretend that the situation is as it should be yet.

TC: I think there's a class dimension to that as well, Dilwar, because I think this is true in well-educated, relatively wealthier sections of some minority communities – just as there are more progressive views among some sections of the white communities. But I think in a lot of minority communities – and not just the Muslim community – there's still a very great reluctance to discuss these issues and to break taboos and tackle some of the unacceptable behaviours. I think we need to think more about the role of women. We think about faith as a male institution and, of course, so many of the faith bodies discriminate against women in so many ways – in terms of representation in church, in churches and in mosques, ordination, and in social and cultural terms. Credence has been given to 'cultural sensitivities' in the past and they have been allowed to conflict with what were in other circumstances fought for as universal human rights.

DH: It's interesting that, within the general underachievement of Pakistani/Bangladeshi communities, the girls are doing far better than boys. For the next generation, you'll have a cohort of much-better-educated girls than boys – a generation that's much more confident and now has the skills to match their aspirations. Now this can go either of two ways, those aspirations can be fulfilled or, if they're challenged, it's going to create all sorts of tensions and dynamics within the Muslim community. So that's yet to come and I think that's going to be an important issue.

Ed: How do you see the role of faith in the public realm in Britain?

DH: My background is in researching Muslim communities across Europe and I think our secular arrangement is quite moderate actually. I know that within a national context sometimes it can look quite materialistic and aggressive but if we compare it to a place like France, you get a sense of perspective and a sense of balance. There is no single model of secular arrangements – every country has its own and usually these things are hugely dependent on history and culture. Had it not been for Henry VIII, we wouldn't have the arrangement that we have between church and state, and so on. So I think, in the grand scheme of things, the British secular model is a fairly positive one and it can always be tweaked here and there in specific places. I would argue for a moderate secularism. And I don't mean anti-faithism or anti-clericalism but a separation of spaces into religious and secular, public and private – a separation of the public sphere and the private sphere but allowing the interjection of faith values and ideas as a point of debate. I think we need to be open to that.

It should not be squashed out of the public sphere and the public arena. At the same time, I think people of faith should not presume a sense of privilege to their interjections. So everyone can come into that open arena and give a reasoned basis for their opinion. Be allowed to argue their cause and get shot down if necessary.

MA: Since 7/7, Muslims are finding a place in public debate. I think we have got enough legislation to give us a freedom of religion under the Human Rights Act. There are enough avenues for the Muslim community to come out and bring their concerns into mainstream forums, rather than keeping them inside the community and blaming the media and others. British Muslims need to be brave enough to take on the criticism. I have a strong belief that Islam, Christianity and Judaism – and other minority faiths – are all quite shock proof: they can take the criticism and have a healthy debate. And there is an expectation now from government that the faiths should contribute – that they can enhance cohesiveness and harmony in society and improve the quality of the life. There is capacity within faith institutions on many issues: environmental issues, flooding issues, animal rights and welfare. In every area of public conflict, faith people need to have a contribution.

TC: There's still some very difficult choices to be made about the space that we give to faith in the public realm. I'm not sure who makes those decisions. So, for example, take abortion, people hosting the debate on TV or whatever, immediately turn to somebody from the Catholic Church as opposed to saying, well actually this debate is entirely an issue to be resolved by various clinicians on the basis of science or medical needs, and/or the choices of the individual women concerned. Who makes the decision to invoke a moral dimension? And if you magnify that into all other areas of debate about ethics and morality – even to questions of what women wear – who is making the decision about the prominence and privilege we give to religious groups? And in a largely secular society, it's possible to say that, if government is meeting with faith groups – obviously it currently gives priority to meeting Muslim groups but has met with other faith groups as well – and faith represents, just for the sake of argument, 10% of the population, surely they should be meeting secular groups 90% of the time and faith groups only 10% of the time? But proportionality – in numerical terms at least – is not the principle that we are working on here. It seems to me these are incredibly difficult decisions and I'm not sure they're ever made as such, and if they are, it is on pragmatic rather than principled grounds.

DH: The narrative of faith communities would be that the public realm has been secular with a small 's' all this time – it's been pitted against us. What we're seeing now is a very slight readjustment of that balance, rather than any special privilege. I think most of the faith activists who do go and meet government would probably say that, in the grand scheme of things, the exposure or input we're having is still marginal as opposed to other, you know, secular worldviews. So there really is this mismatch of faith communities seeing their position as quite marginal, and the other perspective seeing faith groups as having a disproportionate impact. And this happens on different levels, I mean Muslims always say that they are marginal but other faith communities could see the Muslim community as getting disproportionate amounts of funding, time, exposure and so forth. That's part of the competing perceptions and perspectives that we have to constantly negotiate. It's like when Black communities are given funding, people in other parts of the city say, why aren't we getting funding? But multiculturalism is a dynamic process of change, so such questions and priorities will always have to be resolved.

MA: I think the more you separate faith from society, the more it causes misunderstandings and misconceptions. We are so fortunate in Britain to have an open society, and we need an open debate on the place of faith. We simply cannot go back to – let me put it another way – a body without a soul. I think that is how I look at society without faith: it is a soulless body.

Notes

[1] *Faith in the city* was published in the UK in 1985, authored by the Archbishop of Canterbury's Commission on Urban Priority Areas (ACUPA, 1985). The report created controversy because of the link it drew between growing spiritual and economic poverty in Britain's inner cities and Thatcherite policies. In 2003 the Commission on Urban Life and Faith was established to report on the 20th anniversary of *Faith in the city*, publishing its final report *Faithful cities* in 2006 (CULF, 2006).

[2] Selected local authorities were funded during 2007/08 by the Department of Communities and Local Government to act as Preventing Violent Extremism (PVE) Pathfinders. Under the scheme

local authorities have supported capacity-building projects in Muslim communities aimed at building their resilience to extremist ideology and fostering their participation in wider community life (DCLG, 2007). Activities have focused on improving mosque governance and community leadership, and the inclusion of Muslim women and Muslim youth. Following the end of the Pathfinder programme, the Home Office has sought to combine this community-based approach with a tighter security focus, locating PVE firmly within its broader counter-terrorism strategy.

[3] *Face-to-face and side-by-side: A framework for inter faith dialogue and social action* seeks to develop a framework for partnership to support increased inter-faith dialogue and social action (DCLG, 2008).

[4] The EHRC is a non-departmental public body established under the 2006 Equality Act, with the aim of promoting equality and human rights, eliminating discrimination, reducing inequality, building good community relations and ensuring equality of opportunity. It replaces the Equal Opportunities Commission, the Commission for Racial Equality and the Disability Rights Commission (www. equalityhumanrights.com).

[5] Ted Cantle was appointed in August 2001 by the Home Secretary to lead the review of the causes of the urban disturbances in Northern England. The subsequent 'Cantle Report' was responsible for the initial development of the 'community cohesion' policy agenda (Cantle, 2001). Ted Cantle sets the agenda in its wider historical and intellectual context in *Community cohesion: A new framework for race and diversity* (Cantle, 2008).

[6] The Commission on Integration and Cohesion was established by the government in 2006 to look at how local areas can make the most of diversity while being able to respond to the tensions it may cause. Following an extensive consultation process, regional outreach visits, engagement of key stakeholders and local communities and research, the Commission published its final report *Our shared future* in 2007 (CIC, 2007).

[7] The St Philip's Centre, Leicester, is a national ecumenical training centre that provides training for Christians, those of other faiths and civic partners. It is committed to promoting good working relationships and dialogue between people of all faiths (www.stphilipscentre.co.uk). As Chapter Four demonstrates, St Philip's is just one example of many such initiatives across Britain.

[8] London Citizens is a diverse alliance of active citizens and community leaders who campaign on issues around poverty and social justice, and support the development of community groups and local leaders. Faith groups (from different religions) have played an important role in mobilising coalitions including schools, student organisations, trades union branches and residents' groups (www.londoncitizens.org.uk).

[9] Established in 1992, the Muslim Parliament concerns itself with the affairs of Muslims in Britain and abroad by debating issues and championing causes. It is an independent national forum in which Muslims of different denominations and ethnic origins meet. The aim of the organisation is stated as 'Working towards creating an informed, caring and morally upright Muslim community ready to engage with its environment at all levels' (www.muslimparliament.org.uk).

References

ACUPA (Archbishop's Commission on Urban Priority Areas) (1985) *Faith in the city: A call for action by church and nation – The report of the Archbishop of Canterbury's Commission on Urban Priority Areas*, London: Church House Publishing.

Cantle, T. (2001) *Community cohesion: A report of the independent review team*, London: Home Office.

Cantle, T. (2008) *Community cohesion: A new framework for race and diversity* (2nd edn), Basingstoke: Palgrave.

Casciani, D. (2005) 'Analysis: segregated Britain?', *The Guardian*, 22 September, http://news.bbc.co.uk/1/hi/uk/4270010.stm

CIC (Commission on Integration and Cohesion) (2007) *Our shared future*, London: CIC, www.integrationandcohesion.org.uk/Our_final_report.aspx

CULF (Commission on Urban Life and Faith) (2006) *Faithful cities, a call for celebration, vision and justice*, London: Methodist Publishing House and Church House Publishing.

DCLG (Department of Communities and Local Government) (2007) *Preventing Violent Extremism Pathfinder guidance*, London: DCLG.

DCLG (2008) *Face-to-face and side-by-side: A framework for inter faith dialogue and social action*, London: DCLG, www.communities.gov.uk/documents/communities/pdf/613367.pdf

Giddens, A. (2008) 'Multiculturalism', News Update, www.polity.co.uk/giddens5/news/multiculturalism.asp

LGA (Local Government Association) (2002) *Guidance on community cohesion*, London: LGA.

Modood, T. (2007) *Multiculturalism: A civic idea*, Cambridge: Polity Press.

Parekh, B. (2006) *Rethinking multiculturalism: Cultural diversity and political theory* (2nd edn), Basingstoke: Palgrave Macmillan.

Woodhead, L. and Heelas, P. *(2005) The spiritual revolution. Why religion is giving way to spirituality,* Oxford, UK and Malden, MA: Blackwell.

SIX

Blurred encounters? Religious literacy, spiritual capital and language

Christopher Baker

Introduction

This chapter is framed by the idea of 'blurred encounters', particularly the encounters between faith groups, government, academia and other partners in the third sector. These encounters have recently increased in scope and frequency due to current government policy aimed at increasing the role played by the third sector (including faith groups) in key policy areas such as social cohesion, local democracy and public service provision (for example, LGA, 2002; PIU, 2002; Home Office, 2004).

The following discussion first describes the phenomenon of blurred encounters. This provides a basis for the subsequent identification and exploration of different levels of miscommunication that can occur in situations of blurred encounters between faith- and non-faith-based sectors. It is shown that that these miscommunications stem as much from attempts to use shared language and concepts as the use of different ones. This is because faith and non-faith sectors have different understandings and interpretations of key motifs used within government policy, a problem exacerbated by the fact that government interpretations based on secular/modernist assumptions of the importance of neutrality and bureaucratic accountability are usually assumed to be the default ones. These observations stem from qualitative research undertaken by the author and colleagues at the William Temple Foundation (WTF), involving fieldwork with nine church-based congregations and initiatives in three rapidly regenerating areas of Manchester in the period from 2002 to 2005 (William Temple Foundation, 2003; Baker and Skinner, 2005, 2006).

The chapter concludes with, first, the offer of a strategy for addressing this problematic of miscommunication between language and values through a common discourse based on different types of social capital and, second, some comments about what can be defined as 'religious literacy' and whether there is a further need for other bridging concepts or metaphors, apart from 'capital', within public political discourse.

Blurred encounters – good or bad?

Blurred relationships between two individuals or institutions might be interpreted positively as signifying an apparent consensus, a pleasing overlap of ethos, philosophies and methods of working. The parties may enjoy being part of a partnership or network from which they have been previously excluded, as in the case of a faith-based organisation attending a strategic policy meeting previously reserved for secular bodies.

The 'downside' of blurred encounters is that there can be a loss of essential identity or ethos. If this happens, the initial euphoria and excitement of being part of a larger consensus or network can turn to cynicism, frustration and a sense of values, visions and distinctiveness compromised. Indeed, it can turn to anger if it is discovered that, while there is talk of empowerment, the actual reality of how power and resources are shared has not fundamentally changed. It may be found that personal or group identity is being used by *others* in the pursuit of *their* wider political goals. The consequent internalised anger usually produces 'burnout' or depression because motivating visions, values and ideas have been rendered inoperable by the 'fog' of the blurred encounter. At best, there is a sense of a loss of moral bearings and energising ethos. At worst, people may feel conned and even exploited.

This, it is suggested, is how some faith groups feel about the invitation to become co-creators of civil society and joint-providers of social enterprise and social capital. The WTF research certainly found these sentiments within some of the case-study churches with which it worked in 'regenerated' parts of Manchester. As the French philosopher Jacques Derrida (1996) pointed out when discussing the art of hospitality, whenever we have an encounter with another outside our normal experience, there are risks involved. We can either *eat well*, enjoying a rich feast of new experiences and learning, developing our existing understanding of the world; or we can *be eaten*, finding our essential identity consumed within the encounter until nothing of value, with which we entered into the relationship or partnership, is left. In a rapidly changing political and cultural context described by Stoker (2004, p 18) as 'multi-level governance' and 'post-bureaucratic localism', it is suggested here that some faith groups, and indeed some non-faith groups, are asking: 'Are we eating well or are we being eaten?'.

Blurred encounters and regeneration

One major source of blurred encounters between faith-based and other partners is the concept of regeneration, an idea that lies at the heart of the UK government's social and economic renewal of cities and communities. Furbey (1999) has traced some of the origins of the word from Stoic philosophy, Christian Gnosticism and Hindu theology through to the 19th-century liberal socialist tradition of Ruskin and Tolstoy and to recent New Age and postmodern religions that offer psychological pathways to self-development. He concluded that the concept of regeneration offers an 'infinitely inclusive canopy' under which all may shelter and agree (Furbey, 1999, p 422).

This elastic, yet opaque, word certainly caused some confusion within the church groups engaged with the WTF research in Manchester. They were drawn towards its semi-spiritual connotations in the hope that they would be allowed to interpret regeneration in a dynamically religious, as well as utilitarian, way. Yet the frameworks of political discourse and funding opportunities were not established to allow them to express these spiritual and religious aspirations. Many churches and other faith groups have striven hard to reframe how they describe their community work to fit into the technocratic, targets-based language that the regeneration industry requires. They have also created formalised accountability structures that perhaps over-professionalise their more informal ways of operation (see, for example, Locke et al, 2003). The immediate prize for this reordering of priorities can be secular funding. However, the collateral costs can be high. Churches already weakened through a lack of human and financial capital take on tasks they cannot own as a whole. Recent research indicates an over-reliance on one person (usually an ordained leader) and inadequate management structures within which to deploy paid staff. This leads to many smaller church-based projects suffering premature burnout or else the loss of their former support base as they are perceived to adopt an overtly liberal or secular agenda (Orton, 2006).

Thus, the implementation of the language of regeneration has occurred within a dominant one-way discourse. Church and other faith groups have sought to adapt to secular understandings of regeneration, as expressed in policy relating to housing-led regeneration and public service provision, health, crime and education targets. Yet, a strong perception emerged from the Manchester research that churches' understandings of regeneration were not so welcome. They felt that their language and values had been 'hijacked' by other partners for the sake of ticking the right boxes, especially those boxes requiring evidence of 'added value'. The churches judged this tick-box approach as expressing a form of monitoring and evaluation, which ignored the deeper changes in institutional culture required for real regeneration. In the words of one focus group member: 'They've stolen our words, and not recognised us, not recognised what we're doing' (Baker and Skinner, 2005, p 23). Another participant said: 'They [other regeneration agencies] have got to get all these [holistic] words in the document and we're thinking – it's so frustrating. I think it starts to lose its power ... you know, once the language is hijacked then it starts to lose its power' (Baker and Skinner, 2005, p 23).

The Manchester groups also felt that government policy on engaging faith communities, and local government implementation of this rhetoric, remain largely tokenistic since faith communities are still excluded from the 'tables of power'. This perception has been supported by further recent research exploring the mixed experience of faith-based organisations engaging in government-sponsored initiatives at the local level, such as Local Area Agreements and Local Strategic Partnerships. For example, 44% of over 100 faith representatives on Local Public Partnerships interviewed by the Church Urban Fund (2006) felt that their main partners were not open to discussing 'faith' issues. Furthermore, general levels of misunderstanding, together with some instances of overt hostility towards faith members and limited religious literacy, were reported. This resistance by secular partners to consultation with, and the incorporation of, faith groups in the policy frame may reflect ongoing mistrust as well as a lack of religious literacy (see Farnell et al, 2003).

Different conceptual frameworks – transcendent versus immanent

For non-faith-based partners, there is something intrinsic to faith groups that can make communication and understanding difficult. This section of the chapter draws on James Hopewell's (1987) influential analysis of the structure and nature of church congregations. Hopewell conducted in-depth longitudinal studies of three different US congregations, focusing on the stories that they told and the language that they used, shaping their almost unconscious perception of who they are and their role in the wider world. He identified four types of narratives in congregational life: romantic, tragic, comic and ironic.

Romantic stories expressed an heroic sense of adventure and excitement and romantic mission. One example from the Manchester research was from an Eden youth project where team members elect to live in a poorer community for a minimum of five years:

> We would talk about a God whose love and compassion for people is worked out through people, that that mission of God, if you like, doing his missionary bit by coming from heaven to earth is replicated by Christians who will continue to live out that purpose and emulate, in as far as it is possible, to emulate the life of Jesus, you know, showing compassion … putting himself into places, you know of, I suppose darkness, if you like. (Baker and Skinner, 2005, p 41)

Tragic tales portray 'the decay of life and the necessary sacrifice of the self before a resolution occurs' (Hopewell, 1987, p 60). The world is a harsher and more dangerous place and the heroic self must endure death in order to achieve resolution, a story clearly linked to the story of Christ's crucifixion. An example of a tragic story from the WTF research is from an Anglican parish church in Wythenshawe whose attempts to run a Learn Direct programme (a government-sponsored adult education scheme designed to top up their skills and learning) were constantly thwarted by burglaries and carjackings of computer equipment:

> I mean we had all these burglaries last year … and in that I was very aware of the cross and how actually we were called to be faithful in spite of the painfulness of that and I suppose when the Learn Direct Centre, which had been going so well, was closed down by the carjacking in January, that was a real sense of death and of loss and of brokenness … I think the PCC [parish church council] were very clear that actually if we chose to start the Learn Direct Centre up again, we were choosing to be burgled again. Reality is what that means … to take up our cross, but that that was what we as a Christian community were called to do. (Baker and Skinner, 2005, p 41)

Comic narratives are those stories that produce a happy ending in the face of apparent disaster, brought by the realisation of an unknown truth, a revelation (or gnosis) that dispels the crisis as the narrative moves from problem to solution.

Ironic stories are those that challenge the heroic:

> Miracles do not happen; patterns lose their design; life is unjust, not justified by transcendent forces. Trapped in such an ironic world, one shrugs one's shoulders about reports of divine ultimacies and intimacies. Instead of experiencing such supernatural outcomes, one embraces one's brothers and sisters in camaraderie. (Hopewell, 1987, p 61)

Within the WTF research, few narratives emerged that were ironic or comic, perhaps because, in these stories, it is more 'the self' that is in control, either actively resolving the situation or rejecting the transcendent. One quasi-ironic narrative in the Manchester study was a tough critique offered by one church community, which saw the regeneration of East Manchester as a new form of 'colonialism'. The existing white working-class culture was deemed as 'failing' and 'inappropriate' and given targets and tools by which to 'improve'. In this context, the church, ironically, saw itself as a counter-cultural influence against the 'missionary' zeal of the regeneration managers, who were promising the rewards of a new life in exchange for renunciation of old behaviours (Baker and Skinner, 2005, p 76).

Most of the Manchester stories were romantic or tragic narratives in which the self is either reliant on, or fits into, a worldview that is controlled in some way by a transcendent force that is called 'God'. God is present in suffering and will redeem it in some way. Within these narratives, God will lead people on a journey and is worthy of being trusted.

These extracts indicate moments where issues of religious literacy are raised most sharply. How does one reconcile forms of language that express such radically different worldviews? One set of languages and values (faith-based ones) will veer towards the claim to a higher, *transcendent*, authority as the basis for action and for setting benchmarks. As we have seen, this reference to a transcendent force, controlling or engaged in one's personal life, tends towards the romantic and tragic forms of narrative. The other set of languages (academic and policy based) looks to empirical evidence and humanly defined legal structures or market mechanisms to justify its approach. It operates within more *immanent* terms of reference and, within Hopewell's typologies, leans more to the comic (that is, a relentless rhetoric of 'happy' or successful outcomes as a result of policy initiatives) or to the ironic (a realistic assessment of the complexity of real life without recourse to divine intervention by which to resolve loose or untidy ends).

Are we destined to work in parallel languages and discourses that rarely cross over and connect? Or can we create a more dynamic and equal space where values and norms as well as policies and strategies can be explored? Having identified some aspects of the problematic of miscommunicated language, what might be solution? One way forward might be to develop the prevalent theoretical construct of social capital with reference to the role and identity of faiths in civil society.

The rise of spiritual and religious capital

The pervasive growth of *social* capital theory has led to resurgence in capital theory more generally. Thus, within the 'ecology' of the social capital field, *spiritual* and *religious* capitals have emerged as subsets. For example, a literature review by Iannaccone and Klick (2003) as part of a major Templeton Foundation research programme assumes spiritual capital to be: 'The effects of spiritual and religious practices, beliefs, networks and institutions that have a measurable impact on individuals, communities and societies' (cited in Metanexus, 2003). An influential contributor to the field, Pierre Bourdieu (1983), makes no reference to spiritual capital, but sees *religious* capital deployed to maintain the stability of what he calls the *habitus*, the dynamic domain of interpretations held by religious people that are inculcated by transcendent symbols and hierarchies of production in the religious field: for example, the role of priests as guardians of the sources of revelation that are mediated down to laypeople. Thus, religious capital keeps the religious field in good, working order by broadly functioning in similar ways to other forms of capital (for example, economic and cultural) by maintaining control over the means of production in the hands of the elite and at the expense of the masses.

In the light of its research, the WTF defines spiritual and religious capital somewhat differently, recognising the distinction between these two terms, but also their close connection:

- **Spiritual capital** *energises* religious capital by providing a theological identity and worshipping tradition, but also a value system, moral vision and a basis of faith. Spiritual capital is often embedded locally within faith groups but also expressed in the lives of individuals (Baker and Skinner, 2006).
- **Religious capital** is the practical contribution to local and national life made by faith groups.

These definitions distinguish between what *motivates* the engagement of faith-based communities and their *practical* actions. In other words, the *why* and *what* of church (in this case) contributions to their communities. The 'what' we have defined as religious capital: that is, the concrete actions and resources that faith communities contribute. The 'why' we have defined as spiritual capital: that is, the motivating basis of faith, belief and values that shapes the concrete actions of faith communities and individuals.

These concepts were an acknowledged influence in *Faithful cities* (CULF, 2006, p 3), a cross-denominational and cross-faith report by the Commission on Urban Life and Faith, a follow-up to the landmark *Faith in the city* report by the Church of England 21 years earlier (ACUPA, 1985). Its concept of **faithful capital** refers to the two 'distinguishing' elements brought to the public realm by faith groups; namely, their *language* (concepts such as 'love', 'hope', 'judgement', 'forgiveness', 'remembrance' and 'hospitality') and their *practices* (such as 'local rootedness', 'acceptance of failure', 'genuine participation and working together').

The qualities of spiritual and religious capital

Analysis of the WTF Manchester fieldwork permitted the development of a list of key aspects of a spiritual capital approach to the regeneration of poor communities. This list clearly has a Christian bias, since the sample survey were all Christian faith-based organisations. But it is reasonable to expect overlapping responses with other faith traditions, and research (ongoing at the time of writing) by WTF, funded by the Leverhulme Trust, will test concepts of religious and spiritual capital across faith groups and also groups who prefer to define themselves as 'spiritual' rather than religious. Such research also begins to reveal some of the deeper nuances behind existing sets of norms and values that are beginning to be identified (see, for example, Lowndes and Chapman, 2005).

Spiritual capital

Spiritual capital (as explored in the WTF Manchester study):

- focuses on transforming people personally and spiritually, as well as improving their area physically;
- values personal stories, especially about how individual 'regeneration' occurs;

- believes implicitly or explicitly that God is at work within regeneration and civil society;
- accepts that there is considerable and strong emotion experienced and expressed when working for healthy communities (for example: anger, frustration, cynicism, weariness, fragility) and acknowledges the importance and significance of 'feelings';
- introduces the values of self-emptying, forgiveness, transformation, risk taking and openness to learning;
- begins with the intention of accepting those who have been rejected elsewhere;
- values people's inner resources and their capacity to create their own solutions to their problems, ones that constitute a form of *liquid* capital, relating to intangibles such as ideas and visions, not exclusively claimed by a specific religious tradition.

Religious capital

Religious capital, meanwhile, reflects the pragmatic and functional outworkings of institutions and networks inspired by spiritual capital. It can be described, therefore, as a more solid form of capital. Typically, this will include:

- '*economic*' projects, such as local anti-poverty campaigns and the global Make Poverty History movement; measures to counter usurious practices and indebtedness, notably the Islamic practice of interest-free banking, and involvement in human well-being debates and related activities;
- projects contributing to the strengthening of *civil society and urban and rural regeneration*, such as the development of multi-use centres, empowerment networks, and volunteering and service provision schemes;
- involvement in regional *governance*, for example through regional faith forums and through the appointment of church members to relevant committees and boards;
- *educational engagement*, through primary, secondary and tertiary faith-based schools and college chaplains;
- presence in the *criminal justice system* through, for example, prison chaplaincies and restorative justice schemes.

The link between spiritual/religious capital and social capital

Social capital theory stresses the importance of relationships, networks and norms that can be used to enrich individuals and communities. According to now familiar formulations, bonding capital invested in tightly networked and homogenous groups allows people to 'get by', whereas bridging capital enables them to create new relationships and networks with people outside their usual group, creating a form of capital that allows them to 'get ahead' (Putnam, 2000, p 23). Linking capital allows people to span power differentials. As such, it is another form of 'getting ahead' capital.

The added value of religious capital

Faith-based organisations, like all institutions and organisations, can choose to invest their religious capital (buildings, volunteers and so on) either for the good of their own specific community (in which case it may become a form of negative bonding capital) or for the benefit of the wider community. The positive risk to their investment is that they increase their influence, acquire greater networks and secure actual hard economic capital as well. Conversely, the negative risk is that they may become disoriented and burnt out in meeting the extra demands put on them (see Orton, 2006).

The added value of spiritual capital

The spiritual capital of faith-based organisations (that is, the motivation provided by the theological beliefs, values and visions that energise their mission) is a similarly ambiguous form of capital. It can also exert a multiplier effect on existing religious capital. Two recent academic studies of faith-based social enterprises in Manchester refer to the greater commitment, creativity, work ethic and originality that these enterprises exhibit in working within some of the toughest social and economic environments compared with other similar secular or state-led projects (EIUA, 2005; Centre for Citizenship Studies in Education, University of Leicester, 2005). One such enterprise is a community-empowerment network called Community Pride, with clear Christian origins but ones expressed as ethos rather than as 'business statement'. This network operates across the cities of Manchester and Salford and was assessed as having the following strengths:

- a firm value base that allowed it to 'go the extra mile';
- a moral force and impact beyond its numbers;
- a sense of sharing that leads to mutual support;
- a belief in partnership;
- a commitment to trailblazing and identifying needs that are not otherwise being met;
- creating self-sustaining structures, not dependency;
- creating a niche market of operating that mixes both analysis and group work skills;
- recognising the significance of power structures;
- keeping up to date with current policy initiatives;
- translating knowledge and information for those who are affected by the decisions of others;
- feeding intelligence back to the policy makers (EIUA, 2000, p 8).

This evaluation made reference to Community Pride's mission statement, which included the expression of 'a desire to make real the values of the Christian Gospel' (EIUA, 2005, p 6). The link between this statement and qualities of 'going the extra mile', and having 'moral force and impact beyond its numbers', is implicit rather than explicit but the close connections are clear.

However, risks remain when an organisation exposes its spiritual capital to the logic of partnerships with the market or the state. Confronted with pragmatic needs for compromise and accommodation with other viewpoints and perspectives, it can undergo radical mutation. Sustainable spiritual capital requires a certain suppleness and flexibility. If it is too brittle there is the suggestion that it might snap, as the cognitive dissonance experienced by individuals or faith communities increases as the perceived risks associated with continuing engagement with civil society also increase. For example, research by Flint and Kearns (2004, p 12) among Church of Scotland congregations found that the more contentious a particular public partnership project was perceived to be by church communities (for example drug needle exchanges), the more dissent it provoked within congregations, and the more pressure there appeared to be to revert to bonding (that is, members-only care) rather than bridging capital.

Functionalist versus values-driven religious literacy

The remaining discussion is designed to inform future research in this field through reflection on two specific issues: the nature and significance of 'religious literacy' and the adequacy of the language of 'capital'.

Turning to the first of these themes, we can identify two kinds of religious literacy. First, there is 'functionalist' religious literacy, the 'what to do at a civic function and how to get funding' type of literacy (see, for example, Home Office, 2004). This is adequate as a first stage in developing understanding but is unlikely to lead to any deep cognitive or institutional change by faith-based and secular institutions.

Second, there is religious literacy that expresses engagement with others at the level of values and visions, and seeks understanding of the motivation of others. All institutions have values and visions and individuals have 'spiritual capital' whether or not they define themselves as religious or spiritual people. Leonie Sandercock (2006), a postmodern planner who also defines herself as a secular humanist, emphasises the supreme importance of restoring a sense of the sacred, not only within urban spaces but also within the processes of dialogue between different users of the city. She defines what she calls a secular spirituality, a set of values and visions that constitute a form of faith that needs to be publicly shared and delineated for the sake of uncovering a sense of the common good (or common goods) within increasingly diverse but also polarised communities: 'The faith at the heart of planning is very simple. It's our faith in humanity, in ourselves as social beings, in the presence of the human spirit and the possibility of realising/bringing into being the best of what it means to be human' (Sandercock, 2006, p 65).

As a planner she sees the importance of tapping into this faith as the building block for people's visions of the future for cities, and the creation of discourses that will create political partnerships based on more open and flexible communication. She is keen to question the difference between religion and spirituality. For Sandercock, spirituality, as opposed to religion, brings the prospect of a potential consensus around values, creating a shared political and social agenda for civil society:

> The values can be named as respect, caring, neighbourliness; a concern for building connections between people, building a caring human community ... a notion of a service for others. These are all old virtues, discussed by philosophers as well as theologians for thousands of years, but dismissed in the neo-liberal city, which has revived enlightened self-interest as its moral code. (Sandercock, 2006, p 66)

Sandercock's interest in articulating a secular spirituality reinforces the significance of a search for a values-driven religious literacy as a resource for a 'new form of planning action' (Sandercock, 2006, p 67). She is not averse to using a more affective (rather than rational) language. For example, she asks rhetorically: 'Can we explicitly cultivate love in the planning process?' (2006, p 67). Can we legitimately replace the word 'planning' with 'regeneration' or 'social cohesion'? The suggestion here is that we can.

This strongly articulated argument from a highly respected global academic and practitioner signals the importance of seeing *spiritual* capital as a related, but also distinctive, concept to religious capital. Spiritual capital is an inclusive term that expresses the values and visions of those who would define themselves as possessing spirituality, irrespective of an explicit, implicit or non-existent religious 'faith', and see spirituality (and the linguistic concepts associated with it) as an important source of motivation for their role and identity in civil society.

Two further points arise from this discussion. First, we should note that Sandercock's secular 'spiritual' capital works in very similar ways as religious spiritual capital in terms of motivation and action – that is, it energises and motivates action, but does so in the secular rather than religious areas (or fields) of civil society. Second, the concept of spiritual capital, working as it does in both secular and religious fields, could be developed as a tool for highlighting overlapping areas of consensus in terms of values and methodologies. In other words, it could become a 'bridging' tool that highlights commonalities between religions and secular agencies, rather than stressing radical and antithetical differences.

Paradigms beyond spiritual capital

Earlier discussion recognised benefits in using the concept of 'capital' as a way of facilitating conversations between faith-based and non-faith-based actors in civil society. However, metaphors can limit as well as advance understanding and there may be other ideas and frameworks by which to discuss the increasingly significant role of faiths in public life. Thus, Andrew Davey (2007) questions the use of 'faithful capital' (see above) as one of the central motifs in the *Faithful cities* report (CULF, 2006). He suggests that, instead of faiths being 'useful to government', which the use of 'capital' language can imply, faiths should be modelling what he calls 'intuitive models of critical engagement' (Davey, 2007, p 17). He suggests a category of 'everyday faithfulness' (rather than faithful capital), which can impact more on the public stage as 'prophetic faithfulness'. This 'everyday and prophetic faithfulness' is akin to a form of practical and critical wisdom that can invigorate and inspire grassroots communities. Here, Davey directly quotes the Colombian philosopher-theologian Eduardo Mendieta:

> Religion appears as a resource of images, concepts, traditions and practices that can allow individuals and communities to deal with a world that is changing around them by the hour. In the new 'unsurveyability' of our global society, religion appears as a compendium of intuitions that have not been extinguished by the so-called process of 'secularisation'. (Mendieta, 2001, p 20, cited in Davey, 2007, p 17)

Davey's discussion leans towards the theoretical. A more grounded analysis is required to explore those resources and methodologies belonging to faith groups that could be identified as 'intuitive models of creative engagement'. Nevertheless, this type of language shifts the focus from hard-edged outcomes to a more suggestive and symbolic level, emphasising images, symbols and traditional community practices that deepen and critique the current discourses of 'capital' in a more anthropological or person-centred approach.

Marion Maddox, a New Zealand public theologian, offers the metaphor of 'gift', in particular the gift of reconciliation and apology from the faith community on behalf of, and in partnership with, wider society. She traces the emergence of this idea within recent Australian political history and in particular the increasingly contested and controversial decade of work towards aboriginal reconciliation initiated by the Australian government in1992, a development that paralleled similar civil society initiatives in Canada, New Zealand, South Africa and the US). In 2002 John Howard, the Australian Prime Minister, stopped short of offering an apology to members of the 'Stolen Generation' of indigenous children, forcibly removed from families under policies of assimilation between 1900 and 1969. He did so on the grounds that those who carried out these policies at the time did so in 'good faith'. Other elements of Australian civil society intervened in protest. They organised a series of millennium bridge walks between indigenous and non-indigenous Australians. An estimated 400,000 Australians in Sydney alone took part in symbolic marches across local bridges, in a demonstration of apology. The 2000 Sydney Olympics reflected a further public rejection of Howard's stance when the indigenous athlete Cathy Freeman was chosen to light the Olympic Flame and rock band

Midnight Oil played the closing ceremony in black suits with the word 'SORRY' emblazoned on their backs.

Maddox suggests that such efforts to build a progressive politics founded on recognition of difference and a repudiation of past colonial policies are based on 'a religious-redemptive model of reconciliation', which contains the following elements:

- a genuine apology that relies on faith and hope for assurance of forgiveness;
- intergenerational apology (for example, the apology by President Clinton in 1997 for the slavery and ill-treatment of African Americans 200 years previously) that suggests the possibility that forgiveness comes from a more transcendent source;
- the idea of culpability for things you did not personally do has echoes of the Christian idea of 'original sin';
- the process that implies belief in the transformative power of receiving and giving forgiveness (Maddox, 2007, p 96).

This list bears a striking resemblance to some of the elements of spiritual capital identified in the WTF research, particularly the emphasis on the need for forgiveness and reconciliation as a precursor to transformation. 'Transformation' is perceived as deep-seated change that occurs at both individual and community levels. Here, Maddox quotes Australian philosopher Michael Philips:

> In reconciliation politics forgiveness is a transformative political agency which makes possible the restoration of the political community. It puts an end to enmity and makes peace, and hence the future, possible. (Philips, 2003, p 229, cited in Maddox, 2007, p 97)

The language of 'gift' suggests that the contribution of reconciliation to wider society, often derived from the work of religious communities (Maddox, 2007, pp 97-8) and with strong spiritual and religious overtones, is something that is offered freely, without an ulterior motive or the expectation of a return on investment, which the harder-edged language of capital might suggest. However, as some critics point out, these public (and therefore political) symbolic acts of reconciliation can become what Maddox (2007, p 96) refers to as 'crypto-religious events' that have no explicit religious language or ritual but confer a rhetorical, and therefore potentially confusing, experience that does little to change fundamental inequalities. In other words, can the language of gift simply degenerate into the emptiness of gesture politics?

Conclusions: blurred encounters – are we eating well or being eaten?

This chapter started by suggesting that the government's use of semi-religious concepts such as 'regeneration' is unhelpful because it leads to a blurring of boundaries between faith groups and policy strategists, who can have very different ideas of what that word means, and the criteria by which one can measure its outcomes. Discussion then moved to an examination of different types of narrative deployed by Christian faith groups, as a way of helping to explain where this mismatch of understanding and language occurs. The ideas of spiritual and religious capital were then advanced as a possible 'bridging' discourse of language that might help promote religious literacy between faith- and non-faith-based sectors. This discourse was then connected to the emerging concept of 'secular spirituality', which also invokes the heart-driven language associated with religious groups within political discourses in an attempt to improve the quality of urban space and civil renewal. The last sections explored emerging faith-based examples of alternatives to the linguistic paradigm of 'capital' (for example the language of 'intuitive engagement' and the ideas of 'gift') by which to articulate the role of faith in civil society.

The conclusion to be drawn from this debate is that the language of faith, when brought into the arena of policy, is likely to be contested due to the confusion and imprecision of key terms and concepts currently used and the conflict caused by the sometimes opposing use of both transcendent and immanent horizons of language. The blurring of boundaries is therefore a frustrating, but also creative, process which holds promise for a better quality of discourse and political process.

A paramount concern within these 'blurred encounters' is that the type of language used by all concerned moves beyond a *functionalist* level of discourse to one that is more connected with uncovering the values and visions that all people hold dear when engaging in public life. This will involve a commitment to a more profound type of literacy involving deep listening to language that expresses core values and visions, and a commitment to the exploitation of the many points of connection and overlap. In Derridian terms, this is 'eating well', enjoying a wider range of insights and ideas than one normally encounters. However, it is equally important to avoid being 'eaten' in such an encounter. Therefore, individual and partner organisations, both faith and non-faith, need to be clear and confident about the parameters of their identity so that the basis of engagement is both realistic and sustainable.

References

ACUPA (Archbishop's Commission on Urban Priority Areas) (1985) *Faith in the city: A call for action by church and nation – The report of the Archbishop of Canterbury's Commission on Urban Priority Areas*, London: Church House Publishing.

Baker, C. and Skinner, H. (2005) *Telling the stories: How churches are contributing to social capital*, Manchester: William Temple Foundation.

Baker, C. and Skinner, H. (2006) *Faith in action: The dynamic connection between spiritual and religious capital*, Manchester: William Temple Foundation.

Bourdieu, P. (1983) 'Forms of capital', in J. Richardson (ed) *Handbook of theory and research for the sociology of education*, New York: Greenwood Press.

Centre for Citizenship Studies in Education, University of Leicester (2005) *Building a bridge into inclusion for the young people of North East Manchester*, Manchester: The Message Trust.

Church Urban Fund (2006) *Faithful representation: Faith representatives on Local Public Partnerships*, London: Church Urban Fund.

CULF (Commission on Urban Life and Faith) (2006) *Faithful cities: A call for celebration, vision and justice*, London: Church Housing Publishing/Methodist Publishing House.

Davey, A. (2007) '*Faithful cities*: locating everyday faithfulness', *Contact*, no 152, pp 8-20.

Derrida, J. (1996) 'Remarks on deconstruction and pragmatism', in S. Critchley, J. Derrida, E. Laclau and R. Rorty (eds) *Deconstruction and pragmatism*, London and New York: Routledge.

EIUA (European Institute for Urban Affairs) (2005) *Impact Report, 2002–5*, Manchester: Community Pride Initiative.

Farnell, R., Furbey, R., Shams Al-Haqq Hills, S., Macey, R. and Smith, S. (2003) *Faith in urban regeneration?, Engaging faith communities in urban regeneration*, Bristol: The Policy Press.

Flint, J. and Kearns, A. (2004) *The role of Church of Scotland congregations in developing social capital in Scottish communities: enabling and cohesive or irrelevant and divisive?*, Centre for Neighbourhood Research Paper No 16, Glasgow: University of Glasgow.

Furbey, R. (1999) 'Urban "regeneration": reflections on a metaphor', *Critical Social Policy*, vol 19, no 4, pp 419-55.

Home Office (2004) *Working together: Co-operation between government and faith communities*, London: Faith Communities Unit.

Hopewell, J. (1987) *Congregation: Stories and structures*, London: SCM Press.

Iannaconne, R. and Klick, J. (2003) 'Spiritual capital: an introduction and literature review', Prepared for the Spiritual Capital Planning Meeting, Cambridge, MA.

LGA (Local Government Association) (2002) *Faith and community: A good practice guide for local authorities*, London: LGA Publications.

Locke, M. and Lukka, P. with Soteri-Proctor, A. (2003) *Faith and voluntary action: Community, values and resources*, London: Institute for Volunteering Research and University of East London.

Lowndes, V. and Chapman, R. (2005) *Faith, hope and clarity: Developing a model of faith group involvement in civil* renewal, Leicester: Local Government Research Unit, De Montfort University.

Maddox, M. (2007) 'Religion, secularism and the promise of public theology', *International Journal of Public Theology*, vol 1, no 1, pp 82-100.

Mendieta, E. (2001) 'Invisible cities: a phenomenology of globalisation from below', *City: Analysis of Urban Trends, Culture, Theory, Policy, Action*, vol 5, no 1, pp 7-26.

Metanexus Institute (2003), www.metanexus.net/spiritual%5Fcapital/what_is.asp

Orton, A. (2006) 'Contesting "good practice" in English faith-based community work: changing agendas and changing organisations', Unpublished paper prepared for the Faith-Based Organisations and Human Geography paper session of the 102nd Annual Meeting of the Association of American Geographers, Chicago, IL, 7-11 March.

Philips, M. (2003) 'The politics and theology of Aboriginal reconciliation', Unpublished PhD thesis, University of Sydney.

PIU (Performance and Innovation Unit) (2002) *Social capital: A discussion paper*, London: PIU.

Putnam, R. (2000) *Bowling alone: The collapse and revival of American community*, New York: Simon and Schuster.

Sandercock, L. (2006) 'Spirituality and the urban professions: the paradox at the heart of urban planning', *Planning Theory and Practice*, vol 7, no 1, pp 65-97.

Stoker, G. (2004) *Transforming local governance: From Thatcherism to New Labour*, Basingstoke: Palgrave Macmillan.

William Temple Foundation (2003) *Regenerating communities: A theological and strategic critique – end of Year One report – mapping the boundaries*, Manchester: William Temple Foundation.

SEVEN

Religion, political participation and civic engagement: women's experiences

Brenda O'Neill

Introduction

The role that religion plays in shaping political and civic behaviour has received significant attention in recent years (see, for example, Norris and Inglehart, 2005). Religion's influence on political behaviour has been well established (Layman, 1997). Burns et al (2001, p 231) suggest that 'religious institutions are a crucial component of civic society'. Within this area of research, however, women have received less focused attention. This stems perhaps from religion's longstanding negative impact on women's equality, and the traditional roles that it can assign to them in both the public and the private sectors (Woodhead, 2001; Inglehart and Norris, 2003). Extant research has revealed the specific ways in which women are sometimes able to benefit and find individual agency within the most patriarchal of religious institutions (see, for example, Ammerman, 1987). Within many such institutions, women can receive the stimulus and claim the agency necessary for participating in political and civil arenas (Caiazza, 2005; O'Neill, 2006). A comprehensive understanding of the connections between religion, political participation and civic engagement requires an examination of women's experiences in faith communities (Burns et al, 2001; Inglehart and Norris, 2003).

This chapter moves in that direction by examining the connection between religion and spirituality and women's political and civic engagement. The distinction between religion and spirituality is an important one. Much of the research examining political behaviour focuses on *religion*, that is, the set of beliefs and practices related to an organised and communal belief system, rather than *faith* or *spirituality*, which involves the more personal and subjective elements of such organised systems. The former has been shown to affect women's political attitudes and behaviour in multiple ways. Women's private roles as wives and mothers and, more publicly, as protectors of society's morality, reflect the prescriptions found within various religions. First-wave 'maternal' feminism in Canada was intimately connected to women's participation in religious organisations, helping to explain not only their acceptance of private and public roles but also the focus on good works, charity and social reform designed to raise the moral standard of early 20th-century Canada (Newman and White, 2006). Women's memberships of religious organisations continue to account for a large portion of their volunteering activities (O'Neill, 2006). In spite of apparent increasing secularisation and the progressive forces of second-wave feminism, women nevertheless remain more religious than men at the aggregate level (O'Neill, 2001). Spirituality's role in shaping political and civic engagement remains underresearched.

Much research looking at women's religious involvement and its connection to their political behaviour, particularly that employing quantitative methodologies, offers only superficial analysis. The goal of this chapter is to develop our understanding of how women respond to religious influences and how these shape women's decisions regarding active citizenship. Importantly, it focuses on a comparison of the political and civic engagement of women who identify with an organised religion and those who instead prefer to label their religious beliefs and practices 'spirituality'. This distinction was identified in focus groups held with Canadian women in the summer of 2004 (O'Neill, 2007). These focus groups guided the collection of survey data also employed in this investigation: a telephone survey of Canadian women outside of the province of Québec undertaken in the summer of 2007. The survey assesses women's religiosity and spirituality, and includes a battery of questions on a number of political issues and women's political and civic behaviour. The result is a unique opportunity for evaluating the role that religion and spirituality play in shaping women's political behaviour in a modern liberal democracy and, as such, for evaluating whether and how policies ought to consider addressing women's relative underrepresentation in formal political processes.

The focus on Canada provides an important international dimension to the examination of faith in the public sector. The Canadian experience may well differ from that in the UK due, for example, to important demographic, linguistic and religious distinctions. Yet similarities (both are advanced capitalist democracies with parliamentary systems and single-member plurality systems) make the comparison a useful one. And the use of a large-scale opinion survey allows for the development of generalisations regarding the role of religion and spirituality in shaping women's political and civic engagement that cannot be drawn from the more qualitative research undertaken with the focus groups.

Why study women?

A key justification for studying women independently is that their private and public lives remain sufficiently different from men's, raising the possibility that there might exist distinctive explanations for their political participation and civic behaviour (O'Neill, 2002). Research on gender differences in political engagement suggests that generalisations are difficult to make. Women have met and, in some cases, matched men's turnout levels in elections. Women are more likely to be involved in cause-oriented activities such as boycotting (refusing to buy products or services for political and/or ethical reasons), 'buycotting' (choosing specific products and services because of political and/or ethical choices made by the company) and signing a petition (Norris et al, 2004; Stolle and Micheletti, 2006). They do not, however, join political parties or interest groups at the same rates as men (Norris et al, 2004); they reveal levels of political interest, efficacy (belief in one's ability to effect political change) and knowledge that are lower than men's (Gidengil et al, 2006); and they continue to be underrepresented in elected office (Inglehart and Norris, 2003).

Research also reveals that women's and men's opinions differ on certain political issues. Most often cited are differences in attitudes on the use of force (women are less supportive); public safety and regulation issues (men are less supportive); and compassion issues (women are more supportive) (Shapiro and Mahajan, 1986). Explanations have focused on differences in women's and men's values and, in particular, the relative importance that they assign to equality, justice and individual freedom. Gilligan's (1982) work highlights women's concentration on connections and relationships over equality and justice concerns. Structural explanations for differences in political behaviour focus on the role of resources provided by education, income and occupation for the skills, motivation and opportunity that they offer (Schlozman et al, 1994). Women's associational networks, in particular, are also important for the skills that they afford as well as the recruitment potential that they provide (Verba et al, 1995; O'Neill, 2006). Women's involvement in such networks can mirror levels found among men although the types of associations differ substantially (Lowndes, 2006; Norris and Inglehart, 2006). Where men are more likely to participate in professional associations and sports clubs, women are more likely to be found in religious and charitable organisations (Burns et al, 2001; Norris et al, 2004). Socialisation provides an additional explanation for differences in attitudes and behaviour. Gender identity, norms and roles help to explain women's political attitudes and behaviours (Sapiro, 1983; Everitt, 1998).

The importance of religion in women's lives has been well documented and existing research suggests that it is fundamental to understanding women's political behaviour (Inglehart and Norris, 2003; Caiazza, 2005; O'Neill, 2006). Women's attitudes are mobilised and shaped by their memberships in religious organisations (Burns et al, 2001; O'Neill, 2001, 2006; Inglehart and Norris, 2003). Both religious leaders and group memberships serve to provide information that influences political behaviour and attitudes (Layman, 2001). Women are more likely to report religious attendance and greater strength of religious beliefs than men (Burns et al, 2001; Woodhead, 2001). Women in the US have been found to be highly visible as inter-faith group leaders (Caiazza, 2005), while research on faith-based groups in the UK noted the dominance of women at the grassroots level but their increasing absence at higher decision-making levels (Furbey et al, 2006).

Discussions in the focus groups

Women in the focus groups were asked how they defined and interpreted the role of religion in their lives (O'Neill, 2007). Among the themes that developed, three are particularly revelant in the context of the role that religion plays in shaping women's political and civic participation:

- religion as it is practised both privately and as part of a community;
- religion as belief versus religion as action;
- religion versus spirituality.

The first theme relates to the practice of religion. Women identified the many ways in which religion is practised as key to its importance in their lives; religion is, in many ways, the **practice of faith**. For several, religion is a relationship, personally with God and with the faith community. The importance attached to attending organised religious services, however, varied widely. For some, membership in a faith community required not just individual prayer and devotion but also a commitment to the community. For others, the practice of faith could take place individually.

The second theme involved contrasting religious beliefs with religious action. The identification of religion as a set of morals to guide one's actions and as a belief system was repeated in a number of the groups. One participant explained it in the following manner: 'I would say [religions] hold all the same values fundamentally; for instance, forgiveness, mutual help, helping one's fellow man, the idea of believing in something greater than oneself'.

Themes of selflessness, aid to others, humility, love, forgiveness, morality, discipline and patience permeated the conversations. An understanding of religion as a belief system was often combined, although in some instances contrasted, with its depiction as action. Faith is not simply a roadmap that provides direction for living one's life; instead, it also embodies action that helps on a daily basis to bring those beliefs to action. According to another participant:

> 'The active part goes beyond spirituality. With spirituality, I could do that quietly in the privacy of my home but with religion, an organised religion, it calls me to be active in my community. So then I attend the services that they have, I do good deeds in the community, I help the ones who need assistance. Whether it be picking someone up who needs a lift to get there or be it someone who needs food. So my religion calls me to action.'

A number of women identified volunteering activities as key elements of their religious lives, including volunteering for soup kitchens, sponsoring families from abroad, catechism classes, visitation of the sick and elderly, and collecting clothing for the needy. The importance of 'doing unto others' was linked to a norm of reciprocity: by caring for others in the community one could expect that the community would return that care if and when necessary.

An interesting theme that ran through several of the groups relates less to the definition and practice of religion than to reaction to the use of the term 'religion'. For a number of the participants in the focus groups, 'religious' was not an identifier that they were willing to employ to describe themselves even when they exhibited characteristics that one would normally associate with the term. This unwillingness seems to stem from an association of religion with organised religion as an institution as well as from perceived negative stereotypes others had of religious individuals. That is, a number of the women who were unwilling to call themselves 'religious' were, instead, quite happy to adopt the label 'spiritual' because the latter is a more personal identity, while the former is linked to institutions and organisations that are not always seen in a positive light. According to one woman,

> 'I hate the word religion; spiritual maybe is the right word? ... I do attend religious services at a non-denominational [church] a few times a week ... I would be religious in most people's sense of the word, because I believe in the Bible and I'm a Christian and all the rest of it, but I find 'religion', it's just too.... When I think of religion, I think of something that's more organised. With mine, it's more of a relationship with God – it's more spiritual.'

The latter was a particularly stiking finding in that the shift to spirituality has not been adequately addressed in research on women's engagement. These conversations suggest that religion plays an important role in women's lives, although the manner in which it is practised and the degree to which it includes a call to action varies. Also, for some women, the structure and organisation found in established religions led them to adopt a more personal form of faith.

The discussion in the focus groups mirrored the dominant themes found in research on religion and political participation, including thinking of religion as a multidimensional phenomenon and considering beliefs, behaviour and belonging as the key religious dimensions of relevance for politics (Layman, 2001). Nevertheless, processes of secularisation have meant that these dimensions have diminished as important markers of religious commitment, particularly within Western Christian religions (Houtman and Aupers, 2007). Others have countered the general claim of declining religiosity and have focused instead on new forms of religion (sometimes referred to as 'post-Christian spirituality') that are increasingly evident in Western states. This 'relocation of the sacred' (Houtman and Aupers, 2007, p 315) is less structured than traditional religiosity and more individualised (Heelas and Woodhead, 2005). Moral imperatives and practices in this new version of religious belief are subjectively determined, according to what 'works' for each individual, and what allows one to be 'faithful to one's "inner voice" and [to] trust one's "intuition"' (Houtman and Aupers, 2007, p 307).

Research conducted in Kendal, in the North West of England, found that 'much of the growth of associational, holistic spiritualities of life is due to the fact that women have decided to participate' (Heelas and

Woodhead, 2005, p 94), a result the researchers ascribed to women's increased valuation of 'the intimate, expressive, relational path to subjective well-being' (Heelas and Woodhead, 2005, p 100). Others have identified women's adoption of spirituality as being related to detraditionalisation (Houtman and Aupers, 2008); that is, the diminished role of external and authoritative sources of meaning and identity that has occurred in modern societies leaves women more likely to search within themselves for moral compasses.

The shift away from institutionalised forms of worship towards more individualised forms of spirituality is not viewed universally as a move towards a completely individualistic form of worship. Instead, researchers have argued that spirituality is 'socially constructed because people are socialised into a spiritual discourse about the self' (Houtman and Aupers, 2007, p 317) and that it is neither atomistic, discrete nor selfish, but rather holistic (Heelas and Woodhead, 2005). Robert Putnam's (2000) research, on the other hand, has argued that the decline in identification with traditional religious organisations (as a form of associational membership) has led to a decline in social capital and as such helps to explain declining involvement in civic life.

Survey analysis

Given the preceding discussion, the following questions guide the subsequent analysis:

- What relationships exists between religion and spirituality and women's political and civic engagement? To what extent does religious orientiation assist or restrict women's patterns of engagement?
- How do religion and spirituality differ across generational, socioeconomic and minority/dominant group divides? Do these divides minimise the effects of religious orientation on civic and political engagement?

To investigate these questions, this chapter employs the Women's Political Participation Survey 2007, undertaken between July and October 2007. The survey collected information on a set of political attitudes and behaviours, religious and feminist identification, and a battery of sociodemographic variables. The sample included 1,264 women from nine Canadian provinces (the province of Quebec was excluded).

The variables of greatest interest relate to the respondent's religious and spiritual involvement. Women were first asked to identify their religion, if they had one. Women who responded that they had none, did not know, or who refused to answer the question were then asked whether they would consider themselves to be a spiritual person. As such, spiritual respondents include only those women who do not identify with an organised religion, ensuring that the label is not confused with traditional uses of the term within organised religions associated closely, for example, with salvation. The results reveal that more than three in four of the women (77.8%) identify with a religious denomination, the largest being Catholic (34.8%), the United Church (13%), Anglican (10.8%) and unaffiliated Protestant and Christian identifications (12.7%). Importantly, two thirds of the women who did not identify with an organised religion responded that they would nevertheless consider themselves to be spiritual (14.7% of the sample). Around 8% of the sample neither identified with an established religion nor considered themselves to be spiritual. The vast majority of Canadian women in our sample identified with a Christian faith, in keeping with Canadians generally. In the 2001 Canadian Census, 72% of Canadians identified with a Christian religion (Statistics Canada, 2003). As such, the discussion in this chapter of the role that religion plays in shaping women's political participation and civic engagement reflects the dominance of Christian religions. The small proportion of Canadians identifying with non-Christian religions makes it difficult to render any conclusions regarding the role of these religions in shaping behaviour, particuarly with a sample of only around 1,200 women.

Religious identification and professed spirituality are rather blunt instruments to adequately capture the various dimensions of each. The importance that individuals ascribe to religion and spirituality probably determines the relative impact of 'religion' and 'spirituality' on other aspects of their lives. Hence, a typology was created from both religious identification (organised, spiritual, neither) and strength of religion/spirituality (very important and less than very important). The result is a fivefold classification: strong identifier, weak identifier, strong spiritualist, weak spiritualist, and secularist.

The typology breaks the sample of women into two larger and three smaller groups. The two largest groups are composed of women who, first, identify with a religious denomination and, second, either report that religion plays a very important role in their lives (37.4% of the sample) or that it is less than very important (40.8%). The smaller groups consist of spiritual women for whom spirituality plays a very important role in their lives (7.4%), spiritual women who report that it plays a less than very important role in their lives (6.9%) and secular women who report neither religious nor spiritual forces in their lives (7.6%). Thus, although spiritualist women probably differ in many respects from those who identify with organised religions, they are similar in that half in each group suggest that their faith/spirituality is important in their lives.

A first step is to assess differences in attitudes across the typology. Three questions in the survey explore civic-minded behaviour. The first is the degree to which people can be trusted, which relates directly to Putnam's notion of social capital. Associational involvement is said to increase levels of generalised trust. One might expect, given social capital theory, that women who are members of organised religions would exhibit higher levels of trust than spiritual and secularist women. The results suggest that such an assumption would be misplaced. A clear distinction in attitudes on this question is between spiritualist and other women. While over half of spiritualist women believe that people can generally be trusted, roughly 40% of the remaining women respond in a like manner (results not shown). In social capital terms, spiritualist women have higher stores of one element that can lead to greater engagement in the community: generalised trust.

A second question of interest in addressing women's civic behaviour is the degree to which they 'always put the needs of others ahead of their own'. Altrusim has formed a core element of the formal doctrines of many religions, particularly in the role ascribed to women as mothers. For spiritualists, on the other hand, this outward-looking value is unlikely to constitute a key element of what is, at its core, a more self-directed form of worship. The results suggest that this is indeed the case. Women who identify, even weakly, with a traditional religious faith are more likely than other women to believe that they always put others' needs ahead of their own. Whereas roughly a third of identifiers respond in this manner, closer to one in five of the remaining women respond similarly. This may help to explain patterns of civic engagement. Importantly, however, their responses to this question might only reflect the *perception* of selflessness rather than actual behaviour.

The final attitudinal question addresses the importance of tradition. Respondents were asked how well the statement 'Tradition is very important to you' described them. A majority (63.3%) of strong identifiers and just under half of weak identifiers (47.3%) indicated that it described them very well. In contrast, tradition is much less important for the remaining women. For secularist women, in particular, fewer than one in four said that the statement described them very well. Thus, religious identification is associated with a conservative outlook, at least in the importance of tradition. Such an outlook might help to explain the willingness and unwillingness of women to adopt unconventional political behaviours.

The key purpose of the chapter is to assess how religious and spiritual beliefs affect women's political and civic engagement. Table 7.1 provides a breakdown of participation in activities by religious type. The data reveal that spiritualist women are generally more likely to engage in both politics and their communities than other women. Thus, strong spiritualist women are much more likely to be very interested in politics (30.1%) than other women, by a margin of at least 14 percentage points. Similarly, they are twice as likely to have been a member of a political party (27.7%) than strong and weak identifiers (14.4% and 12.4% respectively) and weak spiritualists (14.8%), and more than

Table 7.1: Political and civic engagement by religious typology (%)

	Strong identifier	Weak identifier	Strong spiritualist	Weak spiritualist	Secularist
Very interested in politics[a]	18.7	15.7	30.1	16.1	16.3
Voted in last federal election[a]	82.9	73.7	79.8	81.2	58.4
Member of a political party[a]	14.4	12.4	27.7	14.8	8.3
Member of an interest group[a]	12.9	10.4	23.7	25.3	5.2
Signed a petition in last 12 months	27.9	28.2	41.3	31.0	30.2
Ever taken part in a demonstration[a]	18.8	13.2	35.1	32.2	20.8
Boycotted product in last 12 months[a]	21.7	21.6	37.0	39.1	22.1
Buycotted product in last 12 months[a]	38.3	36.7	57.1	48.9	41.8
Worked to bring about a change in local neighbourhood or school	65.4	65.7	76.6	71.3	63.5
Volunteered for a group	63.1	59.0	57.4	67.0	56.3
Total number (maximum)	*472*	*517*	*93*	*89*	*96*

Note: [a] indicates that differences are significant at the 0.05 level.

three times as likely as secularist women (8.3%). Spiritualist women are also significantly more likely to have been a member of an interest group (roughly one in four). In comparison, roughly one in ten of identifiers and just over one in 20 of secularist women have joined such organisations. Thus, on several measures of traditional religious involvement, spiritualist women exhibit greater levels of engagement than either religious or secular women.

The degree to which spiritualist women reveal distinctive levels of political engagement is particularly pronounced for non-traditional modes of political engagement. Spiritualist women, both weak and strong, are far more likely to have ever taken part in a demonstration, and to have boycotted and buycotted a product in the last year, than other women. Strong spiritualist women are also more likely to have signed a petition in the last year than other women. It appears that women who have adopted a religious outlook that is more individualistic, and which discounts traditional institutions, are more likely than other women to be drawn to political activities that occur on a more individualistic basis, which provide a greater perceived measure of effectiveness, and which bypass traditional political institutions. This finding reflects arguments for the growing strength of post-materialism (Inglehart, 1997) and for the importance of cognitive mobilisation in helping to explain both the decline in deference to institutions and individuals in positions of authority and the desire for more direct and effective forms of political action (Nevitte, 1996).

The trend continues when the lens is turned towards civic engagement. When asked whether they had ever 'worked to bring about some kind of change in your neighborhood or local school', over 70% of spiritualist women responded in the affirmative. Identifiers and secularist women were also very engaged, at over 60% in each case. Rates of more formal volunteering, however, reveal a slightly different pattern in that weak spiritualist and strong religious identifiers exhibit the highest volunteering rates, at 67% and 63% respectively. For both forms of civic engagement, secularist women reveal the lowest rates of participation. However, these differences are not especially large.

The final step is to assess the independent effect of religious identification and spirituality on different forms of engagement. Table 7.2 provides the results of linear regression analyses that include dummy variables for: our religious typology, age categories, immigration status and visible minority status, as well as variables for education and household income (see the Appendix at the end of the chapter for a brief explanation of the regression analyses). The dependent variables are additive variables for traditional political participation, non-traditional

Table 7.2: Determinants of political and civic engagement

	Traditional political participation (1)	Non-traditional political participation (2)	Formal and informal volunteering (3)
Weak identifier	**–0.26**	**–0.23**	**–0.21**
Strong spiritualist	0.09	**0.34**	0.00
Weak spiritualist	0.20	0.21	–0.13
Secularist	**–0.54**	0.04	**–0.20**
18 to 30 years	**–1.84**	–0.09	**0.18**
31 to 40 years	**–1.28**	0.22	0.01
41 to 50 years	**–0.76**	0.12	**0.16**
51 to 60 years	**–0.44**	**0.26**	0.4
Education	**0.14**	**0.16**	**0.08**
Household income	**0.06**	**0.03**	**0.04**
Immigration status	**–0.45**	0.08	**–0.21**
Visible minority status	**–0.76**	**–0.80**	–0.04
Constant	**–0.67**	–0.12	**0.62**
Adjusted R^2	0.293	0.142	0.089
Total *N*	827	883	902

Note: Entries are unstandardised linear regression coefficients; bold entries are statistically significant at $p < 0.05$. Omitted categories for dummy variables are strong identifier, over 60 years of age, non-immigrant and non-visible minority. Education ranges from 1 (some elementary) to 11 (doctorate). Household income ranges from 1 (less than $20,000) to 10 (more than $100,000).

political participation and volunteering (see the Appendix for the construction of these variables). The goal is to determine whether differences across the categories of the religious typology remain after having accounted for the impact of key determinants of political and civic engagement. For example, participation is decreased among younger, poor and less educated women, given the role that income and education play in shaping individual ability, motivation and opportunity to engage in the political and civic arenas (Burns et al,

2001). Also, research has established that immigrant and visible minority women exhibit political and civic behaviours that differ from other Canadians. On the one hand, people born outside Canada often undergo a period of adjustment after their arrival, during which their levels of participation are lower than average. Over time, however, their participation often approaches average levels (Jedwab, 2006; White et al, 2006). Members of visible minorities also often experience levels of marginalisation and discrimination that directly affect their ability to engage effectively with the political system (Burns et al, 2001).

The analyses reinforce existing research findings on the importance of socioeconomic resources, life-cycle and generational effects, and integration for participation patterns. Traditional forms of participation are much less employed by young women, the less educated, those born elsewhere and those of visible minority status. Non-traditional forms of participation are less common among women with less education, lower household incomes and of visible minority status. Interestingly, age matters less for this form of participation: the only age group to stand out in this regard is that of women between the ages of 51 to 60 years who reveal a higher level of participation than all other age groups. The final form of engagement – formal and informal volunteering – also appears to require the resources available to those with higher educations and incomes, and is more likely to be undertaken by Canadian-born than other women. Women below 30 years of age and those between 41 and 50 years of age are also more likely than other women to volunteer.

However, is it the case that religion and spirituality play some independent role in shaping women's civic and political engagement? The analysis suggest that this is the case but their impact varies with the type of engagement in question. In the first regression, strong female 'identifiers' and both strong and weak 'spiritualists' exhibit levels of traditional participation that are significantly higher than those exhibited by secularist and weak religious identifiers, a pattern that is repeated for volunteering activities. Secular women and those with only a weak attachment to an organised religion are less likely to devote time to volunteering. Thus, for conventional forms of political and civic engagement, something associated with identifying as a spiritualist and with a strong religious identity provides an independent participatory boost. For non-traditional participation, on the other hand, the pattern differs. Here we see that strong religious identifiers, weak spiritualists and secularist women are indistinguishable in their participation levels. Weak religious identifiers, on the other hand, are significantly less likely than other women to engage in non-traditional forms of political action while strong spiritualists stand apart for their relatively high propensity to engage in such political acts.

Discussion and conclusion

The goal in this chapter was to evaluate how women's religion and spirituality shape their political participation and civic engagement. Spirituality is distinguished from religion as a more recent and less organised form of worship that has received relatively little focused research attention. The results suggest that spirituality ought not to be overlooked as roughly 15% of women display a willingness to identify themselves by this label. While 15% may seem relatively insignificant compared with the 78% who identify with a religious denomination, the fact that the larger group may be shrinking while the smaller one is growing underscores the importance of understanding the role that such an identity plays in shaping citizen engagement (Heelas and Woodhead, 2005).

Religion shapes political and citizen engagement in multiple ways: by developing a value system that encourages community involvement; by providing opportunities for participation; and by encouraging the development of skills that provide the ability to participate. In short, it encourages thinking about the community and one's responsibility to it. Religion is often a call to action. Its impact on engagement depends, not surprisingly, on the relative importance that it plays in an individual's life. The greater its importance, the greater its impact. Its impact also varies according to the type of engagement in question. Religion is most likely to encourage traditional forms of participation such as political party and interest group membership and formal and informal volunteering. It tends to have little effect in encouraging protest and consumer-based political activity.

The results of this investigation also suggest that spirituality plays a similar role in shaping political and civic engagement. 'Spiritualists' are often indistinguishable from women with a strong religious faith in their engagement. They are as likely to vote, join parties and interest groups, and to volunteer. They differ, however, in the lack of differentiation in the participation rates between those for whom spirituality plays an important, rather than a less important, role in their lives. All women who identify as spiritual are as likely to engage in traditional and formal and informal volunteering as strong religious women. An additional exception lies in their non-traditional political participation. Whereas strong religious, weak spiritualist and secular women display indistinguishable levels of involvement in these activities, strong spiritualist women are unique in their significantly higher levels of participation in protest, demonstrations and consumer-based political action. Understanding why spirituality leads to enhanced political activity requires further study. How identification with the newer, more self-directed and less group-based forms of worship enhances the ability, motivation and opportunity for participation can only be a matter of speculation here. One possibility lies in the higher levels of generalised trust that these women exhibit; quite simply, trusting your neighbours encourages social interaction and civic action. Another possibility is the low level of importance assigned to tradition. Political action that eschews traditional political channels would seem tied to such beliefs. At the very least, it would appear that the greater focus on individual needs exhibited by spiritual women does little to diminish their political and civic engagement overall.

These results can assist in the development of policy designed to encourage women's engagement. Women's political and civic engagement are key policy concerns given women's consistent underrepresentation in positions of political and civic authority. Religious organisations provide a tremendously important route to women's engagement. Women are present in large numbers in these organsations, they assist in the development of the skills, values and efficacy that encourage their participation in and with their communities in multiple ways, and religious women are more engaged in and with their communities than other women. Importantly, the participatory boost provided by these organisations assists women in overcoming the barriers erected by social and economic forces such as income, education and ethnicity. As such, governments ought to be encouraged to seek women's participation where they *are*, whenever possible by encouraging participatory democratic practices that involve religious organisations. Such efforts would undoubtedly result in a direct increase in women's representation but could also result in indirect effects such as greater numbers of women running for office. The importance of motivation in encouraging women's political involvement should not be understated (Lawless and Fox, 2005).

The degree to which policy decisions can harness the potential that exists in spirituality's connection to increased engagement is more speculative given the relatively limited research that exists on the question. The project may be made more difficult by the fact that 'spiritual' women are less likely to be easily identified given the relative lack of identifiable organisational structures. What is more certain is that this nascent form of faith encourages an active form of citizenship among women that may offset recent trends towards disengagment in traditional political processes. As such, religion and spirituality combined offer important untapped avenues for encouraging women's participation in more formal political processes that could result in greater political responsiveness to their values.

References

Ammerman, N. (1987) *Bible believers: Fundamentalists in the modern world*, New Brunswick, NJ: Rutgers University Press.

Burns, N., Schlozman, K.L. and Verba, S. (2001) *The private roots of public action: Gender, equality, and political participation*, Cambridge, MA: Harvard University Press.

Caiazza, A. (2005) *The ties that bind: Women's public vision for politics: Religion and civil society*, Washington, DC: Institute for Women's Policy Research.

Everitt, J. (1998) 'The gender gap in Canada: now you see it, now you don't', *Canadian Review of Sociology and Anthropology*, vol 35, no 12, pp 191-219.

Furbey, R., Dinham, A., Farnell, R., Finneron, D. and Wilkinson, G. (2006) *Faith as social capital: Connecting or dividing?*, Bristol: The Policy Press.

Gidengil, E., Goodyear-Grant, E., Nevitte, N. and Blais, A. (2006) 'Gender, knowledge and social capital', in B. O'Neill and E. Gidengil (eds) *Gender and social capital*, New York: Routledge, pp 241-72.

Gilligan, C. (1982) *In a different voice: Psychological theory and women's development*, Cambridge, MA: Harvard University Press.

Heelas, P. and Woodhead, L. (2005) *The spiritual revolution: Why religion is giving way to spirituality*, Malden, MA: Blackwell Publishing.

Houtman, D. and Aupers, S. (2007) 'The spiritual turn and the decline of tradition: the spread of post-Christian spirituality in 14 Western countries, 1981-2000', *Journal for the Scientific Study of Religion*, vol 46, no 3, pp 305-20.

Houtman, D. and Aupers, S. (2008) 'The spiritual revolution and the New Age gender puzzle: the sacralisation of the self in late modernity (1980-2000)', in G. Vincett, S. Sharma and K. Aune (eds) *Women and religion in the West: Challenging secularization*, Aldershot: Ashgate.

Inglehart, R. (1997) *Modernization and postmodernization: Cultural, economic and political change in 43 nations*, Princeton, NJ: Princeton University Press.

Inglehart, R. and Norris, P. (2003) *Rising tide: Gender equality and cultural change around the World*, New York: Cambridge University Press.

Jedwab, J. (2006) 'The roots of immigrant and ethnic voter participation in Canada', *Electoral Insight*, vol 8, no 2, pp 3-9.

Lawless, J. L. and Fox, R. L. (2005) *It takes a candidate: Why women don't run for office*, New York: Cambridge.

Layman, G.C. (1997) 'Religion and political behaviour in the United States: the impact of beliefs, affiliation and commitment from 1980 to 1994', *Public Opinion Quarterly*, vol 61, no 2, pp 288-316.

Layman, G.C. (2001) *The great divide: Religious and cultural conflict in American party politics*, New York: Columbia University Press.

Lowndes, V. (2006) 'It's not what you got, it's what you do with it: women, social capital, and political participation', in B. O'Neill and E. Gidengil (eds) *Gender and social capital*, New York: Routledge, pp 213-40.

Nevitte, N. (1996) *The decline of deference*, Peterborough, Ontario: Broadview Press.

Newman, J. and White, L.A. (2006) *Women, politics and public policy: The political struggles of Canadian women*, Toronto, Ontario: Oxford University Press.

Norris, P. and Inglehart, R. (2005) *Sacred and secular: Religion and politics worldwide*, New York: Cambridge University Press.

Norris, P. and Inglehart, R. (2006) 'Gendering social capital: bowling in women's leagues?', in B. O'Neill and E. Gidengil (eds) *Gender and social capital*, New York: Routledge, pp 73-98.

Norris, P., Lovenduski, J. and Campbell, R. (2004) *Gender and political participation* [online], The Electoral Commission, Available at: www.electoralcommission.org.uk

O'Neill, B. (2001) 'A simple difference of opinion? Religious beliefs and gender gaps in public opinion in Canada', *The Canadian Journal of Political Science*, vol 34, no 2, pp 275-98.

O'Neill, B. (2002) 'Sugar and spice? Political culture and the political behaviour of Canadian women', in J. Everitt and B. O'Neill (eds) *Citizen politics: Research and theory in Canadian political behaviour*, Toronto, Ontario: Oxford University Press, pp 40-55.

O'Neill, B. (2006) 'Canadian women's religious volunteerism: compassion, connections, and comparisons', in B. O'Neill and E. Gidengil (eds) *Gender and social capital*, New York: Routledge, pp 185-211.

O'Neill, B. (2007) 'Exploring the religious and feminist beliefs of women' [online], American Political Science Association Annual Meeting, Chicago, IL, 30 August-2 September, Available at: http://convention2.allacademic.com/one/apsa/apsa07/index.php?cmd+apsa07&id

Putnam, R. (2000) *Bowling alone: The collapse and revival of American community*, New York: Simon and Schuster.

Sapiro, V. (1983) *The political integration of women: Roles, socialization and politics*, Urbana, IL: University of Illinois Press.

Schlozman, R.L., Burns, N. and Verba, S. (1984) 'Gender and the pathways to participation: The role of resources', *Journal of Politics*, vol 56, pp 963-90.

Shapiro, R.Y. and Mahajan, H. (1986) 'Gender differences in policy preferences: a summary of trends from the 1960s to the 1980s', *Public Opinion Quarterly*, vol 50, no 1, pp 42-61.

Statistics Canada (2003) *Religions in Canada*, [Online], Ottawa, Ontario: Statistics Canada, Available at: www12.statcan.ca/english/census01/ Products/Analytic/companion/rel/contents.cfm

Stolle, D. and Micheletti, M. (2006) 'The gender gap reversed: political consumerism as a women-friendly form of civic and political engagement', in B. O'Neill and E. Gidengil (eds) *Gender and social capital*, New York: Routledge, pp 45-72.

Verba, S., Schlozman, K.L. and Brady, H.E. (1995) *Voice and equality: Civic voluntarism in American politics*, Cambridge, MA: Harvard University Press.

White, S., Nevitte, N., Blais, A., Everitt, J., Fournier, P. and Gidengil, E. (2006) 'Making up for lost time: immigrant voter turnout in Canada', *Electoral Insight*, vol 8, no 2, pp 10-6.

Woodhead, L. (2001) 'Feminism and the sociology of religion: from gender-blindness to gendered difference', in R.K. Fenn (ed) *The Blackwell companion to sociology of religion*, Malden, MA: Blackwell, pp 67-84.

Appendix

Dependent variable construction and wording

The three dependent variables are indexes that add together responses to several questions regarding engagement. If the respondent participated in an activity in the index, they received 1 point on the index.

Traditional political participation variable

- Did you happen to vote in the last federal election in January 2006?
- What about the last provincial election in [*fill PROVINCE*]? Did you vote?
- And did you happen to vote in the last municipal election?
- Have you ever been a member of a political party?
- Have you ever been a member of an interest group working for change on a particular social or political issue?

Non-traditional political participation variable

- In the last 12 months, have you signed a petition?
- Have you ever taken part in a demonstration?
- In the last 12 months, have you boycotted any products for political, ethical or environmental reasons?
- In the last 12 months, have you bought any products for political, ethical or environmental reasons?

Volunteering variable

- Have you ever worked with others to bring about some kind of change in your neighbourhood or local school, for example raising money to pay for playground equipment?
- Have you volunteered time for a group or organisation other than a political party in last 12 months?

Methodological note regarding regression analysis

Linear regression is a statistical tool that assesses the independent effects of independent variables (X) on a dependent variable (Y). Table 7.2 presents the results of three separate regression analyses: column 1 is for traditional political participation, column 2 for non-traditional political participation and column 3 for formal and informal volunteering. The set of variables in the column on the left includes the independent variables. The individual entries in columns 1 to 3 are regression coeffients, which represent:

- the difference in the dependent variable resulting from a one-unit difference in the independent variable or;
- the difference in the dependent variable between an omitted category of a variable and the category that appears in the regression (referred to as a dummy variable).

Each coefficient is assessed on two dimensions: substantive significance (how much of an impact does it have on the dependent variable?) and statistical significance (how certain are we that the results that have been obtained from a sample of respondents are also found in the population?).

On the first dimension, the first entry in column 1 (−0.26) suggests that a weak identifier comes in 0.26 units lower on the traditional political participation scale than a strong identifier (note: strong identifier is the omitted dummy variable category for the religious typology variable; all four categories of this typology are compared to this omitted category).

The ninth entry in column 1, on the other hand, suggests that the score on the traditional political participation variable is 0.14 units higher with every 1 unit increase in education. The second dimension is assessed on a purely statistical basis; entries in bold represent those coeffecients that are likely to exist in the population 19 times out of 20 (or in 95% of the samples pulled from the population). As such, coefficients in bold are more robust and stable than others and can be discussed with a greater level of certainty.

EIGHT

Young people and faith activism: British Muslim youth, glocalisation and the *umma*

Richard Gale and Therese O'Toole

Introduction

In this chapter, we examine a case study of faith activism among young Muslim men in Birmingham, UK, exploring how faith identity frames their public engagement and political activism. The chapter engages with two core concerns raised in this volume: the ways in which faith frames or orientates public action; and how we should conceptualise the public realm as a site of faith activism.

Our case study arises from a two-year qualitative study of black and minority ethnic young people's political engagement, in the course of which we worked with young members of a locally based Muslim 'justice movement'. This movement organises around a political and social agenda that is concerned with increasing public and political participation among Muslims, as well as achieving goals of 'social justice'. In relation to the latter, this involves both mobilising around notions of justice for Muslims, and the articulation of Muslim notions of justice more generally. We explore how faith identity and values animate these young men's political activism and the different scales (ranging from the local to the global) at which this is expressed. In particular, we see the articulation of a highly 'glocalised' political sensibility, which shapes both their political concerns, and the terrains on which they are active. These expressions of the 'global in the local' are apparent in their use of a variety of 'grammars' of action, ranging from mobilisation within local neighbourhood and community contexts, to engagement in global debates over the politics of Muslim identity. In exploring these intersections between the local and the global, we reflect on how identification with the *umma* (the global community of Muslims) forms an important dimension of young Muslims' renegotiation of their identities in relation to familial and cultural heritage and their localised lived experiences.

We begin by highlighting some of the ways in which young British Muslims have featured in the public domain – particularly in relation to debates on political and civic participation and social and community cohesion, before setting out some observations we consider key to our consideration of political participation and notions of the public. Following this, we discuss recent research on forms of political and public engagement among Muslims, particularly in relation to contemporary expressions of global Islam, which points us to the significance of understanding the 'glocal' forms of engagement that lie at the core of our case study of the Muslim Justice Movement (Anderson, 2003; McDonald, 2006; Mandaville, 2007). Finally, our case study explores how young activists relate to the public sphere by focusing on their personal engagement with faith and how this informs their identities and political action.

Young Muslims in the public realm

Recent decades have witnessed mounting public concern in the UK and across a number of advanced democracies over declining levels of citizen participation in formal political processes (Norris, 2002). While explanations of this trend vary considerably, there is now a widely held view, focused largely on analyses of electoral turnout, that conventional forms of political participation are following a pattern of persistent decline, discernible from the early postwar period to the present day (Norris, 2002, p 1).

An important aspect of this concern is expressed in relation to groups such as young people, who are thought to be even less likely to engage in formal politics. Notably, there has been considerable public debate on the disengagement of young Muslims from mainstream political and civic life, prompted by the disturbances of 2001 in Bradford, Burnley and Oldham, and the fallout from the attacks on New York and Washington in September 2001 and the bombings in London on 7 July 2005. With regard to the official reports on the disturbances of 2001, the disengagement of Muslims and especially Muslim youth from local democratic processes was identified as a key background factor contributing to the events (Cantle, 2001). Subsequently, Muslims in the three affected urban areas and elsewhere in Britain were accused of social and cultural 'introspection' and 'self-segregation' (see Simpson, 2004; Phillips, 2006). Furthermore, in the wake of the 7/7 attacks, the Preventing Extremism Together Working Group, which was set up by the Home Office in August 2005 to consider ways of engaging Muslim youth, commented that 'Participation by young Muslims in civic and political activity is lower than the national average', attributing this to their lack of confidence in mainstream Muslim organisations, as well as to low levels of political efficacy in relation to UK political and civic institutions (Home Office, 2005, p 14).

We argue, however, that there are two significant problems with these narratives of political disengagement as they play out in relation to young British Muslims and young people of other religious and ethnic minorities. The first of these is empirical, and concerns the dearth of existing data from which it is possible to robustly assess the relationships between religion, ethnicity and age when accounting for patterns of participation in the political mainstream. The second problem is more fundamental, and concerns the way in which politics and political participation are conceptualised. Not infrequently, in public and academic debates, 'politics' is equated narrowly with mainstream 'arena-based' politics (Marsh et al, 2007), referring predominantly to party political identification and voting behaviour. In our research, in contrast, we develop a substantive yet broadened definition of 'the political', which also encompasses action in a variety of alternative 'public spheres', ranging from locally focused community engagement to network-based mobilisation and internet activism. This conception of participation recognises the growing literature that focuses on an increasing array of 'postconventional' forms of participation that take place outside of the realm of electoral and party politics (Norris, 2002; Micheletti et al, 2004). In the case study explored in this chapter, a range of political modes ('grammars of action') are clearly at work (McDonald, 2006).

Our approach is informed by the contention that the public domain should be recognised as a differentiated realm for a variety of reasons. First, many commentators argue that, historically, political mobilisation among black and minority ethnic groups in the UK and elsewhere has been most intensively located within 'alternative' public spheres (such as local and grassroots community organisations), as a result of exclusion from 'mainstream' public spheres (Gilroy, 1987; Black Public Sphere Collective, 1995; Solomos et al, 2003). The emergence of self-organisation within alternative public spheres can be seen as a response on the part of marginalised groups to counter political, social or public exclusion (Fraser, 1997). Second, it is suggested by some that there has been a proliferation of public spheres because of increased social complexity, whereby contemporary social movements constitute autonomous spheres of action that permit the public articulation of interests, identities and demands that cannot any longer be addressed within the mainstream public sphere or via the state (Melucci and Avritzer, 2000). Third, it is argued that the rise of new technologies has facilitated the emergence of global and virtual publics. Significantly for our research, it is suggested that this has found particular expression within global Islamic movements and networks that, by recourse to global media, have constituted heterogeneous transnational Muslim publics.

Drawing on this broadened conception of participation and a pluralistic understanding of the public realm, we are particularly interested in how young people relate to mainstream, alternative and global politics and how these intersect with their everyday political experiences and imaginaries.

Islam, transnationalism and alternative public spheres

In this section we develop these themes in a review of the emerging research literature on Muslim youth identities and political imaginaries, teasing out the ways in which these are presently taking shape in the context of globalisation. Particular reference is made to the role of new information and communication technologies in transforming the public expression of aspects of faith, the emergence of global Islamic movements, and the impact of these developments for the identities of young Muslims living in diaspora.

An emerging theme within the recent literature on Muslim youth has focused on the role of new telecommunications media in facilitating a global intensification of the promulgation of Islamic knowledge, and in expanding public deliberation over matters of Islamic tradition and belonging. Building on Benedict Anderson's (1991) classic analysis of the relationship between print capitalism and the spread of nationalism, several analysts argue that the increasing prevalence of the internet, enabling not only the consumption but also the production of knowledge and information, acts as a conduit for the emergence and multiplication of alternative 'public spheres', including the means of imagining a global Muslim 'public sphere'. In Jon Anderson's (2003, p 887) words,

> Opening the social field to new spokes-people and new discursive practices not only challenges authority long since thought settled to interpret what religion requires, but also blurs boundaries between public and private discourse and

fosters new habits of production and consumption tied to media, and particularly to new media.

In this way, 'electronic communication' is 'moving Islamic discourse into the marketplace and aligning its practices, range of choice, and alternatives both metaphorically and literally with additional means to service these demands' (Anderson, 2003, p 889).

Importantly, in terms of our case study, Jon Anderson regards the intersection between new media and Islam as having significant implications for the engagement of young Muslims (Anderson, 2003, p 891). Thus, there are numerous instances in which electronic media are being used to develop and/or sustain new forms of religious networking and group formation, particularly among young people. One example is the Forum of European Muslim and Youth and Student Organisations (FEMYSO), a federation of Muslim groups within the European Union that aims to be 'an international network which can facilitate in providing services and global links to youth organisations', and which explicitly fosters a 'European identity' among young Muslims in different European societies. This organisation incorporates the use of a website, as well as an online newsletter with electronic subscription, to support its activities (FEMYSO, http://p9445.typo3server.info/home.0.html).

Other authors question the implicit normative assumption at work in this type of account, that is, that the expansion of the 'Muslim public sphere' through use of telecommunications media is an inherently desirable phenomenon. For instance, Peter Mandaville (2007, p 102) argues that although globalisation has promoted debate on the meaning and nature of the authoritative in Islam, 'the mere fact alone of more people being able to serve up a wider range of ideas about religion – that is, a widening of the public sphere – does not in itself produce more pluralistic (in the sense of being more tolerant or open-ended) knowledge'. Nevertheless, he suggests that, just as it cannot be assumed that a global expansion of 'Muslim politics' generates more 'tolerant', 'progressive' strands within Muslim thought, neither can it be crudely assumed that such expansion entails a greater tendency to embrace 'politically extreme idioms of Islamism', noting in this context the rise of distinctively progressive Muslim youth organisations (Mandaville, 2007, p 112).

These debates are taken up and developed further in Kevin McDonald's recent (2006) work on contemporary global movements. McDonald takes issue with accounts that see global Islamism as an inevitably defensive reaction to processes of globalisation in the era of late modernity. Specifically, his arguments take the form of a challenge to Manuel Castells (2000), who, in his writings on the rise of the 'network society', characterises the many global Islamic movements that have emerged since the Iranian revolution as defensive responses to the totalising effects of global information networks: as 'cultural communes' that seek to stand outside of globalised networking logics. While McDonald accepts much of Castells' argument concerning the rise of the network society, he suggests that contemporary articulations of global Islam and identification with the *umma* are manifestations of alternative, rather than culturally defensive, global movements. From this perspective, new forms of commitment to Islam are not straightforward entrenchments of tradition that are opposed to the erosive effects of modernity and networking, but in fact utilise and express the logics of the network society. In this context, he underscores how, in the identities of young Muslims in particular, consciousness of globalised Muslim experience dovetails with a new emphasis on personal piety that registers as social, religious and political engagement in local contexts (McDonald, 2006, pp 184-208). Following Kepel, he cites this as an example of 're-Islamicisation from below' (2006, p 184). For some young Muslims, particularly those living in diaspora, identification with the Muslim *umma* becomes a key modality in which identities are renegotiated, with forms of personal piety providing a source of challenge to familial and communal 'traditions' (McDonald, 2006, pp 192-6).

In the British context, this argument is supported by ethnographic research, which has shown an increase in the importance of religion in the identities of young British Pakistanis, with the suggestion that faith identifications are increasingly seen as distinct from, and more significant than, ethnic affiliations (Jacobson, 1997, p 239; Mirza et al, 2007). Such distinctions are also observed in Muslim diasporas in other European societies (Bowen, 2004; Grillo, 2004). For instance, the French anthropologist Dounia Bouzar (2001) reports on the experiences of a young Turkish woman in France, whose increasing personal knowledge of the texts of Islam provide her with a means to counter parental expectations, which she felt were a manifestation of cultural 'tradition' rather than religious commitment:

> When I discovered my religious sources and I had the chance to study them, I realised that Islam gave me rights that my father had forbidden me: studies, my assent for choosing a husband who was not necessarily Turkish, etc. This provoked a revolution in the house.... I proved to

my parents that they had confused the traditions of their little village with the religion. I succeeded in realising my own values without having to leave the home, as my big sister had been obliged to do. (Bouzar, 2001, p 47, authors' translation)

The recent resurgence and differentiation of Islamic identities, in Britain and elsewhere, has developed in tandem with the global expansion of telecommunications networks and informational exchange, and not necessarily in reaction against it. This raises important sociological questions about how faith in general and Islam in particular is expressed at the level of 'the global' and 'the local', as well as about the implications of these changes for patterns of participation in the existing institutional arrangements of (secular) democratic societies (on this, see particularly Bowen, 2006). These intersections between globalisation and Islam have particular implications for young Muslims who are engaged in the ongoing negotiation of diasporic identities, while increasingly animated by global events such as the Iraq War and the publication of cartoons of Muhammad in Denmark and elsewhere in late 2005. The themes of local and transnational allegiance and an emphasis on faith that is distinct from culture can be clearly discerned in the activities of the Muslim Justice Movement (MJM).

Glocalised faith activism and the Muslim Justice Movement

In this section, we present our case study of the MJM, a network-based organisation in Birmingham, exploring how the transnational articulations of faith discussed in the previous section manifest themselves as part of the political imaginaries of young Muslims. The MJM comprises an organisational core of young Muslim men who met at a further education college in Birmingham, and who came together as an organisation when two of them were expelled from the college in late 2005. We examine how the Movement combines new 'grammars of action' with more conventional political modes to realise simultaneously global and local sets of political concerns. In particular, this 'glocalised' political sensibility fuses members' global '*ummatic*' identity with local community engagement, helping to forge an alternative (Muslim) public sphere that references, but is not enfolded within, the political mainstream.

The case study draws together a range of ethnographic materials. Research with the group was primarily with five of its members, aged between 19 and 23, and took place in two stages: first, a focus group explored the nature and range of activities of the group, their attitudes towards mainstream politics and institutions and their perceptions of/relationships to their local areas; second, a series of individual in-depth interviews were held with the focus group participants, exploring their routes into political activism and following up on themes that had emerged in the focus group. These encounters were supplemented by emails and telephone contacts, as well as consideration of their website, newsletters and blog.

The MJM is organised and led by its youth members, and its foundations lie in a campaign for the establishment of a prayer room for students on the premises of a local college, at which a number of MJM members were students. This campaign brought the activists into confrontation with the college principal, and culminated in the expulsion of two students who had been at the forefront of the campaign for the prayer room. At the same time that they had been engaged in this campaign, the students had also been engaged in college-based anti-war activities, which again brought them into confrontation with the college authorities, particularly in relation to a planned visit of former Prime Minister Tony Blair to the college. Their opposition to this visit was inevitably cited as a factor in their expulsion from the college, and these linkages brought the campaigners to the attention of local anti-war groups, who joined the students in expressing outrage over the conduct of the college. The college campaigns and the students' expulsion began to feature in Stop the War Coalition debates, and was the focus of a Channel 4 feature. Out of these activities, the group began to cohere around opposition to the war on Iraq and Afghanistan, forging links with a range of anti-war organisations, including Respect, Stop the War Coalition and the Socialist Workers Party, although without becoming absorbed into any of them. Their activities began to diversify around concern with a range of social justice issues, while their desire to express these remained foregrounded by a political consciousness that was engaged with questions of Muslim identity and values, and a critique of mainstream political institutions' responses to Muslims in the UK and abroad. To this end, the group has engaged with organisations such as the Muslim Public Affairs Committee (MPAC), but has chosen to form itself into an autonomous group, inspired by Muslim notions of justice. As we shall see, however, there has been vigorous debate within the group about the role of faith in framing conceptions of 'justice'. The MJM draws on a range of repertoires of action, including local community activism, involvement in protests and demonstrations and e-activism.

MJM perspectives on faith, culture and political engagement

The members of the MJM articulated a commitment to religion that they consciously decoupled from ethnic identification. Thus, while acknowledging a continuing 'connection' to Pakistan, the following member of the group laid claim to a hyphenated 'British Muslim' identity, suggesting that loyalties attached to place of birth and those relating to faith are not mutually exclusive:

> 'I think … the youngsters are more attached to Islam, more, the, that's more of their identity, [of] Muslims, British Muslims, and they don't [paint] themselves as to be, kind of, … Pakistanis as much, you know, they know that they've got some connection with Pakistan, … those kind of things, but I think, it's, it, that they've come to the conclusion that they're more British Muslim. And … I don't think the two clash, one's where you're born, the other thing is what you believe in.'

The respondent went on to contrast this sense of the mutuality of faith and belonging with what he perceived as his parents' more latent commitment to religion:

> '[I]t wasn't like they [his parents] forced me how to pray or something, … you know, wake me up at, in the morning, those kind of things. It's kind of left down to me, if you know what I mean, that if I wanna do it, you do it.… Obviously, if I wanted they encouraged me … you know. Um, they, they'd be there for me … it's more me now telling them, rather than them, them … telling me. 'Cause again there's, like, kind of typical story of them coming from Pakistan, they weren't exactly religious, but their kids turned out more religious than they are.'

For these and other respondents in our sample, the emphasis placed on faith as something standing apart from more immediate ties of family and ethnicity was closely entwined with their political engagement. Thus, recalling the words of the Turkish young women cited by Bouzar (2001) (see above), one member of the group stated explicitly that not only had his faith encouraged him to distinguish between cultural practices and religion but also that Islam encouraged his political activity:

> 'My religion has given me more freedom than anyone. I mean things like arranged marriages which is more culture than religion, I mean parents they bring up their kids more culturally, especially Pakistani, Indian and Bangladeshis. It's quite, I don't know, when they read Islamically it's, it's, it gives them more freedom the way I see it, and it's given me more freedom to do things, and more freedom to speak out. It's like when my parents say to me, "Don't go to a protest, they're gonna arrest you", but Islamically it tells me to, yeah, go to a protest and I see the word of God greater than my dad's any day.'

Another member of the group drew a similar contrast between his own religiosity and that of his parents, indicating that his faith was a source of motivation for his political engagement:

> '[T]hey want you to go and practise your religion, they want you to pray five times a day, but they don't want you to do anything else other than [that].... Islam is a way of life, it's not just, it's, it's about the way you speak, your manners and everything, but they [the respondent's parents] don't want to see anything of that. They just want me to pray five times a day, come home, don't get involved in anything.'

Faith in action: origins of the MJM

There are important ways in which these perceived interlinkages between faith and political action thread through into both the political grammars of the MJM and their perceptions of mainstream politics. However, in each of their activities, this coupling of faith to politics is open-textured rather than exclusive. While members' commitment to faith galvanises their politics, the programmatic aspects of their engagement countenances cooperation with non-Muslim organisations, and, more importantly, is not solely focused on 'Muslim causes'.

As noted above, the MJM emerged when two of its future members were expelled from a Birmingham further education college. The issue at stake was that members of the group wanted to establish a student Islamic Society and associated prayer room on the college premises. The management of the college opposed this initiative, allowing neither Islamic nor other faith societies on the college premises. Later, the college shifted its position to allow a multi-faith, as opposed to a Muslim, prayer facility. As the issue developed, the group began to suspect that the decision of the college was not anti-faith per se, but that it had distinctively Islamophobic connotations. As one of the members of the group commented in an interview:

> 'I mean the college, it was proper ... that college is Islamophobic as hell. They actually thought we were, they made it out like we were trying to start an organisation, some sort of HT [Hizb-ut Tahrir] organisation but ... we didn't want that, we just wanted a prayer room, really, and a big enough [one], they gave us, okay, they go, "Okay, we won't give you a prayer, we'll give you a multi-faith room", which means that any religion ..., okay, we were like fine with that ... but they gave us like, one that was, it's probably like half the size of this room [a small interview room], if not smaller, to pray in and it was a bit ... it was a bit dodgy.'

It is significant in terms of the subsequent orientations of the MJM and its members, that the case for opposing the college's policy was supported through the use of rights-based arguments as opposed to particularistic religious claims, and was distinguished from more religiously separatist campaigns of Hizb-ut Tahrir based on college campaigns for prayer rooms for exclusively Muslim use (Hussain, 2007). Specifically, the group began to circulate an unofficial college newsletter, which, as well as carrying articles on current affairs topics such as the Iraq War and Anglo-American foreign policy, also contained articles that were critical of the college's decision on faith societies. One of these, entitled 'God Can't Come to College', began by observing that the college was 'refusing to allow any religious societies to be formed on its premises, be they Muslim, Christian or Jewish, despite the fact that most other higher education facilities have them'. The piece went on to bolster its argument through reference to the 1998 Human Rights Act, although not Article 9 on freedom of religion and conscience, but Article 11 on freedom of association. The article continued:

> So what exactly is the real agenda behind this blatantly discriminative policy the college has in place and are they aware that they are in breach of the Human Rights Act of 1998, Article 11, which states that everyone has 'the right to freedom of peaceful assembly'? ... Whatever people's

opinions are about religion it doesn't change the fact that Britain is a country that allows individuals to practise and express their beliefs, and by the looks of things this college expects people to just shut up and leave their religion and God at the College entrance, or just simply shut up and leave the College.

The second (and ultimately final) issue of the newsletter contained a further critique of the college on the grounds of its restrictive security arrangements. Subsequently, two of the students responsible for producing the newsletter were suspended 'with immediate effect for an indefinite period' and later expelled. They were joined by others in a public demonstration outside the college grounds to protest at the action of the college. It was at this point that the group came together as the MJM. While locally focused, the demonstration was multi-organisational and multiply scaled: as well as enlisting the support of students from a local university, the action was supported by national organisations in the form of the National Union of Students and Stop the War Coalition, the latter with an internationally focused agenda.

The issue of how faith values and perspectives were expressed in the activities of the MJM was inherent to the decision over the most appropriate name of the group. Indeed, the decision to call the organisation the Muslim Justice Movement was not unanimously agreed on by its membership, in that some members clearly felt that it could be taken to imply too narrow a focus on Muslim interests and concerns. The emphasis they intended, and thus the reason the name was adhered to, stressed the idea of Islamic notions of justice being drawn upon and mobilised in a movement that construed itself as having a more broadly 'progressive' political agenda. As was commented by one member of the movement during the focus group discussion:

> 'Yeah, it's ... it's called the Muslim Justice Movement, but it's for everyone. [Everyone is supposed to be involved], it's not just for Muslims and it was a bit of a talk about the name and it being a bit too exclusive.... That's the, the only part I agree on in the name.'

The view that the movement should be oriented towards an inclusive notion of justice, and that this should be harnessed to the political activity of the group, is most clearly expressed in the way they have approached anti-war campaigning. On the one hand, the group clearly felt that the texts of Islam – including the traditions of the prophet

Muhammad (*hadith*) – enjoined them to political action over the military campaigns in Iraq and Afghanistan. As one individual put it:

> '[I]f you don't get involved it's a bit like … you're just staying quiet while like millions or hundreds of thousands are getting killed around the world. And it's, it's like a crime in itself, you just don't get involved. And if you don't speak out, um, Islamically we're supposed to speak out, if, our prophet, peace be upon him, he said that if you see something wrong you either fix it with your hand, and if you can't do that you fix it with your mouth, you speak out against it and if you can't do that then you hate it in your heart, and that's like one of the traditions [*hadith*] of the prophet, and, well, I'd like to say I'm trying to fix it with my hand or my mouth, I mean, I can't exactly go over there and do anything about it, so with the mouth it is then.'

On the other hand, referring to the coordinated anti-war effort of the Stop the War Coalition and the Respect Party, this interviewee also clearly welcomed the ways in which Muslim and non-Muslim groups have coalesced in their opposition to the Iraq War, not only on account of the mobilisation itself but also because of the promise this cooperation seemed to hold out for social relations more broadly:

> 'It's nice to be involved in all non-Muslim groups and it's just nice to know non-Muslims as well, because we live in like a largely Muslim area and I don't know many non-Muslims as well, and it's a nice feeling to know that there's actually non-Muslims out there and they're not all against Muslims, whereas Muslims that don't go out protesting and don't see none of this, 'cause the news don't show the protesting …, the non-Muslims kind of think "Oh…", no the Muslims kind of think that, "Oh, it's all non-Muslims against us", but if they actually went to these protests and seeing that there's more non-Muslims than Muslims, you get about a hundred Muslims at a protest and about a thousand, two thousand, three thousand non-Muslims. They seeing that, that the British people are actually behind them, there'd be kind of [a] whole different point of view from them. It kind of changed my view.'

Indeed, it is clear from other statements made by members of the MJM that inter-group mobilisation and alliance-building is not simply harnessed on pragmatic grounds, but because it coheres with an ultimately 'universalistic' conception of justice that extends well beyond Muslim interests alone. For instance, elaborating on his anti-war stance in relation to the conflicts in Iraq and Lebanon, another member of the group revealed clearly how his political concerns were not restricted to the Middle East, but corresponded to a much broader ethical and geographical worldview. This encompassed a concern with poverty in, and lack of fair-trade arrangements with, Africa, as well as a broader focus on the relationships between globalisation and (neo-)imperialism:

> 'I mean, [it's like] the Iraq [war] happened, campaigning against that, then the Lebanon war happened again, you know, and, and it does seem to be happening all around the Middle East, but … I think that, you know, more kind of attention should be given to the conflict in Africa and, and the poverty, and why these kind of things are happening. Why, they say that they give debt relief, but what about fair trade, you know? They've, they've got the rights to, kind of, extract their own resources and … do trade, you know, rather than Western companies coming in and taking their resources, … so those kinds of things, also [we] might, kind of, start campaigning for, you know, getting involved in any war that really happens, I'm basically against it, you know … globalisation kind of imperialism and those kind of things…. And just as much as any bombs going off in, in Baghdad also, you know, [I] don't want them happening in, in London as well.'

A key consideration in this linkage between commitment to Islamic values and engagement in the public realm was the perception that the political terrain on which the group engage has fundamentally changed. Thus, their expressions of personal piety and identification with Islam ran alongside a consciousness of how the situation for young Muslims had been altered by 9/11 and the 7/7 bombings:

> 'The Muslims, yeah, the Muslim youths, the Muslim youth, 'cause they've always been talked about, the Muslim youth and this and that and, you know. So, like, they're like this and they're like that and we're like, "Are we?" [laughter] I don't

think we are, you know what I mean? ... And some of them are like, that doesn't represent my views, some of them are, you know, it's, it's the opposite end of, some of them are, I don't really care, why is he talking about this and that, you know. He's, he's on, on the news, for example, somebody saying that, they're getting all extreme or radical and this and that, those kind of things. And ... I can't ... even know about all these kind of situations. The other one's like, "No, I'm not, ... I'm not radical or anything like", those kind of things, like, he has ... his own political opinion.... But definitely ... it's now from that group where they don't have any, that they're being forced almost to get an opinion on ... the situations that are going on at random.'

Glocalisation and alternative (Muslim) public spheres

A key consideration in relation to the development and ongoing activities of the MJM is that the Movement reflects the changing relationships between the scales of the 'global' and the 'local'. This is evident from the activities of the Movement in two intersecting ways. First, from the point of view of their faith commitment and the orientation towards social justice to which this gives rise, the members of the MJM perceive clear lines of continuity between a range of local issues and global processes and events (the Iraq War, poverty in Africa and so forth). Second, the MJM makes extensive use of new communication media, not only as consumers but also as producers of networked information.

The perceived continuities between the scales of the 'global' and the 'local' are expressed in the MJM's combination of different repertoires of action, which include providing a social and welfare service to people at the local level, and taking a stand against UK foreign policy:

'It was the war, it was the war on Palestine and everything, but ... we'd start off from sorting out everything in our little communities because they reckon that the government is not doing anything. So, if it's just like ... a woman that just needs her shopping done, we'll just get it done for her. We'll go to shops and, like, if she hasn't got transport we'll help her out. It's just, it started off with little things like that, that was the idea and that is still the idea. That we'll start off and when they need us for a protest, um, Anti War

Coalition, what Anti War Coalition do is they call us up and then we'd go down with them in their coaches.'

In terms of the engagement of the MJM with different forms of global media, the focus group discussion revealed the keen critical sense each of the participants had in relation to the normative positions and 'trustworthiness' of different media outlets. In this context, the group made a series of counter-positions of different news stations, including the BBC, Sky, al-Jazeera and a range of Asian and Arab channels, which did not simply cast the group in the role of discerning media consumers, but also underpinned their website and blogs, in which they set out what they saw as an alternative, less biased account of events such as the Iraq War and the conflict between Israel and Lebanon in July 2006. As the participants made clear during the course of the focus group, an important component of their action takes place at the level of discursive politics, through an inherently global medium:

> **Respondent 1:** 'That's …what we see as our only effective means for doing something.…But in, in order to … to draw people to come and protest with us, or to take on board the issues that we are trying to portray, and to let people know about, it's, it's difficult because it's hard to defeat the logic behind what Bush and Blair are doing over in the Middle East. And, and the whole war on terror. The … whole lot, we have to defeat the logic of the war on terror before we can get the real points across. Because they, like he said, they portray it as like a clash of cultures. Bush would say, you know, "they hate our values, that's why they are doing this", you know, and "they don't like our way of life" and all that crap.'

> **Several:** 'Yeah, yeah, yeah, yeah.'

> **Respondent 1:** 'But it's, … it's not that. They don't like your actions, what you're doing, your government. They, they mix up the issue, and so when the public see it, the few individuals can see it for what it is, but the rest of them they just … so when we are protesting [… Lebanon], you know …'

> **Respondent 2:** 'Extremism is going on over there!' [Laughter]

Respondent 1: 'They don't wanna, they don't even [debate] the issue. Talking about Palestine and Israel, you know, the standard conception that you have of Palestine and Israel, is that these "terrorists" [are] terrorising the Israelis. And that's, that's the common understanding.... so ... we have to defeat the logic behind these stories....'

The website of the MJM (http://mjmuk.org/links.php) confirms their intention to use their webpage as a nexus for linking local and global concerns as they affect Muslim groups: 'This site will be updated with news from around the world that concerns Muslims here in the UK and abroad. Ranging from your local communities all the way to politics, the scope will include anything which affects us large or small.'

In the political imaginaries of the MJM membership, there is no contradiction between forms of political action expressed at these different scales. In this context, the operative terms 'Muslim', 'communities' and 'us' is instructive, in that their use implicitly transcends distinctions of space: the linkages facilitated by the availability of new technology are rendered meaningful, by allowing for a collapsing of 'spatial scales'.

Conclusion

Official commentary and much of the research literature on the political participation of young people has seen the presumed withdrawal of young people from the mainstream public sphere as evidence of a more generalised waning of interest in 'the political'. Such a view, we suggest, overlooks the range of public domains within which young people may seek to express and realise their political concerns and goals.

Moreover, this unduly narrow construction of politics is particularly problematic in relation to current debates over young Muslim engagement. As several studies have recently testified (for example, Birt, 2005), many young British Muslims evince suspicion over the motives and efficacy of institutions of the state, as a result of British foreign policy in relation to the Middle East. While this has not necessarily resulted in a jettisoning of conventional forms of participation (Birt, 2005), our research findings suggest that the adoption of more direct modes of participation, such as locally focused 'community' action and worldwide website construction, coincide with frustration over 'unresponsive' mainstream institutions.

The chapter has also shown that the adoption of new 'repertoires' of political action has an intimate relationship to globalisation, in both its technological and cultural guises. Important here, from the point of view of both the emerging literature on Muslim youth identities and our own findings, are the processes in which the public realm is re-imagined and the new forms of political action that are opened up, which include participating in the public articulation of Islamic practice, principles of justice, and democratic accountability. The parallels between expressions of global Islam among young Muslims and other global social movements are recognisable and made possible through shifting relations between scales and communication flows that have been enacted by globalisation.

These new repertoires sit alongside more continuous forms of political action in 'alternative public spheres' relating to community engagement and self-help strategies, however. The significance of our case study of the MJM is that it constitutes an example of organisations that are both responsive to, and expressive of, aspects of the changing relationships between the scales of the 'global' and the 'local'.

It is clear that faith identities serve to animate engagement at these levels and in campaigns for social and political justice. In part, this articulation of faith through public engagement and new repertoires of action is based on a re-imagining of the relationship between faith identity on the one hand and ethnic and cultural identities on the other – a process that also finds resonance in a range of empirical studies of Muslim youth identities (for example, Jacobson, 1997).

In the current climate, marked as it is by public concern over young Muslims' political engagement, it is thus important to recognise that the intertwining of faith, politics and public engagement can find expression in a range of political responses – and not simply in violent *jihadi* politics.

References

Anderson, B. (1991) *Imagined communities: Reflections on the origin and spread of nationalism*, London: Verso.

Anderson, J. (2003) 'New media, new publics: reconfiguring the public sphere of Islam', *Social Research*, vol 70, no 3, pp 887-906.

Birt, Y. (2005) 'Lobbying and marching: British Muslims and the state', in T. Abbas (ed) *British Muslims: Communities under pressure*, London: Zed Books, pp 926-106.

Black Public Sphere Collective (1995) *The black public sphere*, Chicago, IL: University of Chicago Press.

Bouzar, D. (2001) *L'Islam des banlieues – Les predicateurs Musulmans: Nouveaux travailleurs sociaux?*, Paris: Syros la Découverte.

Bowen, J.R. (2004) 'Beyond migration: Islam as a transnational public space', *Journal of Ethnic and Migration Studies*, vol 30, no 5, pp 879-94.

Bowen, J.R. (2006) *Why the French hate headscarves*, Princeton, NJ: Princeton University Press.

Cantle, T. (2001) *Community cohesion: A report of the independent review team*, London: Home Office.

Castells, M. (2004) *The power of identity*, Oxford: Blackwell.

Fraser, N. (1997) *Justice interruptus: Critical reflections on the 'post-socialist' condition*, London: Routledge.

Gilroy, P. (1987) *There ain't no black in the Union Jack*, London: Hutchinson.

Grillo, R. (2004) 'Islam and transnationalism', *Journal of Ethnic and Migration Studies*, vol 30, no 5, pp 861-78.

Home Office (2005) *'Preventing Extremism Together' Working Groups: Working Together to Prevent Extremism*, London: Home Office.

Hussain, E. (2007) *The Islamist*, London: Penguin.

Jacobson, J. (1997) 'Religion and ethnicity: dual and alternative sources of identity among young British Pakistanis', *Ethnic and Racial Studies*, vol 20, no 2, pp 238-56.

Mandaville, P. (2007) 'Globalization and the politics of religious knowledge: pluralizing authority in the Muslim world', *Theory, Culture and Society*, vol 24, no 2, pp 101-15.

Marsh, D., O'Toole, T. and Jones, S. (2007) *Young people and politics in the UK: Apathy or alienation?*, Basingstoke: Palgrave Macmillan.

McDonald, K. (2006) *Global movements: Action and culture*, Oxford: Blackwell.

Melucci, A. and Avritzer, L. (2000) 'Complexity, cultural pluralism and democracy: collective action in the public space', *Social Science Information*, vol 39, no 4, pp 507-27.

Micheletti, M., Follesdal, A. and Stelle, D. (2004) *Politics, products, markets: Exploring political consumerism past and present*, New Brunswick: Transaction Publishers.

Mirza, M., Senthilkumaran, A. and Ja'far, Z. (2007) *Living apart together: British Muslims and the paradox of multiculturalism*, London: Policy Exchange.

Norris, P. (2002) *Democratic phoenix: Re-inventing political activism*, Cambridge: Cambridge University Press.

Phillips, D. (2006) 'Parallel lives? Challenging discourses of British Muslim self-segregation', *Environment and Planning D: Society and Space*, vol 24, no 1, pp 25-40.

Simpson, L. (2004) 'Statistics of racial segregation: measures, evidence and policy', *Urban Studies*, vol 41, no 3, pp 661-81.

Solomos, J., Keith, M. and Shukra, K. (2003) *Democratic governance and ethnic minority political participation in contemporary Britain*, ESRC L215252046, London: ESRC.

NINE

Faith-based schools: institutionalising parallel lives?

John Flint

Introduction

The impacts of education policy and faith-based schools in particular, have constituted a central element of contemporary debates about community cohesion and national identity in the UK. This chapter begins by describing the provision of state-funded faith-based schooling in the UK and how faith-based schools have been conceptualised within public policy discourses around cohesion. It then explores the evidence regarding the impact of faith-based schools on three key dimensions of social cohesion: the inculcation of values; sociospatial segregation; and disparities in educational attainment. This informs an assessment of whether such schools are institutionalising 'parallel lives'. The discussion then addresses the educational policy challenges related to faith-based schools and provides a comparative summary of policy frameworks and issues in other nations. The chapter concludes by suggesting that state-funded faith-based schools may and should be accommodated within a multicultural society but that this necessitates a greater degree of pragmatism and compromise among faith communities.

Background

Churches were the predominant providers of schooling in the early stages of the move towards universal education in Britain (Meer, 2007). The current arrangements in the constituent parts of the UK are the result of a complex series of historical conflicts and compromises (Judge, 2001). There are currently 4,700 Church of England, 2,400 Catholic, 37 Jewish, 28 Methodist, seven Muslim and one Seventh-day Adventist state-funded schools in Britain, and the first state-funded Hindu school opened in London in September 2008 (Doward, 2006; Meer, 2007). The Labour government has promoted the expansion of faith-based schools in England and Wales and has encouraged independent faith schools to enter the state system (DfES, 2001). Similarly, the Scottish Executive retains its support for state-funded Roman Catholic schools (see Flint, 2007).

England and Wales

In England and Wales the historical position of the Church of England has remained the dominant factor 'in determining the contours' between the state and faith-based schools (Judge, 2001, p 466; see Chadwick, 2001, for a detailed account). Throughout the 19th century, Protestant churches were major providers of elementary education, with funded support from the state (Grace, 2001). From 1870 a 'dual' system of church and state schools was developed. The 1944 Education Act enabled independent schools to become voluntary aided (facilitating denominational education and worship and religious authority in school administration, including teaching appointments) or voluntary controlled (where there were no financial responsibilities but no denominational worship). The 1993 Education Act provided the potential for individual sponsors, including faith-based organisations, to apply to establish state-funded grant-maintained schools, although the impact of the Act on religious educational institutions was limited and the legislation was superseded by the 1998 Schools Standards and Framework Act. This incorporated grant-maintained schools within a realigned voluntary-aided sector (Walford, 2001).

There are 5,000 (including independent) Church of England and Church of Wales schools, providing education to one quarter of primary school pupils and 6% of secondary school pupils. Catholic schools were not part of early state–Church settlements and relied on financial support from relatively deprived Catholic communities for their maintenance. The eventual incorporation of Roman Catholic schools into the state-funded sector resulted in the retention of considerable religious identity and governing autonomy for these schools (Grace, 2001). The Catholic school system serves around 10% of the school population in England and Wales (Grace, 2001). State funding was first provided to Jewish schools in 1835 (see Miller, 2001). State-funded Jewish schools are mostly located in the major cities, educating around 12,000 pupils (Valins, 2003). Although the 1944 Education Act provided a framework for state-funded Muslim schools, only a very small number have been established, reflecting the increasingly rigorous processes and regulations governing transfer into the state sector compared with previous historical periods.

In addition to state-funded faith schools there are an estimated 160 fee-paying independent Catholic schools; 115 independent Muslim schools, primarily located in inner-city areas, educating 14,000 pupils; 101 independent Jewish schools educating 11,000 pupils; and at least 70 independent Evangelical Christian schools (Grace, 2001; Walford, 2001; Valins, 2003; Meer, 2007). Significant numbers of Christian, Jewish and Muslim children also receive supplementary religious education in evening or weekend schools. Debates about the (lack of) contribution of faith schools to social cohesion were reignited by disturbances in the North of England in 2001 and the wider problematisation of Islam within British society.

Scotland

Church of Scotland schools were established in almost all parishes by 1750. During the 19th century, limited state funding was given to religious schools, including Roman Catholic and dissenting Protestant educational establishments. The current dual system of non-denominational and Roman Catholic state schools in Scotland stems from the 1872 Education (Scotland) Act, which incorporated Church of Scotland and other Protestant denominational schools into the state sector, while Catholic schools remained outside this settlement until the 1918 Education (Scotland) Act, which resulted in 226 Catholic schools transferring to the state sector. This lack of Church of Scotland schools creates a binary division between non-denominational and Roman Catholic schools, which is one explanatory factor for the frequent challenges to the legitimacy of Roman Catholic schooling in Scotland since the 1920s (Conroy, 2001; Flint, 2007). There are 418 state-funded Catholic schools, providing education to 16% of the Scottish school-age population.

Northern Ireland

Although there were attempts to encourage a multi-denominational school system in Northern Ireland in the 1920s, Catholic schools did not join the state sector as they did in Scotland. State funding of Catholic schools was delayed until 1947 and local authority schools were largely Protestant in character. This resulted in a parallel state-funded school system, which mirrors the residential segregation between the two religious communities, with less than one in ten pupils being from the respective minority religious tradition (Gallagher et al, 2003). The establishment of state-funded integrated schools has been facilitated since the 1977 Education (Northern Ireland) Act. Five per cent of pupils in Northern Ireland attend integrated schools, although there is greater demand than there are school places (Gallagher et al, 2003; McGlynn et al, 2004). In addition, the 1989 Education Reform (Northern Ireland) Order established the duty of the Department of Education to support the development of integrated education. Northern Ireland also maintains a state-supported grammar school system. In 2001, protests against children walking to a Catholic primary school in North Belfast became international news and appeared to symbolise both the conflict in Northern Ireland and the role of the education system within it (Judge, 2001).

Faith schools and community cohesion

Contemporary debates about faith-based schools in the UK occur within a wider historical, international and political context. Concerns about the divisive nature of faith-based education in Europe date back to the Reformation (MacCulloch, 2003). In France throughout the 19th century, schools run by religious orders were regarded as divisive and raised the spectre of the *deux jeunesses* (two youths) (Burleigh, 2005, p 343). Faith-based schools were one site of a wider contestation between secular and religious authorities, with consecutive waves of state support for, or suppression of, religious schooling in Western Europe from the 17th century (Burleigh, 2005). These conflicts have always concerned citizens' allegiance to the nation state as well as divisions between citizens. This explains why schools are such high-profile arenas for debates about social cohesion in European polities: they are perceived to play a key role in the inculcation of civic ideals and national identity and thereby to act as the crucibles for the forging of the relationship between (future) citizens and the state (see Underkuffler, 2001).

The immediate catalyst for reignited concerns about faith-based schooling and community cohesion in England was the serious urban disorder in Bradford, Burnley and Oldham in the summer of 2001 between Asian and white youths and the police. The 'Cantle Report' into the disturbances, although it did not directly link the disorders to faith schools, developed the powerful paradigm of 'parallel' lives to depict the sociospatial segregation of ethnic and religious groups within 'enclave' neighbourhoods and did implicate educational processes as contributing to this segregation (Cantle, 2001). This manifested itself in ethnically divided schools, linked, through school catchment geographies, to increasing residential segregation. In a two-way process, increasing ethnic polarisation within schools results in households seeking to live within the catchment areas of schools predominately attended by pupils from their own ethnic background, which then reinforces ethnic congregation within particular neighbourhoods. The Cantle Report was careful to note that the 'drift' towards mono-ethnic or mono-cultural educational establishments was not confined to faith-based schools. The report also accepted that Muslim communities could not be denied the right to state-supported Islamic education when this was provided to Christians. However, in January 2005, the Chief Inspector of Schools in England argued that many pupils in faith-based schools had 'little appreciation of their wider ... obligations to British society', which provided 'a challenge to our coherence as a nation' (Bell, 2005). This was widely interpreted as referring specifically to Muslim/Asian-majority schools.

Opponents of faith-based education usually limit their criticism to the state support provided to these institutions, rather than calling for a prohibition on independently funded schools or the supplementary religious education that is an important element of many Christian, Muslim and Jewish children's upbringing. Judge (2001, p 469) argues that 'there are powerful and potentially dangerous tensions between the (publicly funded) nurturing of distinct cultural identities within a heterogeneous society and an orderly process of integration'. For some commentators, any further extension of state funding to faith-based schools will entrench or deepen fragmentation and segregation in society, thereby institutionalising 'parallel lives' (Humanist Philosophers' Group, 2001; Judge, 2001). There are two commonly debated hypotheses applying to faith-based schools and social cohesion: first, a cultural impact of divergent curricula, educational ethos and values; and, second, a social and geographical impact of sociospatial segregation (Gallagher, 1998). These are now discussed in turn, along with the impact of faith schools on educational attainment.

Institutionalising parallel lives?

Teaching, ethos and values

The evidence base for assessing the impact of teaching practices within faith-based schools on social cohesion at local and national levels is weak (Grace, 2003). Indeed, it is not even obvious to what extent faith-based schools are actually different from secular institutions in their interpretations of the curriculum beyond the provision of religious education classes, assemblies and the celebration of religious events. The guidelines within the National Curriculum in England and Wales and the Education for Mutual Learning and Cultural Heritage, introduced in the 1989 Education Reform (Northern Ireland) Order, provide a regulatory framework for teaching standards. The majority of faith-based schools pass state inspections, although a small number of Muslim, Jewish and Evangelical Christian schools have been cited as failing to teach 'tolerance' (Valins, 2003; Meer, 2007). Recent controversies about values in religious teaching have focused on an alleged 'rise of creationism' in some UK schools (Randerson, 2006), in particular the Emmanuel College in Gateshead, funded as a state-supported city technology college by Reg Vardy (further Vardy-funded schools are now established in Doncaster and Middlesbrough). Although the National Curriculum requires the teaching of evolution, it does not proscribe creationism, and the government's programme for City Academies could facilitate an expansion of the number of schools 'favourable' to creationist or intelligent design theories.

These important cases aside, some commentators argue that the ethos and practices within most Anglican, Roman Catholic, Muslim and Jewish schools promote a tolerance of diversity, particularly a respect for other religious traditions (Miller, 2001; Grace, 2003; Association of Muslim Social Scientists, 2004; Billings and Holden, 2007). They achieve this partly through the tradition of critical reasoning and self-reflection within religious teaching practices. This reflects the importance of the active agency of individual children, which is often neglected in debates around faith-based schools, as is the agency of some parents in their resistance to, or bypassing of, the religious ethos of faith institutions (Valins, 2003; Bruegel, 2006). It would appear that there is nothing inherent to faith-based schools that would prohibit them from providing an ethos that is compatible with a multicultural citizenship and inculcating 'a preparedness always to seek justice and integrity within one's own bounded spaces' (Conroy, 2001, p 555). However, it is this very construction of 'bounded spaces' that has been at the heart of concerns about the potential social divisiveness of faith-based schools. It is argued that it is the lack of inter-faith social interaction, rather than the particular teaching ethos or practices of faith-schools, which inhibit more positive attitudes to other religious and non-religious groups (see McGlynn et al, 2004).

Segregation and social networks

The charge that faith-based schools result in circumscribed cultures and fragmented social networks (Humanist Philosophers' Group, 2001; Meer, 2007) also faces the challenge of a limited evidence base (although, see Smith's 2005 study of school, neighbourhood and family influences on children's social interactions). However, research evidence on integrated schools in Northern Ireland does challenge proponents of faith-based schools. The research suggests that integrated schools have impacted positively on identity and out-group attitudes, with one study showing the proportion of pupils with 'mixed friendships' rising from four in ten to two thirds before and after attending an integrated school. These contacts were maintained outside as well as within schools (McGlynn et al, 2004). Another study found that one in ten pupils attending integrated schools had no friends from the other religious tradition, compared with three in ten and four in ten pupils who attended 'Protestant' and 'Catholic' schools respectively. Moreover, comparatively more positive perspectives of the other religious group were evident among integrated school pupils (Schubotz and Robinson, 2006). Integrated schools also managed to retain their balanced pupil intake despite growing residential segregation (Gallagher et al, 2003). These findings are supported by recent research in England that found that it was day-to-day contact between children that was required to break down barriers between communities. This can also bring parents together across ethnic/religious divides (Bruegel, 2006). The debates around sectarianism in Scotland have also focused on the social separation of pupils and parents arising from the dual system of non-denominational and Roman Catholic schools, although evidence about social networks and how these are maintained into adulthood is not available (see Flint, 2007).

Religious institutions themselves appear to accept some of these arguments. The Church of England has stated that its new (but not existing) schools will offer at least one quarter of places to non-Christian pupils (a recommendation of the Cantle Report) and the Catholic Church has also stated that it will be 'more open' about the proportion of non-Catholic pupils in its schools, estimated to be one quarter (Grace, 2001; BBC News, 2006). Muslim and Jewish schools are more religiously stringent in allocations policy where demand from within their own religious community is often high. In other localities there are larger proportions of non-Muslim or non-Jewish pupils, although some Orthodox Jewish schools do explicitly aim to socialise children within single-faith environments as a means of protecting and sustaining faith identities and community allegiances (Valins, 2003; Meer, 2007).

Once more there is a need to conceptualise children as active agents and appreciate the complexity of children's social relations in and out of school that includes both clustering by ethnicity/faith and interaction with 'others' groups (Bruegel, 2006). The relative importance of the school environment on social networks and perspectives is also uncertain. A large majority of respondents in Northern Irish studies believed that family and the maturation process were more important influences on their perspectives on community relations than their schooling (McGlynn et al, 2004; Schubotz and Robinson, 2006). Equating physical proximity in schools with enhanced cohesion also negates the potential for isolation and conflict, which has been a central element of the critique of the government's community cohesion agenda and its assumptions about the positive social benefits of 'mixed' neighbourhoods (Amin, 2002).

It has been argued that the provision of more state-funded minority-faith schools would address the heavy oversubscription to these establishments and would facilitate the accommodation of more pupils of other or no faiths within them (Hewer, 2001). It may also be suggested that further provision of Muslim day education would reduce the present propensity for supplementary Islamic education that may inhibit children's inter-faith social interaction outside of school hours. However, this is countered by Bruegel's research (2006, p 13), which found that primary-aged Asian children did not often identify close friendships outside their school class, casting doubt on the idea that they operate in 'tight ethnic enclaves' around after-school religious activities.

Narrowing gaps in educational attainment

An important, but less prominent dimension of faith-based schooling and social cohesion is the extent to which faith-based schools reduce gaps in levels of educational attainment between different religious, ethnic or income groups. Educational attainment is closely related to social class, race, ethnicity, household structure and gender (Butler and Hamnett, 2007). Faith-based schools, including Anglican, Roman Catholic and Jewish state-funded establishments are generally very successful in terms of academic achievement, although the extent to which this may be attributed to their religious character is less certain (Judge, 2001). Certainly, Church of England and Roman Catholic schools are often regarded as 'the repository of high standards' and utilised by middle-class parents (Butler and Hamnett, 2007, p 1167). Indeed, the argument has been made that faith-based schools contribute to social divisiveness by providing a further vehicle for the reproduction of class advantage (Butler and Hamnett, 2007). Research in London found that many faith-based schools were not serving the most disadvantaged pupils, and also reported evidence of social selection between schools within the faith sector (Allen and West, 2007). The Church of England has responded to this allegation by highlighting that most of its new schools will be located in deprived neighbourhoods (BBC News, 2006). However, Allen and West (2007) also found that faith-based schools' pupil intakes were significantly more affluent than the neighbourhood in which the schools were located.

Many parents from minority faiths also elect to send their children to Church of England or Roman Catholic schools due to their high educational outcomes and the provision of a religious ethos (Bristol City Council and MORI, 2004; Flint, 2007). High educational and disciplinary standards are regularly cited as the reason for the Scottish Executive's support for Roman Catholic schools (see Flint, 2007). The historic comparatively poor educational qualifications of the Roman Catholic population in Scotland have disappeared among more recent generations, and many state-funded Roman Catholic schools are among the highest achieving and oversubscribed in the country. However, Bruce et al (2004) argue that, while the increasing numbers of teachers and improved buildings and teaching materials provided to Roman Catholic schools through state funding has played a role, it was the introduction of the comprehensive education system in 1967 that had the biggest impact. This significantly improved the educational attainment outcomes of working-class children, among whom Roman Catholics were disproportionately represented.

Concerns about lower educational attainment among minority groups are usually based on ethnicity rather than religion, and in particular the poor performance of Pakistani, Bangladeshi and African Caribbean boys (Hamnett et al, 2007; Meer, 2007). It may be argued that the incorporation of some independent Muslim schools into the state system will facilitate additional resources and improved teaching standards, as in the situation of Roman Catholics in Scotland. However, as in the Scottish case, raising educational achievement in all deprived neighbourhoods will have a more significant impact on Muslim children than the provision of further Muslim schools. The additional classes run in mosques and Islamic centres to boost levels of achievement in core curriculum subjects as well as delivering religious instruction also have a role to play in reducing the social divisiveness of differential educational outcomes (Hewer, 2001).

The policy challenge of institutionalised religious diversity

Religious diversity, institutionalised through state-supported faith-based schools, raises considerable policy challenges. One high-profile attempt to mitigate any social and cultural segregation effects of state-funded faith-based schools involves twinning schools. Twinning arrangements to counter ethnic and religious division were recommended in the Cantle Report and have been strongly promoted in Scotland. More recently, the UK government has also suggested stronger twinning linkages between state and independent schools. Twinning involves a spectrum of activities from joint arts and local history projects, through collective sports and drama events to shared physical campuses. Evidence from Scotland suggests that twinning activities have had positive impacts on the social relations and out-group attitudes between pupils in Roman Catholic and non-denominational state schools and between their parents (Scottish Executive, 2006). However, critics have argued that such activities are inadequate and that twinning has little positive effect on diversifying children's social networks (Bruegel, 2006). In addition, the establishment of shared campuses has been controversial and problematic, particularly in Scotland. A proposed programme of shared campuses in North Lanarkshire was halted due to opposition from parents and the Catholic Church. High-profile media coverage of the shared campus in Dalkeith in Midlothian reported conflict between pupils and disputes over the placing of religious icons (Mackinnon, 2004). While these conflicts appear to have been largely resolved (Dick, 2006), they reflect the challenge of governing a diversity that is manifest in physical and symbolic separation.

A key issue is whether the religious requirements of pupils or their parents can be met within 'mainstream' secular schools. Many non-denominational state schools have sought to accommodate the religious needs of their pupils (including those from various Christian denominations) through measures such as respecting religious observance and festivals, providing for pupils' dietary requirements, adapting school uniforms, and sensitive provision of sex and physical education lessons. As Judge (2001) points out, for some non-denominational schools with large numbers of Jewish or Muslim pupils this has resulted in adjustments to their fundamental character and a gradual transformation of every aspect of the educational provision.

Often these changes have resulted in tensions among the parents of pupils from other or non-religious backgrounds. Most famously in Dewsbury in 1987, 26 (white) parents refused to send their children to the local state-run primary school because of its 'Muslim' character and attempted to establish their own alternative schooling arrangements (Naylor, 1989). These tensions are not confined to a secular/religious faultline, as evidenced by controversies over the campaign, supported by the Muslim Association of Britain, to change a state-funded Roman Catholic school in Glasgow with an 80% Muslim pupil intake into a voluntary-aided Muslim school (Meer, 2007).

There is evidence that even pragmatic and extensive strategies of compromise and accommodation by secular state schools may not be sufficient to ameliorate the demand among some parents for a faith-based schooling for their children. A study for Bristol City Council in 2004 found widespread support among Muslim parents for an Islamic secondary school in the city, offering a greater role for Islamic teaching in their children's education and a means of 'resolving' pupils' identity crisis (Bristol City Council and MORI, 2004). In Scotland, the proportion of pupils attending Roman Catholic schools matches the representation of Catholics in the Scottish population and it is claimed that 90% of Catholic parents send their children to Catholic schools where these are available (see Flint, 2007).

Although Muslim parents in the Bristol study recognised that dress codes, diet and observance of holy days had been accommodated in existing state schools, the study concluded that anything short of a new Islamic school would not meet demand. One parent described how, 'If you are talking about Islam, it's not just what they are going to be doing at school, it's their whole way of life. So the teachers will be acting different, the students will be acting different, everything is going to be different' (Bristol City Council and MORI, 2004, p 26).

In this understanding, there is no division between the religious and secular aspects of education, rather all aspects of study would be permeated by Islamic values in a faith-centred integrated system (Hewer, 2001). There is an expectation that all teachers will be committed to, embody and exemplify the *sunnah* (good life of the prophet) rather than being neutral communicators. This would create considerable challenges around equal opportunities, employment, religion and belief legislation, for example in the non-recruitment of homosexual teachers (Hewer, 2001).

There are clearly limitations in the extent to which secular schools can adapt and accommodate some religious demands. For example, the Muslim Parents Association was formed in Bradford in 1974, focusing on the issue of single-sex schooling and leading to the establishment of a number of independent schools (Meer, 2007). Similarly, the majority of parents in the Bristol study desired that boys and girls should be taught separately on the same site and that prayer should be part of the school day (see Hewer, 2001, for similar findings in Birmingham). There have also been several controversies and legal cases about the right of pupils (and teaching assistants) to wear the *niqab* in contravention of schools' uniform policies, which in the two most high-profile cases did permit the *hijab* (Bright and Peters, 2005; BBC News, 2007). The wearing of Islamic headscarves in schools has been an even more controversial issue in France.

Despite these controversies, it is important to note that the Bristol study found that the teaching of Islam in school was more important to parents than any cultural practices. Only six out of 289 respondents disagreed with the school's inclusion of non-Muslim teachers and only two did not want their children to be taught about other faiths (Bristol City Council and MORI, 2004). It is not a religious isolationism and cultural monopolisation that is being demanded here, rather a greater emphasis on faith. Nonetheless, this raises considerable practical challenges for education authorities as well as equity issues around the school experience of non-religious children and how additional religious requirements should be funded. The fact that Muslim parents did not object to non-Muslim teachers is important. Also noteworthy is the fact that many independent Muslim schools also employ non-Muslim teachers (Hewer, 2001), certainly in a context where differential teacher recruitment and promotion practices favouring Roman Catholic individuals in state-funded Roman Catholic schools have been a central cause for opposition to such schools, including opposition by high-profile teaching trade unionists (Flint, 2007).

The comparative international experience

Given the complexities of debates around state-funded faith-based schooling, it is instructive to examine how the politics of faith-based schools play out in other national contexts.

In the US, the Supreme Court interprets the First Amendment to the Constitution as requiring a separation of state and religion and therefore proscribes the state funding of religious institutions including schools (Underkuffler, 2001). However, the issue remains controversial, with over 30 Supreme Court rulings since the 1940s. In a famous case, the Supreme Court ruled that the Amish religious belief in the discontinuation of a child's education after elementary school took precedence over the state's requirement for universal childhood education (Underkuffler, 2001, p 580). The US also allows the discriminatory employment of teachers on faith grounds within faith-based educational institutions.

The debates in the US have focused on religious practices and the content of teaching within faith-based schools, linked to the requirement for adherence to mainstream values deemed critical to the formation of future citizens (Underkuffler, 2001). Less attention has been given to the sociospatial segregation that may arise from faith-based schooling: this in a context where racial segregation dominates the political agenda and where the Supreme Court ruled in 1954 that separate but equal schools, on the basis of race, were not acceptable. A key lesson from the US is that, while religious freedom and equality and the separation of church and state are founding myths, the historical reality is one of religious discrimination and the predominance of white, Anglo-Saxon and Protestant elites (Underkuffler, 2001). Although not directly comparable, this is relevant to the disparities in economic, social and cultural power between ethnic and religious groups in the UK.

In Canada, some provinces offer separate, publicly funded schooling to defined religious groups including Protestants, Catholics and French Catholics. Importantly, such provision is located within the wider context of the extent of state control of education and the varying levels of state-facilitated diversity between the provinces. For example, Alberta not only supports faith-based schooling, but also subsidises home schooling, independent and charter schools within a very pluralistic education system (Hepburn and Van Belle, 2003).

In the Netherlands, state and private schools have received equal state funding since the 1917 Constitution, and two thirds of pupils attend state-funded 'private schools', including Catholic, Protestant, Jewish, Sikh, Seventh-day Adventist, Muslim and Hindu schools (Walford, 2001). The context for this funding arrangement was the pillorisation of Dutch society, which continued into the 1960s, in which cultural, political and religious subgroups operated parallel but separate social institutions, including hospitals, newspapers, television channels and trades unions as well as schools. At its peak in the 1950s it could be argued that 'A Catholic would have lived his or her life within the confines of a homogenous Catholic subculture and its organisational infrastructure' (Andeweg and Irwin, 1993, p 20). Such sociospatial segregation would epitomise the negative consequences for social cohesion emphasised by many critics of faith-based schools.

Faith-based private schools in the Netherlands retain the right to an admissions and teacher recruitment policy based on religious orientation. However, the rapid secularisation of Dutch society and greater state control over required teaching content have diluted the religious dimension of some of these schools such that Walford (2001, p 532) argues that many nominally Christian schools are almost indistinguishable from their state counterparts. In addition, declining pupil numbers in some areas have resulted in the merger of some Roman Catholic and Protestant schools. Despite a common perception that establishing new religiously based schools is comparatively straightforward in the Netherlands, only a very small number of Evangelical Christian schools have been founded (Walford, 2001).

In France, legislation in 2004 prohibited the wearing of conspicuous religious signs in public schools, including Islamic headscarves (*foulards*), a culmination of events since the *affaire des foulards* in 1989 (Thomas, 2006; Salvatore, 2007). These developments need to be framed within French republican history and the principle of *laïcité* (secularism) aimed at freeing the state from undue religious influence. Secularism is understood as a vehicle for ensuring social cohesion, requiring citizens to distance themselves from religious identity, at least in the public realm, including public schools (Thomas, 2006; Salvatore, 2007). The dominance of *laïcité* means that France has been less accommodating of Islamic institutions, including schools, than other European nations, including the UK (Fetzer and Soper, 2005). The French situation illustrates how schools cannot be conceived of as 'pure' spaces devoid of political meaning but are subject to organising principles and political projects, including secularism. The debates around the wearing of Islamic headscarves in France also highlights the agency of young Muslim women and the various interpretations, practices and resistances that they enact, contrary to the notion of a religious subservience and determinism (Laborde, 2006; Salvatore, 2007). Finally, French *laïcité*, which extends to prohibiting the collection of Census data on ethnicity as well as faith, did not prevent serious urban disorder among ethnic and religious minorities in November 2005.

Conclusions

The politics of faith–based schools are dominated by a conceptualisation of schools as sites of 'community interface' (McGlynn et al, 2004, p 148). Although the controversy over state funding dominates the debates, schools are also cultural institutions that belong to the private and civic, as well as public realm (Parekh, 2000, p 202).

There are several weaknesses in the arguments against state support for faith schooling. Judge (2001, p 464) states that parents should have the right to pay for the independent religious education of their children but that the state, and thereby other citizens, should not have to pay for it. However, the state already subsidises independent education through the charitable status it accords many private schools. The idea that religious education should only be available to those who are able to afford it is incompatible with social justice or equity principles. Indeed the struggles of comparatively impoverished Irish/Roman Catholic and, more recently, of Asian/Muslim populations to sustain their own schools are testament to this (see Flint, 2007).

The British education system is already highly segregated and it is parental strategies based on socioeconomic background, rather than ethnicity or faith, that are the largest drivers of educational segregation (Butler and Hamnett, 2007). Although only 5% of pupils are educated in the 'social enclaves' (Ball and Vincent, 2007, p 1183) of fee-paying independent schools nationally, this rises to 20% in cities such as London and Edinburgh. This segregation is not confined to the independent school sector, as house price premiums in residential areas linked to the catchment areas of high-performing state schools serve to exclude many middle- and low-income households. Unless the argument is made that all fee-paying independent schools should be abolished and access to high-demand housing made more equitable, then a focus on faith schools as creating 'educational apartheid' (Cohen, 2007) limits the state's role to preventing social separation on the basis of religion but not doing so on the basis of parents' economic (and indeed social and cultural) capital.

In a wider sense, the specific criticism regarding Jewish, Muslim and Roman Catholic schools as institutions and mechanisms for the transmission of religious identities to new generations (see Conroy, 2001; Judge, 2001; Valins, 2003) neglects the extent to which the secular school system serves as a vehicle for the social reproduction of class advantage and values (Ball and Vincent, 2007). Finally, it is evident that schools in urban areas in Denmark, Germany, the Netherlands and the UK – countries with very different accommodation settlements for faith schools – are becoming increasingly ethnically (and, by default, religiously) segregated (Butler and Hamnett, 2007). These developments highlight how schools are sites where wider social, economic and cultural forces play out rather than schools themselves being the sole, or even primary, drivers of these forces.

There are also contradictions in the arguments of proponents of faith schools. Conroy (2001, p 555) argues that the Scottish state should support the continued existence of Catholic schools 'as a sign of its inclusiveness coupled with its willingness to support autonomous moral and social thinking'. But in the same article he then criticises Scottish local authority publications on sex education as being 'overtly libertarian' (p 556). Similarly, Modood and Ahmad (2007) acknowledge the contradiction of Muslims demanding respect (rather than mere tolerance) for their religious values and lifestyle while at the same time being unable to extend this respect to other minority groups, most notably homosexuals. Walford (2001) found that a concern about the potential requirement to employ homosexual teachers was a barrier to Evangelical Christian schools in both England and the Netherlands seeking state funding. If various religious traditions assert the right to analyse and challenge the positions of the state and lay them open to alternative perspectives and critiques (Hewer, 2001) then a similar right pertains to secular authorities with regard to religious institutions. Accommodating religious schools within the state sector actually enhances the power of the state to regulate their activities and to ensure that some of the considerable achievements of a secular-based citizenship, such as more equal opportunities for women and gay rights, are maintained. There is also a pressing need for a greater flexibility and compromise among faith institutions in acknowledging the equity issues involved in the state accommodating and funding religious requirements and in accepting the legitimacy of attempts to foster social interaction between pupils and teachers of different schools. The Catholic Church's opposition to shared staff facilities in the twinned campus at Dalkeith is a particularly stark example of unnecessary intransigence.

Judge (2001, p 469) argues that in the Dutch model 'a virtue is made of the *magnification* of differences and therefore of segregation' (emphasis added). However, his argument is based on two premises. First, that the Dutch system seeks to promote the increase of difference, rather than positively embracing existent social diversity. Second, that institutionalised diversity (through state-funded faith-based schools or other means) is linked in a linear process to increased social segregation. The evidence that does exist about the impact of faith-based schools on social cohesion in the UK suggests a far more complex relationship, although the important findings from integrated schools in Northern Ireland should not be ignored.

Placing contemporary developments in their wider historical and international context illustrates how the politics of faith-based schools are linked to various and competing authorities that seek to generate a centrifugal force towards a particular concept of the good citizen (Conroy, 2001, p 550). If we return to a multicultural definition of national identity, then faith-based schools may be conceptualised as integrating religious minorities (including actively practising Christians) into a matrix, rather than mould, of British citizenship (Meer, 2007). This matrix would recognise and accommodate a diversity of mechanisms for enacting civic engagement and expressing national identity and allegiances, rather than a uniform, static and exclusionary mould of citizenship. Reaching a settlement on faith-based schools may also enable a focus on the disparity in the levels of economic, social and cultural capital available to different groups within British society, which is the principal barrier to a more socially cohesive education system in the UK.

References

Allen, R. and West, A. (2007) 'Religious schools in London: school admissions, composition and selectivity?', Paper presented at the British Educational Research Association Conference, London, 7 September.

Amin, A. (2002) 'Ethnicity and the multi-cultural city: living with diversity', *Environment and Planning A*, vol 34, no 6, pp 959-80.

Andeweg, R.B. and Irwin, G.A. (1993) *Dutch government and politics*, London: Macmillan.

Association of Muslim Social Scientists (2004) *Muslims on education: A position paper*, Richmond: Association of Muslim Social Scientists.

Ball, S.J. and Vincent, C. (2007) 'Education, class fractions and the local rules of spatial relations', *Urban Studies*, vol 44, no 7, pp 1175-89.

BBC News (2006) 'Church schools in "inclusive" row', *BBC News*, 3 October.

BBC News (2007) 'Schoolgirl loses veil legal case', *BBC News*, 21 February.

Bell, D. (2005) Speech to the Hansard Society, London, 17 January.

Billings, A. and Holden, A. (2007) *The Burnley project: Interfaith interventions and cohesive communities: The effectiveness of interfaith activity in towns marked by enclavisation and parallel lives*, Lancaster: University of Lancaster.

Bright, M. and Peters, M. (2005) 'We still feel cheated and segregated', *The Observer*, 6 March, p 14.

Bristol City Council and MORI (2004) *Demand for a Muslim school in Bristol*, Bristol: Bristol City Council.

Bruce, S., Glendinning, T., Paterson, I. and Rosie, M. (2004) *Sectarianism in Scotland*, Edinburgh: Edinburgh University Press.

Bruegel, I. (2006) *Social capital, diversity and education policy*, London: London South Bank University.

Burleigh, M. (2005) *Earthly powers: Religion and politics in Europe from the Enlightenment to the Great War*, London: Harper Perennial.

Butler, T. and Hamnett, C. (2007) 'The geography of education: introduction', *Urban Studies*, vol 44, no 7, pp 1161-74.

Cantle, T. (2001) *Community cohesion: A report of the independent review team*, London: Home Office.

Chadwick, P. (2001) 'The Anglican perspective on Church schools', *Oxford Review of Education*, vol 27, no 4, pp 475-86.

Cohen, N. (2007) 'Stop this drift into educational apartheid', *The Observer*, 13 May, p 12.

Conroy, J.C. (2001) 'A very Scottish affair: Catholic education and the state', *Oxford Review of Education*, vol 27, no 4, pp 543-58.

DfES (Department for Education and Skills) (2001) *Schools achieving success*, London: DfES.

Dick, S. (2006) 'Going into battle for shared campus', *The Evening News*, 27 February, p 12.

Doward, J. (2006) '£10m state cash for first Hindu school', *The Guardian*, 24 December, p 6.

Fetzer, J.S. and Soper, J.C. (2005) *Muslims and the state in Britain, France and Germany*, Cambridge: Cambridge University Press.

Flint, J. (2007) 'Faith schools, multiculturalism and community cohesion: Muslim and Roman Catholic state schools in England and Scotland', *Policy & Politics*, vol 35, no 2, pp 251-68.

Gallagher, A. (1998) 'Religious divisions in schools in Northern Ireland', Paper presented at the Annual Conference of the British Educational Research Association, Queens University Belfast, August.

Gallagher, A., Smith, A. and Montgomery, A. (2003) *Integrated education in Northern Ireland: Participation, profile and performance*, Coleraine: University of Ulster.

Grace, G. (2001) 'The State and Catholic schooling in England and Wales: politics, ideology and mission integrity', *Oxford Review of Education*, vol 27, no 4, pp 489-98.

Grace, G. (2003) 'Educational studies and faith-based schooling: moving away from prejudice to evidence-based argument', *British Journal of Educational Studies*, vol 51, no 2, pp 149-67.

Hamnett, C., Ramsden, M. and Butler, T. (2007) 'Social background, ethnicity, school composition and educational attainment in East London', *Urban Studies*, vol 44, no 7, pp 1255-80.

Hepburn, C. and Van Belle, R. (2003) *The Canadian Education Freedom Index*, Vancouver, BC: Fraser Institute.

Hewer, C. (2001) 'Schools for Muslims', *Oxford Review of Education*, vol 27, no 4, pp 515-27.

Humanist Philosophers' Group (2001) *Religious schools:The case against*, London: British Humanist Association.

Judge, H. (2001) 'Faith-based schools and state funding: a partial argument', *Oxford Review of Education*, vol 27, no 4, pp 463-74.

Laborde, C. (2006) 'Female autonomy, education and the hijab', *Critical Review of International Social and Political Philosophy*, vol 9, no 3, pp 351-77.

MacCulloch, D. (2003) *Reformation: Europe's house divided 1490–1700*, London: Penguin.

MacKinnon, S. (2004) 'Religious icons removed from shared wall in mixed campus', *The Scotsman*, 13 February, p 8.

McGlynn, C., Niens, U., Cairns, E. and Hewstone, M. (2004) 'Moving out of conflict: the contribution of integrated schools in Northern Ireland to identity, attitudes, forgiveness and reconciliation', *Journal of Peace Education*, vol 1, no 2, pp 147-63.

Meer, N. (2007) 'Muslim schools in Britain: challenging mobilisations or logical developments?', *Asia Pacific Journal of Education*, vol 27, no 1, pp 55-71.

Miller, H. (2001) 'Meeting the challenge: the Jewish schooling phenomenon in the UK', *Oxford Review of Education*, vol 27, no 4, pp 501-13.

Modood, T. and Ahmad, F. (2007) 'British Muslim perspectives on multiculturalism', *Theory, Culture and Society*, vol 24, no 2, pp 187-213.

Naylor, F. (1989) *Dewsbury and the school above the pub*, London: Claridge Press.

Parekh, B. (2000) *Rethinking multiculturalism: Cultural diversity and political theory*, New York: Palgrave.

Randerson, J. (2006) 'Revealed: rise of creationism in UK schools', *The Guardian*, 27 November, p 9.

Salvatore, A. (2007) 'Authority in question: secularity, republicanism and communitarianism in the emerging Euro-Islamic public sphere', *Theory, Culture and Society*, vol 24, no 2, pp 135-60.

Schubotz, D. and Robinson, G. (2006) *Cross-community integration and mixing: Does it make a difference?*, ARK Research Update Number 43, Available at: www.ark.ac.uk

Scottish Executive (2006) *Building friendships and strengthening communities: A guide to twinning between denominational and non-denominational schools*, Edinburgh: Scottish Executive.

Smith, G. (2005) *Children's perspectives on believing and belonging*, York: Joseph Rowntree Foundation/National Children's Bureau.

Thomas, E.R. (2006) 'Keeping identity at a distance: explaining France's new legal restrictions on the Islamic headscarf', *Ethnic and Racial Studies*, vol 29, no 2, pp 237-59.

Underkuffler, L.S. (2001) 'Public funding for religious schools: difficulties and dangers in a pluralistic society', *Oxford Review of Education*, vol 27, no 4, pp 577-92.

Valins, O. (2003) 'Defending identities or segregating communities? Faith-based schooling and the UK Jewish community', *Geoforum*, vol 34, pp 235-47.

Walford, G. (2001) 'Evangelical schools in England and the Netherlands', *Oxford Review of Education*, vol 27, no 4, pp 529-41.

TEN

Faiths, government and regeneration: a contested discourse

Richard Farnell

Introduction

The engagement of faith communities in regeneration and community renewal is a matter of keenly contested debate. Stakeholders bring varying, and not always compatible, perspectives to the table (Dinham and Lowndes, 2008). Leaders of faith groups aspire to a recognised role in regeneration but are liable to resist uncritical co-option into government agendas. Conversely, the pronouncements of national politicians and senior civil servants often assume that, with a little encouragement, people of faith will participate in the implementation of official policies and plans. Many professionals at the local level, whether in local authorities, regeneration agencies or third sector bodies, view faith organisations with a degree of suspicion and experience some difficulty in developing and maintaining good, productive relationships.

This chapter uses the concept of discourse to capture and explore these diverse stakeholder perspectives. Stakeholders develop a discourse concerning the events they experience and the debates in which they engage, a discourse that is also informed by their particular purposes and assumptions. Beliefs, experiences, stories, images and metaphors provide a framework of meaning, which, together, produce a particular version or discourse of events and how they should be interpreted (Burr, 2003; Butcher et al, 2007). A discourse provides an everyday, often unquestioned, way of thinking and speaking about situations and policies. The concept is used here in the singular to refer to the engagement of faiths with regeneration, but this discourse has various strands, aspects and elements that contribute to the whole.

The following discussion unravels the strands of this discourse on faiths, government and regeneration to develop better understandings and foundations for policy and practice. First, the discussion outlines a series of propositions regarding the elements of the discourse, defined in relation to the main stakeholders. These propositions are then given further assessment through the exploration of a case study based on primary research for the London Borough of Lewisham in 2006-07.

Stakeholder discourse

The policy discourse surrounding community involvement in regeneration has a long history (Fagence, 1977; Banks et al, 2003; Chanon, 2003). However, it was only in the 1990s that this 'community' focus extended to the participation of people identifying by their religion. The formation of the Inner Cities Religious Council in 1992 could be seen as a significant stimulus to this shift. The essential message from central government regarding engagement with faith communities in regeneration has not shifted significantly since the 1990s and the guidance given at that time retains its ring today: 'Faith communities should be involved because they have sizeable memberships and have good local contacts: they are important community based organisations and have resources that they can invest in regeneration projects' (DETR, 1997, pp 149-60).

While the precise wording might change, the basic message – that faith groups have resources and should be networked appropriately – has not. For example, in the late 1990s neighbourhood renewal policies were developed by the Labour government, through the Cabinet Office, and in 2001 the government released its National Strategy Action Plan for neighbourhood renewal (Cabinet Office, 2001). Commitment 91 of this document states: 'Faith groups may offer a channel to some of the hardest to reach groups. A pragmatic approach will be taken to funding faith groups, recognising that they may be the most suitable organisation to deliver community objectives' (Cabinet Office, 2001, p 52).

Similarly, in 2004, David Blunkett, then Home Secretary, looked for productive and respectful engagement between public authorities and faith communities (Home Office, 2004). The Faith Communities Capacity Building Fund (see www.cdf.org.uk) was launched the following year with the aim of supporting faith and inter-faith organisations to strengthen their capacity to play a fuller part in civil society and community cohesion. Examples of government pronouncements could be multiplied. A notable publication is a good practice guide for local authorities, marking a significant translation of government advice at the local level (LGA, 2002).

Government approaches to the engagement of faith groups in regeneration and renewal focus on 'delivery'. From this perspective, faith groups, along with other voluntary and community groups, are instruments for achieving the government's aims. For the purposes of this chapter, therefore, this aspect of the discourse is labelled **'instrumental'**.

These national aspirations for regeneration practice have not always been noticed at a more local level. When they have, the reality of implementation has not proved straightforward. Officials with responsibility for these programmes and projects express mixed responses to their task (see, for example, Farnell et al, 2003; Furbey et al, 2006). A potentially negative discourse about working with faith groups has been observed:

> Among some professionals there is scepticism concerning the motives of Faith groups, which reveals itself in the search for hidden agendas. For others there is the view that faith groups sometimes have unrealistic expectations, have undertaken insufficient investigation of their situation, and lack clarity about their basic aims. (Furbey et al, 2006, p 36)

In addition, officials report pressures of work with faith organisations, which prompt obsession with crisis management rather than a more positive, face-to-face, engagement in the form of collaborative strategy and implementation. A lack of religious literacy, a failure to distinguish between ethnic and faith communities, differing views on the nature of equal opportunities, worries about how funding for faith groups will be used and issues of accountability all add to a **'sceptical'** discourse among some regeneration professionals. The large number of faith groups in a locality, their diversity, sometimes conflicting approaches and the potential for competition, within as well as between such groups, reinforce the reluctance to engage more fully (Farnell et al, 2003).

These two elements of the discourse on faith communities in regeneration, labelled here as 'instrumental' and 'sceptical', would be incomplete without substantial reference to the discourse of a third set of stakeholders, the people of faith themselves (Lowndes and Chapman, 2005). For the purposes of the present discussion the discourse of faith may be resolved into two main elements. First, those with extensive experience of engagement reflect that they are not, and do not intend to be, delivery agents for government. These people of faith have their own worldviews and notions of purpose and mission, whether clearly articulated or not. For many groups that have a strong 'calling' to work in and with their neighbourhood, 'Involvement in publicly funded projects and programmes is just a small part of their contribution to the wider community' (Farnell et al, 2003, p 13).

Some faith leaders have questioned what the government means by 'faith communities'. Is it a synonym for 'black and minority ethnic' communities? Does it refer primarily to minority religions in the UK? And does it include Christianity? The following quote sums up the response of one woman minister and community leader with insight into the way that political and bureaucratic agendas often distort initiatives to improve the life and well-being of disadvantaged people and communities: 'It's lunacy! It's lunacy! It's another injustice because you set up people who have failed to fail further because of the expectations of these programmes. You can't apply targets and outcomes in an area like this. What you need to nurture is process and people, and people are trying!' (Farnell et al, 2003, p 13).

This discourse demonstrates a desire on the part of some faith communities to challenge government's approaches and the outcomes for people struggling with disadvantage. This discourse can be designated as **'critical'**.

Nevertheless, the discourse within faith circles is far from simple. Faith groups also often attempt to secure recognition for the contribution made to local communities and neighbourhoods through social action projects of various types. Studies in a growing range of cities and regions provide evidence of the very substantial activity in civic and civil society by faith groups, principally Christian churches but not exclusively so. The earliest publications were in London (London Churches Group, 2002), followed by Yorkshire and the Humber (Yorkshire Churches, 2002), the North West of England (Northwest Regional Development Agency, 2003) and Leicester (Ravat, 2004). The conclusion of *Faith in England's Northwest* (Northwest Regional Development Agency, 2003, p 45) illustrates the main conclusion of these four studies and the many others completed subsequently: 'The report demonstrates that the major contribution is, by far, the impressive range of community projects undertaken by faith communities and wholly funded and staffed by them'.

A later recent study, funded by the government's Department for Environment, Food and Rural Affairs, investigated the contribution of people of faith to rural community vibrancy and underlined calls for the recognition of the positive contribution of faith communities and assessed its strengths and weaknesses (Farnell et al, 2006, p 47).

This aspiration is also identified in reflections on Local Strategic Partnerships and regional assemblies. If city and regional representatives of the major faiths wish to be involved in policy making and the creation of strategies that have a significant impact on whole communities rather than just in local neighbourhoods, then involvement in the decision-making boards of these partnerships becomes important. Several issues have presented themselves. Should there be 'faith sector' representatives on these partnerships? If so, how many would be appropriate, bearing in mind the size of the boards? Should they be elected or nominated? If so, who should nominate them? To whom should they be accountable? Preliminary answers have focused on the development of 'faith forums' involving leaders from the main religions in the area. Thus, for example, one of the aims of the West Midlands Faith Forum is 'To interface with regional agencies delivering government policies in the West Midlands and advise them on the impact of such agendas on faith communities' (West Midlands Faith Forum, 2006, p 1).

This willingness to engage is further revealed in a study, funded through the government's Department of Communities and Local Government, by the Church Urban Fund and the Faith Based Regeneration Network (Berkeley et al, 2006), which investigated the experience of 'faith representatives' on Local Strategic Partnerships and regional assemblies and recommended support of such presence and involvement. This desire for recognition, an **'aspirational'** discourse, is rooted in a desire to make a more significant contribution to community renewal and in a wish not to be ignored.

What conclusions might be drawn from this analysis? First, this aspirational discourse is not unproblematic. Different players have different perceptions of the reality of faith engagement. While there may be some commonality within the discourse across the three main sets of stakeholders, they nevertheless have different priorities. Should attempts be made to create a better understanding between stakeholders? If so, how might this be achieved? This internally variegated discourse has developed over more than a decade. It may now be time for these stakeholders to reflect critically on past understandings and approaches in their quest for better outcomes for disadvantaged communities (Furbey and Macey, 2005). How might these outcomes be articulated? What insights might be gained from wider debates about faith and civil society that could inform new and positive effects on the development of policy and practice for regeneration? How might the dangers inherent in other discourses about extremism and the genesis of terrorism (DCLG, 2007a) be prevented from undermining practical cooperation in regeneration and community renewal?

These questions are now addressed through a case study that allows a deeper assessment of the relationship between faith groups and one local authority, the London Borough of Lewisham.

Faith communities and the London Borough of Lewisham

This case study was developed through a qualitative research strategy. Group discussions and semi-structured interviews were the main data sources, augmented by internal and published documents provided by the local authority. Thirty-three people agreed to discuss the relationship between the local authority and faith groups. One third of participants were from the local authority, including the Mayor and two executive directors, and half were from faith groups. Most of the latter were people with leadership roles. The remaining voices were from voluntary sector agencies in the Borough.

Most religious organisations and places of worship in Lewisham are Christian, as indicated by the database of faith contacts built up over the years by the Council. Of the 158 current contacts only five are of faiths other than Christian. Of course, there are many expressions of Christianity. It should not be assumed that their understanding and approaches to faith and their views of public authorities are uniform.

The Mayor of Lewisham, on his re-election in 2005, initiated a 'Commission on Community and Neighbourhood Empowerment'. Simultaneously, an evaluation was undertaken of the Borough's engagement with faith groups to inform recommendations about future approaches (Farnell, 2007). The following discussion reports the story revealed by this study.

Although relationships between some Christian churches and the local authority in the early 1990s were strained because of differing views on equal opportunities and sexual orientation, by the late 1990s a new period of cooperation began. The first Having Faith in Lewisham conference took place in March 1999 with over 120 delegates from a wide range of faith organisations. Through the workshops, participants were able to share information about the social action projects in which they were engaged. Ideas for networking and communication were suggested and a follow-up conference was held in the following year.

Another development was the appointment by the Council of a Faith and Social Action Officer to facilitate these developments and create a fund to support the social action initiatives of faith groups. From 2001 onwards £50,000 was allocated each year to provide small grants to assist in developing projects. Those groups in receipt of grant funding were seen as sharing the same general goals as the Borough in terms of community development. In March 2002 consultants recommended the development of an umbrella organisation to enable faith groups to develop partnerships with each another and with statutory bodies and to undertake a complete audit of all faith groups to assess their services, resources and community impact.

The third Having Faith in Lewisham conference in June 2003 brought over 150 people together to assess progress and to build on activity since the previous conference in 2000. Chaired by the Mayor, it attracted 50% of its participants from black and minority ethnic groups, with the majority coming from the Christian churches and some from the Muslim communities. The conference recommended the involvement of faith groups in the design and delivery of services with access to mainstream resources. It was also agreed that the Faith in Lewisham Network should be used as a vehicle for supporting faith groups in the development of expertise around key regeneration themes.

Following the conference, work on the Faith in Lewisham Network commenced with the aim of facilitating effective networking among Lewisham's faith groups, through a website, newsletter and periodic events to encourage the development of faith-based community initiatives through training, sharing expertise and promoting models of best practice. The Faith and Social Action Officer continued to provide one-to-one support for faith groups developing community projects. However, at the more strategic level, the conclusion shared by most of the interviewees by 2006 was that the network was not developing as intended. The idea of a faith network had been promising initially but it then stalled for reasons discussed below. Although some committed members continued to meet occasionally, the website attracted little interest and became dormant.

An instrumental discourse

Recent governmental commitment to engage faith communities in regeneration and in broader aspects of service delivery is clear. The aim is to assemble a significant group of interests otherwise missing from the table. Within this context, government wishes to relate to a defined 'faith sector' rather than religious groups, organisations and communities in all their diversity. This construction of a faith sector suggests a quest for a more united voice and the formation of forums that bring all the faiths together. In these arenas, so it is assumed, faiths will be able to mitigate their differences and create a common set of views about policies and practices, which will engage neatly with the processes of governance. These forums are presented as accountable by reference to their elected or appointed nature. Such government proposals in the early 2000s were prompted by existing inter-faith and multi-faith organisations in cities and towns, supported by the Inter Faith Network for the UK. The government's Department of Communities and Local Government continued to reinforce this thinking with the publication of its draft Inter Faith Strategy (DCLG, 2007b).

This is not to suggest that the delineation of a faith sector and the potential of inter-faith initiatives are of no relevance or importance, but it is to say that such a discourse of faith engagement and integration and its component concepts have exerted a particular influence on policy and practice since New Labour came to power in 1997. This instrumental discourse has created space for intermediate or infrastructure organisations to flourish and has accorded more voice for 'faith' in an increasingly diverse public realm. Organisations such as the Church Urban Fund and the Faith Based Regeneration Network play an important role in facilitating research and capacity-building with regard to faith groups in regeneration and community renewal.

These debates have resonance in the Lewisham story. Faith in Lewisham is quoted as a model of good practice in an influential publication by the Local Government Association (LGA, 2002). Table 10.1 compares the recommendations made to local authorities and the recorded activity in Lewisham.

The initiatives taken by the London Borough of Lewisham during the first five years of the current decade are strongly congruent with the LGA recommendations. The decision to set up a specific fund for faith groups and to establish a website suggests commitment beyond that of the LGA advice and, on balance, it is fair to say that Lewisham made, certainly from an official perspective, a more than satisfactory start in developing its relationships with faith communities. In particular, from the end of the 1990s the Borough's approach has been to establish a network of faith groups, brought together in a more or less formal partnership or forum. This network and a series of inter-faith conferences, supported by the Faith and Social Action Officer, formed the core of the strategy. In one sense it should have been easier for Lewisham to achieve these things than for some other local councils because the vast majority of faith groups in the Borough are of one faith: Christianity. Yet the common judgement of research respondents is that by 2005/06 these initiatives had disappointed.

Table 10.1: National guidelines and local practice on faith engagement: the performance of Lewisham

LGA recommendations, 2002	Activity in Lewisham, 1999–2005
Map faith leaders and places of worship	Database created
Allocate officer responsibility and define a contact point in the authority	Faith and Social Action Officer appointed in 1999 within what became the Community Services Directorate
Create an internal champion	Faith and Social Action Officer
Define a remit for a Cabinet member	The elected Mayor
Make full use of existing activity	Recognised in part
Focus on issues of particular significance	Examples include: • Faith in Education projects (2003) • Response to London bombings (2005)
Encourage small informal meetings	Regular pattern of meetings for borough deans and others
Encourage learning, both ways	Commitment to learn through conferences
Be inclusive	Improved diversity of people attending the 2003 conference
Use a range of consultation exercises	Undertaken in part
Form a steering group	Faith in Lewisham Network launched in 2004
Hold conferences	'Having Faith in Lewisham' conferences, 1999, 2000 and 2003
Faith representatives on Local Strategic Partnership	No formal representation but Mayor's Adviser for Faith attends
Contract faith groups to provide public services	• Financial support for projects initiated by Faith Groups, such as 'Street Pastors' • Faith in Lewisham Fund, 2001 onwards, providing £50,000 each year • www.faithinlewisham.org.uk established in 2003

Why did this happen? Was there an assumption that all faiths would see things in the same way? Is it more realistic to start from an acknowledgement that faith groups are characterised by diversity and difference, within faiths as well as between them? Some are more inclined than others to engage with the local authority and to dialogue and partner. Yet it is difficult to predict which groups will want to participate. For some it will be historical events that have influenced current involvement. For others it will be their theological understanding that will have inclined them towards or away from engagement. The passage of time will inevitably bring about changes in attitude and approach.

A second issue concerns the government's initiative to develop the capacity of faith communities to relate to government and its agents. The national Faith Capacity Building Fund was launched in 2005 to support hundreds of faith groups to develop their skills and understandings of regeneration and community renewal, often through action and development projects as well as direct training. This may be welcomed, but it has often been suggested (Farnell et al, 2003) that it is the professionals and politicians who need to be much more understanding of religions, their culture and organisations if meaningful engagement is to occur. Hence, both official religious literacy and capacity-building among faith groups are required. Present instrumental assumptions have produced unbalanced responses with little emphasis on improving the religious literacy of professional officials.

Recognition of this instrumental discourse highlights a third element in the government's approach to faith groups: the assumption that improved engagement between faiths and local authorities will result from improving relationship between the religions. This reflects an assumption that people of different faiths are, by definition, likely to be in conflict with one another. Misunderstanding and potential for disagreement across faiths should not be underestimated. Nevertheless, research on community participation suggests that adherents to the major world faiths have very similar approaches and values, which are articulated and enacted in community development and action in places of disadvantage (see, for example, Furbey et al, 2006). Obstacles to engagement may stem more from different attitudes and perceptions between faith and non-faith actors than between people of different religious faiths.

The preceding observations challenge the government's instrumental relationship with 'faith'. Simultaneously, however, the discussion indicates significant scope for learning *within* this official discourse. Particular benefits may stem from a much fuller awareness of religious diversity, the identification of shared values and the need for less universal, more locally attuned approaches, which discard simplistic notions of a monolithic 'faith sector'.

Critical and aspirational aspects of the discourse

The initial approach to faith and community in Lewisham focused on the development of good personal relationships between people of faith and local authority personnel. This produced greater trust and understanding on which to build. Thus, stronger bridges and links were secured between local authority officers and faith leaders; the Mayor and other councillors became committed to the engagement with faith communities and organisations; and there was much greater awareness of the large number, wide range and substantial activity of faith groups in the Borough. In turn, recognition of local faith activity and its contribution to the well-being of Lewisham residents placed issues of support and partnership on the political agenda.

Despite these developments, however, faith leaders central to this process were disappointed that engagement had little impact on regeneration and community renewal policy or on the major strategic decisions of the Council. They perceived a continuing lack of understanding of the diversity and characteristics of faith communities, especially at middle and senior management levels of the Council. The potential policy-making influence of the Faith and Social Action Officer was also limited, especially in relation to directorates other than Community Services.

There was general agreement on the challenges facing the Borough and its faith groups if engagement was to be developed further:

> 'The work has reached a plateau and this review needs to help in finding the next level.' (Council officer)

According to faith leaders, movement to this next level required recognition of some fundamental matters. Specifically, a unified faith sector did not exist in Lewisham and some people of faith did not wish to be involved with the local authority. They had their own agendas on which they wanted to focus. Others had involvement in the past and were no longer interested or had moved on to other things. Finally, tensions were present both within and between religions. These divisions are not necessarily the most significant in debates on community cohesion. However, this nevertheless raises awareness of the potential for conflict within communities where religion is one marker of 'difference'.

Of course, developments in Lewisham occurred within a constantly shifting national regeneration agenda, impelled by political necessity and continuing gaps between expectation and achievement (Parkinson et al, 2006). Hence, at the time of this case-study research, policy initiatives on Sustainable Community Strategies, Local Area Agreements and 'double devolution' meshed with the Mayor's Commission on Community and Neighbourhood Empowerment, the Borough's commitment to extending neighbourhood management and its aim to promote cohesive communities. Amidst a perplexing complexity, the engagement of faith communities in regeneration and community renewal was at least one part of the answer.

The perspectives of faith leaders can be summarised through their responses to questions about identity, relationships, community needs and their willingness to work to meet these needs, especially with the local authority. How did these faith leaders see themselves and the groups they lead? They saw themselves as the 'unsung heroes' whose initiatives, local knowledge and volunteering were not really recognised:

> 'We are not just churches or mosques. We are community groups and social enterprises. We have a business approach to our activities. We employ staff. We have assets and significant turnovers. We are substantially self-funded.' (Independent Church leader)

> 'People get converted to Christianity or Islam. This has a positive effect on the community at large.' (Muslim interviewee)

How did these people see one another? How did they see people who share a religious perspective on life? They recognised that they do not all have the same agenda and that they were not able to cooperate with everyone, but:

> 'The idea that we fall out with each other is not really true; for most others we have a real respect.' (Anglican Church leader)

On the other hand, there were those who saw their mission solely as one of proselytising. Others simply decided to work in relative isolation.

What views of the Council were held by these faith leaders? How did they perceive the Council's perception of them? Faith leaders often commented that the Council expected that they could devote time and resources to networking, discussion and partnership, yet there was no consideration of expenses and compensation:

'Everyone is so busy. How can we find the energy to engage?' (Christian youth worker)

While they sensed some degree of recognition from the Council, interviewees commented that this did not always translate into respect and a feeling of being valued. Others were liable to question the local authority's motives for engagement:

'After the London bombings was the authority's motive really about providing us with protection or was it more to do with control?' (Muslim interviewee)

The majority of those interviewed from faith communities had strong feelings regarding the needs of their neighbourhoods and the Borough. They were particularly concerned about young people and the potential for violence and drug abuse. They wanted to do more to help:

'Many of the initiatives to work with people in the most difficult circumstances are motivated by the churches. We have programmes with those who are not seen or heard.' (Independent Church leader)

Faith leaders argued that faith organisations are often the first point of call for the most vulnerable. The more aware groups provided signposts to mainstream services. They also reported times when speedy dialogue is needed between faith groups and public authorities, following the London bombings in 2005 for example. Simple structures for dialogue need to be in place so that there can be positive responses to unexpected events.

Finally, faith leaders identified a willingness on the part of most faith groups to develop relationships with the Borough:

'We believe that our faith affects everything we do and so has a relevance to every area of policy in the Borough.' (Church leader)

Some believed that they could help the Borough achieve its aims, contributing, for example to Local Area Agreement targets. Another contribution may stem from independent church leaders, some of whom are actually employed by the local authority. This may enable them to broker relationships.

It was noted earlier that faith groups at a regional and national level seek greater recognition for their efforts in regeneration and community renewal, while emphasising their resistance to incorporation into the government's agenda. This desire to maintain critical distance and to challenge the instrumental discourse of other stakeholders also finds expression in Lewisham. This suggests a need to deconstruct the concept of the 'faith sector' in the face of religious diversity and differing conceptions of mission. It also underlines the challenge to the inter-faith model as the dominant means of engaging with people of faith and asserts the primacy of addressing social disadvantage and exclusion as the primary motivation of faith groups in partnership work.

A sceptical discourse

In conversations with local authority and voluntary sector interviewees on the place of faith communities in regeneration, many, sometimes contradictory, viewpoints were expressed. Varying degrees of acceptance were also indicated. What did Council officers think of engagement with faith groups? Their responses to this question were marked by some confusion, partly because of the lack of understanding of faith groups and their social action reported earlier in this chapter. Some officers expressed frank scepticism:

> 'Many don't actually contribute very much wider community benefit. You've got to be careful working with religious people.' (Council officer)

For others, however, the independence of faith groups was not just recognised but valued. There was a sense that faith groups have a pre-existing degree of empowerment deriving from 'knowing who you are and what you want to achieve'. Thus, other actors within the Council regarded faith groups as making an invaluable contribution to community life and well-being, one that should be encouraged. As the Mayor commented:

> 'I love it when faith groups come and see me because they don't whinge and complain.'

What issues are perceived in the local authority in engaging with faith groups? Interviewees acknowledged that they had probably missed opportunities for collaboration and engagement, using, for example, faith groups to communicate their message about environmental sustainability or their policy to encourage the adoption, rather than the fostering, of children. They recognised that offers of involvement by faith groups should be accorded an appropriate and positive response.

Finally, what opportunities were identified by Borough staff for faith engagement? Some reiterated the ideas tried earlier in the decade, such as the presence of a faith forum or network. Others sought a situation where faith groups are more fully integrated into the voluntary and community sectors, making use of those structures, processes and personnel. Yet others reflected the sceptical officers' discourse identified above. Scepticism in relation to faith engagement in public policy may be well placed and prompt necessary critical reflection on what is possible in partnership activity and the obstacles that faith participation may present. Conversely, the origins of scepticism themselves require exploration. Is it based on evidence-free prejudice against any religious involvement in the public realm? Is it an attitude that has been reinforced by media coverage of religious fundamentalisms or by the debates around religion stimulated by publications presenting a secularist interpretation of life (British Humanist Association, 2007)? On the other hand, is the scepticism informed by experience of particular groups and their behaviour? Is there evidence of misuse of funds, lack of accountability, struggles to meet health and safety requirements or issues surrounding equal opportunities? Such latter issues, essentially empirical, seem most authoritative in determining the involvement of faith in regeneration partnership. The Lewisham case study provides evidence of both 'philosophical' and 'experiential' scepticism on the part of local authority officials. Some officials were reluctant to engage with people of faith because of their own secular beliefs. Other interviewees described difficult practical issues that they confronted in working with faith groups.

Two examples illustrate important practical difficulties. First, there is the question of the appropriateness of public funding for faith groups. Generally speaking, professionals look for what they regard as clear criteria for awarding public funds to faith groups. They desire to minimise risk and to be confident that, if called to account, they would be able to justify their decisions. One of the guidelines that officials use relates to the purposes of funding. Public funds should not be used for the furtherance of religion, the recruitment of new believers or the support of worship and prayer. Funds may be used for social care and social action projects of benefit to the community. For some, these guidelines might seem clear and helpful. Others are reluctant to divide behaviours in this way, accepting the holistic nature of faith. In this view, social action projects are inseparable from expressions of worship and the desire of groups to share their faith. In this situation, some officials ask for firmer guidance, while others accept responsibility for making necessary judgements.

A second example presents itself in relation to the community cohesion agenda. Is the funding of single faith groups for the provision of services and support just for their own people legitimate? Does this reinforce separation between groups? Should there be a requirement to fund only those projects initiated on a multi-faith basis? In the case of Lewisham this was not a major consideration as the Faith in Lewisham Fund was quite small. Evidence from the first round of the Faith Capacity Building Fund confirmed that many single faith groups supported by the fund were 'reaching out to a diverse user base' (CDF, 2007, pp 9, 21). Nevertheless, the government's Commission on Integration and Cohesion (2007) recommended that 'single-faith funding' should be avoided. A continuing debate on this issue was indicated by the Secretary of State for Communities and Local Government's (2007) response expressed in a letter to Darra Singh that 'we are primarily interested in the activities being funded rather than the groups delivering them'.

Conclusion

This chapter has identified the primary stakeholders in the relationship between faith communities and government in regeneration and community renewal. It has identified a dominant discourse, comprising several elements, in which this relationship is expressed. These elements are labelled instrumental, sceptical, aspirational and critical. They have been explored and then illustrated by case-study research in the London Borough of Lewisham.

Should greater awareness of these differing elements of the discourse be sought, as part of a more open dialogue between stakeholders? If so, how might this be achieved? How might the character of the discourse be shifted from a predominant emphasis on processes towards a more substantive concern with the delivery of desired outcomes for people living in disadvantaged and poor communities? (Dinham and Lowndes, 2008). How might some of the more frenetic debates concerning extremism, fundamentalism and the threat of terrorism, which prevail in the media and occupy some politicians, be prevented from undermining practical cooperation between faiths and between faith and secular agencies in local communities?

Some lessons can be drawn from the previous discussion. Faith contributions to regeneration will only happen if some of the assumptions outlined within the instrumentalist approach are challenged, including prevailing conceptualisations of the faith sector and models that give undue emphasis to inter-faith activity. Approaches characterised as sceptical should be encouraged, provided that the scepticism is based on evidenced reflection and not prejudice. The aspirations of faith groups to recognition of their present contribution to regeneration are legitimate but such recognition will reveal inadequacies as well as quality in their practice. The maintenance and development of a critical approach by faith communities to engagement with local authorities will offer stronger prospects for benefiting deprived and excluded people and communities than acceptance of the co-option by public agencies. Demonstrable success in engaging faiths and authorities will be the most significant way of keeping at bay the fear and mistrust generated by the actuality of terrorism and the debates about extremism.

The Lewisham study suggests some ways forward in order to achieve this. A new mindset on the part of both the Borough and its many faith groups was requested (Farnell, 2007). This new understanding was informed by the Local Government White Paper (Secretary of State for Communities and Local Government, 2006) with its emphasis on community involvement and 'double devolution' from central to local government and from local government to local communities and neighbourhoods. In summary, the Lewisham study suggested that people of faith and the local authority should see the basis for engagement around three themes.

First, people of faith, like everyone else in the Borough, are consumers of services provided by the Borough. The channels for communication, feedback and the monitoring of customer satisfaction provided by faith groups offer an opportunity for local authorities to develop their customer service quality.

Second, there is scope to build on existing partnerships that have been established where faith groups provide services, with or without funding from the local authority. Delivering desired outcomes together tends to generate more energy than endless consultations.

Finally, the potential for people of faith to engage as citizens in the governance of their neighbourhoods has never been stronger. The experience of working within their own faith organisations, having to make decisions with limited budgets and without total unanimity, should provide skills and capacity to contribute to neighbourhood management in all its forms. The potential to contribute to defining local targets for Local Area Agreements and to meeting those targets needs to be recognised by both faith groups and local authorities.

References

Banks, S., Butcher, H., Henderson, P. and Robertson, J. (2003) *Managing community practice: Principles, policies and programmes*, Bristol: The Policy Press.

Berkeley, N., Barnes, S., Dann, B., Stockley, N. and Finneron, D. (2006) *Faithful representation: Faith representatives on Local Strategic Partnerships*, London: Church Urban Fund.

British Humanist Association (2007) *Quality and equality: Human rights, public services and religious organisations*, London: BHA.

Burr, V. (2003) *Social constructionism*, London: Routledge.

Butcher, H., Banks, S., Henderson, P. and Robertson, J. (2007) *Critical community practice*, Bristol: The Policy Press.

Cabinet Office (2001) *A new commitment to neighbourhood renewal: National Strategy Action Plan*, London: Cabinet Office, Social Exclusion Unit.

CDF (Community Development Foundation) (2007) *Report on self completion questionnaires – round 1, wave 1*, www.cdf.org.uk/faithcapacitybuildingfund

Chanon, G. (2003) *Searching for solid foundations: Community involvement and urban policy*, London, ODPM (Office of the Deputy Prime Minister).

Commission on Integration and Cohesion (2007) *Our shared future*, London: Commission on Integration and Cohesion.

DCLG (Department of Communities and Local Government) (2007a) *Preventing violent extremism: Winning hearts and minds*, London: DCLG.

DCLG (2007b) *Face-to-face and side-by-side: A framework for inter faith dialogue and social action*, London: DCLG.

DETR (Department for the Environment, Transport and the Regions) (1997) *Involving communities in urban and rural regeneration: A guide for practitioners*, London: DETR.

Dinham, A. and Lowndes, V. (2008) 'Religion, resources and representation: three narratives of faith engagement in British urban governance', *Urban Affairs Review*, vol 43, no 6, pp 817–45.

Fagence, M. (1977) *Citizen participation in planning*, Oxford: Pergamon.

Farnell, R. (2007) *Faith in Lewisham: A review and evaluation of partnership work between the London Borough of Lewisham and local faith groups*, www.coventry.ac.uk/surge

Farnell, R., Furbey, R., Shams Al-Haqq, S., Macey, M. and Smith, G. (2003) '*Faith' in urban regeneration? Engaging faith communities in urban regeneration*, Bristol: The Policy Press.

Farnell, R., Hopkinson, J., Jarvis, D., Martineau, J. and Ricketts Hein, J. (2006) *Faith in rural communities: Contributions of social capital to community vibrancy*, Coventry: ACORA Publishing.

Furbey, R. and Macey, M. (2005) 'Religion and urban regeneration: a place for faith?', *Policy & Politics*, vol 33, no 1, pp 95-116.

Furbey, R., Dinham, A., Farnell, R., Finneron, D. and Wilkinson, G. (2006) *Faith as social capital: Connecting or dividing?*, Bristol: The Policy Press.

Home Office (2004) *Working together: Co-operation between government and faith communities*, London: Faith Communities Unit, Home Office.

LGA (Local Government Association) (2002) *Faith and community: A good practice guide for local authorities*, London: LGA Publications.

London Churches Group (2002) *Neighbourhood renewal in London: The role of faith communities*, London: Greater London Enterprise.

Lowndes, V. and Chapman, R. (2005) *Faith, hope and clarity: Developing a model of faith group involvement in civil renewal*, Leicester: De Montfort University.

Northwest Regional Development Agency (2003) *Faith in England's Northwest: The contribution made by faith communities to civil society in the region*, Warrington: Northwest Regional Development Agency.

Parkinson, M. et al (2006) *State of the English cities: A research study*, London: ODPM.

Ravat, R. (2004) *Embracing the present, planning the future: Social action by faith communities in Leicester*, Leicester: Leicester Faiths Regeneration Project.

Secretary of State for Communities and Local Government (2006) *Strong and prosperous communities: The Local Government White Paper*, London: DCLG.

Secretary of State for Communities and Local Government (2007) *Letter to Darra Singh, Chair of the Commission on Integration and Cohesion*, London: DCLG.

West Midlands Faith Forum (2006) *Key issues for faith-based regeneration*, Coventry: West Midlands Faith Forum.

Yorkshire Churches (2002) *Angels and advocates: Church social action in Yorkshire and the Humber,* Leeds: Churches Regional Commission for Yorkshire and the Humber.

ELEVEN

Faith and the voluntary sector in urban governance: distinctive yet similar?

Rachael Chapman

Introduction

The engagement of voluntary and community sector (VCS) organisations is an important strand in government policy agendas on sustainable communities (DCLG, 2007a; HM Treasury and Cabinet Office, 2007). The sector's contribution stems from its values, philanthropy, resources and social capital, all of which inform a range of activities including welfare provision, campaigning, advocacy and interest representation. More recently, the government has drawn increasing attention to the potential for faith communities to contribute in similar and, in some cases, distinctive ways to this agenda. A growing body of research confirms that faith-based organisations have much to contribute, not least through their spiritual and religious values, beliefs and resources (see Farnell et al, 2003; Baker and Skinner, 2005; Furbey et al, 2006; Grieve et al, 2007; Lowndes and Chapman, 2007). However, little is understood about how their contribution and experience of engagement in urban governance relates to, and compares with, the wider VCS in Britain. Yet, such an understanding is important for debates on the appropriate and effective role, nature and balance of faith-based and 'secular' VCS engagement in governance.

Drawing on primary and secondary research, this chapter examines the role of faith-based organisations in British urban governance from the 1990s onwards. It addresses the question as to whether faith-based organisations have characteristics or experiences that distinguish them from VCS organisations of a more secular nature. The chapter begins with a brief review of the policy and research context as it applies to faith and VCS engagement in civil society and urban governance. After addressing various definitional and conceptual issues, the chapter compares the contribution and experiences of faith-based and secular

VCS organisations in urban governance. Here urban governance refers specifically to the engagement of statutory and non-governmental partners in the design and delivery of public policies and services in British cities and towns; that is, through participation on public partnerships, consultations and the delivery of publicly funded activities. The chapter concludes by arguing that there are many similarities in the general contribution and experiences of faith-based and secular VCS organisations in this context. However, there are also differences relating to the extent and nature of links to a faith tradition.

Background and context

The role of religious and voluntary institutions in British society has changed over the centuries. Following the Reformation in the 16th century, the Church of England played a central role in exercising social control and in providing education, health and social care. The role of the state was seen to be minimal and regulatory (Taylor, 2004). By the 20th century, the balance shifted towards a more secular welfare state whereby: religious organisations became more subordinate (Farnell et al, 2003); the state played an increasing role as a regulator, funder and then provider; and traditional voluntary organisations (for example, cooperatives and mutual enterprises) maintained a specialist role in some fields. This trend cumulated in the establishment of a comprehensive welfare state in the 1940s, in which the state took major responsibility for welfare, and the VCS provided services complementing state provision and acted as a government 'watchdog' with a view to improving state policy and services (Taylor et al, 2004).

An enhanced role for the VCS later emerged following the election of the Conservative government in 1979, with its commitment to roll back the frontiers of the welfare state, and the 1997 election of the New Labour government, with its emphasis on democratic renewal, partnership and participation. As part of this, the VCS has become increasingly engaged in the delivery of public services, and is a key partner on various public partnerships at the local, regional and national level. A greater role for faith-based organisations has also emerged, particularly from the 1990s onwards. This reflects broader trends towards partnership and a mixed welfare state, together with growing concerns over polarisation and religious extremism and perceptions of 'untapped' faith group resources and capabilities in building sustainable communities. At the national level, the Inner Cities Religious Council was established in 1992 as a forum for partnership working between faith representatives and the government on issues such as urban regeneration, neighbourhood renewal and social inclusion. This was replaced in April 2006 by the Faith Communities Consultative Council, which is additionally concerned with issues of cohesion, integration and sustainable communities.

At the local level, Local Strategic Partnerships are required to make specific efforts to involve and consult faith communities, alongside the wider VCS, including in the development of Community Strategies and Local Area Agreements (Geddes et al, 2007). Statutory authorities have also been encouraged to engage faith communities in developing local compacts alongside the VCS, and to consult with them on various policy issues through standing advisory councils on religious education, inter-faith forums and neighbourhood-level governance structures and initiatives.

A specific role is also outlined for faith groups in building stronger and more cohesive communities and in preventing religious extremism (Commission on Integration and Cohesion, 2007; DCLG, 2007b). In relation to this, the government established the Faith Communities Capacity Building Fund, investing £13.8 million in the first and second round of funding to support capacity-building, inter-faith programmes and faith participation in civil society. A greater role for faith groups in social action, regeneration and welfare delivery was also implied in policy documents and ministerial speeches (DCLG, 2007b; Murphy, 2007a, 2007b). In parallel with these developments, faith communities themselves continue to review their contribution to civil society and have expressed the importance of faith in modern urban life, for example in relation to poverty, community cohesion, social capital and partnership (see CULF, 2006).

These developments raise fascinating questions about the relative role, contribution and experiences of faith-based and wider VCS engagement in the public realm. Do faith-based organisations, for example, offer a distinctive contribution to urban governance in Britain? If so, on what basis and in what ways is it similar to or different from that of the wider VCS more generally? Furthermore, do faith-based organisations experience similar or distinctive challenges and tensions compared with the wider VCS?

These questions have significant implications for policy debates on the appropriate role, scope and mechanisms of faith-based and secular VCS engagement in governance. Despite this, little research has been undertaken on this subject in Britain, as opposed to other countries such as the US (see Edaugh et al, 2005; Kearns et al, 2005). One exception is a report by the National Council for Voluntary Organisations[1] (NCVO, 2007), which draws on UK-based evidence to explore faith and voluntary action. While acknowledging differences in the contribution and experiences of secular and faith-based organisations in civil society, this report concludes by emphasising similarities in terms of their activities, limitations and the challenges and opportunities they face. As such, it marks an important step towards addressing the above questions. However, it does not provide definitive answers. As the authors acknowledge, 'the case for the distinctiveness of faith-based organisations is unresolved'; further analysis and clarity is required concerning the nature of distinctiveness and whether it relates more to process than outcomes (NCVO, 2007, p 55).

This chapter is offered in this spirit. It draws on 36 interviews undertaken in Leicester and London to provide additional and deeper insights into the similarities and differences of faith-based and secular VCS engagement in urban governance. Interviews were undertaken between 2005 and 2007 with: national faith leaders and civil servants in the Home Office and the Department of Communities and Local Government; faith leaders and activists from Bahá'í, Christian, Jain, Jewish, Hindu, Muslim and Sikh communities; and representatives from the wider VCS and statutory bodies in Leicester, including the local authority and constabulary. In addition to primary research, the chapter also draws together and compares findings from existing literature on faith engagement with that of the wider VCS more generally. As already established, the chapter focuses on urban areas, reflecting the importance of towns and cities in the lives of the millions of people living and working within them (that is, around 90% of the population in England and Wales live in urban areas[2]). While some of the findings may apply in a rural setting, there is scope for differences resulting from the specific challenges and socioeconomic characteristics of rural communities, which may in turn shape the relative contribution and experiences of faith-based and secular organisations in governance (see, for example, Farnell et al, 2006; Grieve et al, 2007).

Concepts and definitions

Comparing faith-based and secular VCS organisations poses significant challenges, particularly as there is no agreed way of defining or distinguishing between them. Difficulties stem from the complex array of organisations described under these and other labels (see Halfpenny and Reid, 2002), together with the blurring of boundaries between the public, private and voluntary spheres. Indeed, some definitions of the voluntary sector include certain types of faith-based voluntary action. For example, the Scottish Council for Voluntary Organisations (SCVO,

2007, p 1) defines voluntary organisations as 'non-profit driven, non-statutory, autonomous and run by individuals who do not get paid for running the organisation'. This excludes faith-based organisations that are charitable but have a primarily religious motivation of an exclusive and private nature. However, it includes faith-based organisations with separately constituted projects addressing specific social needs. The UK Charity Commission also recognises the advancement of religion as an eligible activity for charitable status, with the 2006 Charities Act imposing an additional requirement, enforced from 2008, for organisations to also demonstrate public benefit, rather than this being assumed.

With these complexities in mind, it is important to be clear about what is meant by faith-based organisations and the secular VCS. At this stage it is useful to emphasise the chapter's focus on collective action by faith-based and secular organisations, as opposed to individual volunteering. This distinction is important as people of faith and, possibly no faith, are active within both types of organisation. Therefore, it is the organisational, rather than personal connection to faith or otherwise that is important here. Having clarified this, VCS organisations are defined as those that are essentially non-profit-distributing, self-governing, significantly voluntary and have, or are working towards, some formal institutional existence, with the exception of trades unions (based on Kendall and Anheier, 1999). Such organisations are considered secular where there is no reference to religion or associated commitments in their mission, founding history, governance or project content. Faith-based organisations, on the other hand, refer to worshipping communities as well as VCS organisations that are to some extent grounded in a faith tradition.

Sider and Unruh (2004, pp 119-20) offer the following fivefold typology for identifying and classifying the degree to which organisations are linked to faith:

(1) **Faith-permeated** *organisations:* where the connection with religious faith is evident at all levels of mission, staffing, governance and support. Social action projects incorporate extensive and explicit religious content.
(2) **Faith-centred** *organisations:* which are founded for a religious purpose and remain strongly connected with the religious community through funding sources and affiliation. The governing board and most staff share the organisation's faith commitments. Social action projects include explicit religious references or activities, although allow for opt-out of religious content by participants.

(3) *Faith-affiliated organisations*: which retain some influence of their religious founders, such as their mission statement, but do not require staff to affirm religious beliefs or practices. Social action does not typically incorporate explicit religious content, although religious tenets may be included in a general way, for example by making spiritual resources available to participants or through conveying religious messages through nonverbal acts of compassion.

(4) *Faith-background organisations*: which tend to appear secular although they may have an historical tie to a faith tradition. Some personnel may be motivated by religion, but faith commitments are not part of the selection process for staff or boards. Social action projects contain no explicit faith content, besides perhaps their possible location in a religious setting.

(5) *Faith–secular partnerships*: which arise where a secular organisation joins with one or more explicitly religious organisations. The organisation is typically secular in its administrations but it relies on the religious partnership for volunteers and other support.

This typology provides a useful reminder of the diverse nature of faith-based organisations. However, Sider and Unruh (2004) acknowledge that such organisations are more complex than their typology suggests and may exhibit characteristics of different categories. The purpose of their typology is to capture general trends, and the categories should be viewed as points along a spectrum rather than discrete entities.

The remainder of this chapter explores potential similarities and differences in the contribution and experiences of faith-based and secular VCS organisations in urban governance. Three units of analysis are investigated through which these organisations are known to contribute to governance (see Lowndes and Chapman, 2007). The first is termed 'lifeviews', which, adapting Wright and Dalenius's (nd) definition, refers to values, identities, rules of life, beliefs or philosophies that may or may not be directly linked to a faith tradition. An organisation or individual may have various lifeview influences, including culture, law, family and religion. The second is resources, which focuses on organisational capacity arising from members' skills and knowledge, mobilisation of volunteers and staff, fundraising and venues. The third is representation, which refers to the participation of faith and secular VCS representatives in public partnerships and consultations. It is important to note that, while analysed separately, the three units of analysis are not discrete entities. For example, organisational and individual lifeviews and resources are likely to shape the nature and extent of interest representation (to be discussed later).

Lifeviews: values, identities and beliefs

A key similarity between many faith-based and secular VCS organisations involved in urban governance is their value-driven motivation. To elaborate, a defining feature of the third sector generally is the desire to promote social, economic and cultural objectives in pursuit of citizen well-being and better governance. This is often linked to an organisation's founding values, which commonly include social justice, equity, mutuality and solidarity (Taylor and Warburton, 2003; HM Treasury, 2004). A similar value-driven basis can be identified in the commitment of many faith-based organisations to social action and engagement in public partnerships and consultations. Interviews with faith leaders and activists in Leicester and London, for example, revealed a range of founding values and principles, such as justice, equity and solidarity, which were recognised as being similar to those of secular VCS organisations.

Similarities may also be encountered in relation to beliefs, ethics and vision. In their research on the contribution of churches to social capital, Baker and Skinner (2006, p 12) identify a range of lifeviews shaping the contribution of Christian organisations to society. These include:

(1) a focus on hope and transformation of people and places;
(2) the value of 'personal stories';
(3) the belief implicitly or explicitly that God is at work within regeneration and civil society;
(4) an acceptance of strong emotion when working towards healthy communities;
(5) the importance of values such as 'self-emptying, forgiveness, transformation, risk-taking and openness to learning';
(6) beginning with the intention of accepting those who have been rejected elsewhere;
(7) the importance of valuing 'people's inner resources' and seeing people as capable of creating their own solutions to their problems.

Questions were asked in Baker and Skinner's (2006, p 24) research as to whether these aspects were evident within secular groups, with the possibility raised that strand (3) may be the only distinctive contribution of Christian organisations. Such contentions suggest that it is the religious basis on which values, beliefs and identities are founded that forms a distinctive characteristic of faith-based participation, motivation and social action, particularly among organisations where faith is more deeply embedded (see also Finneron, 2007, p 41). Interviews with four faith leaders and activists in Leicester and London provide some support of this. As a faith regeneration officer of Christian faith commented:

> 'I guess at the heart of it, the difference between other voluntary organisations and faith groups is a sense of otherness ... people of faith believe that there is something else, something higher and greater than they are ... you are not just serving others because you think it's right to serve others, you're serving others because you're commanded to do so or that it's the right thing or somehow it enhances your relationship with God.... It's that serving of others, being of service to God, that differs and that commitment to God provides you with that sense of commitment to others.'

Even so, it is important to recognise that voluntary action within faith-based organisations is motivated and informed by a range of factors, not all of which are associated with faith (see Lukka et al, 2003). As Farnell et al (2003) suggest, the positive contribution of faith communities is sometimes linked more to wider social and political principles shared with non-religious people than to specific religious or spiritual qualities and values.

Where religious commitments are important, the question arises as to whether this lends itself to contributions of a similar or distinctive nature to other VCS organisations. On the one hand, faith-based organisations, particularly those of a more faith-permeated or faith-centred nature, can be viewed as distinctive on the grounds that they address people's spiritual and other needs through religious expression (see also Grieve et al, 2007). By way of an example, the strong link between spiritual and practical life within the Bahá'í faith is a core belief underlying a project in Swindon to develop a 'healthy human spirit' in young people through various practical measures (Bishop and Chorley, nd). The active and physical presence of faith-based organisations within local communities may also have a distinctive contribution in facilitating a sense of identity, place and belonging among some people, as highlighted in Leicester by Wright and Dalenius (nd).

Beyond meeting spiritual and religious needs, perspectives on distinctiveness varied, with several interviewees in Leicester and London emphasising similar commitments between faith and non-faith-based organisations (for example, provision of services, fundraising, advocacy and campaigning), and others highlighting potential, sometimes subtle, differences. A bishop within the Pentecostal Church, for example, argued that:

> 'I think a lot of what we do in intent are the same. A lot of the conditions that we then face are the same. The rain falls, it falls on all of us.... I hope what happens to a faith-based group is what I described a while ago; that we would be somewhat more zealous about ensuring that those God-given and God-directed values that we hold dear are lived out.'

Other interviewees suggested that faith groups reinforce and complement other civil society groups through, for example, a holistic commitment to the well-being of communities, a predisposition towards engaging socially excluded people or a speedy and proactive response to changing needs. As one member of a Christian organisation put it:

> 'We're about whole health because we're made as whole people, therefore it's as much about environmental health and educational health as it is about physical health, spiritual health, mental health and vocational health.'

Such a holistic approach is not necessarily unique to, or evident in, all faith-based organisations. Many secular community sector groups are involved in a broad range of activities including relief of poverty, education, environment and health. These groups, whether faith based or otherwise, can complement wider voluntary organisations that focus on a particular issue or service. Similarly, faith-based organisations share a predisposition towards engagement with socially excluded people with the wider VCS. However, previous research indicates that faith groups may have a distinctive role in engaging with 'people who would not trust, and would not approach, or even think of going to a statutory or another voluntary organisation' (Lowndes and Chapman, 2005, p 17). Clearly, this may also work the other way around; secular VCS organisations may have a distinctive role in engaging those that would not trust or approach a faith-based organisation. Interviewees also gave examples where faith-based organisations have made a distinctive contribution through their quick and proactive response to changing needs, which, in Leicester, took the form of mobilising volunteers and support for asylum seekers, refugees and new arrivals (employee of a VCS organisation).

Finally, faith-based organisations may face distinctive challenges associated with their religious beliefs, identities and norms. Interviewees identified tensions arising from a lack of understanding or acceptance of faith-group values, practices and language among policy makers and practitioners. Faith groups may also find it difficult to express religious values, beliefs and principles in a more secularised policy context due to fear of sounding 'a bit weird' or because they themselves take them for granted. A member of the Salvation Army who was interviewed highlighted a need to adopt a more 'secularised language' in this context, using terms such as 'honesty, tolerance and the importance of relationships', as opposed to more instinctive Christian language of 'grace, peace, joy and love'. This led to concerns about what is 'lost in translation'. Previous research also highlights the potential for negative attributes to emerge from faith-based activities where religious doctrines act as simplification, distortion or controlling devices (see Farnell et al, 2003). As Furbey (2007, p 38) suggests, 'faith can be interpreted and used to generate negative social capital and fear and hatred of "the other"'. Even so, not all challenges faced by faith-based organisations engaging in urban governance are distinctive. They, like their more secular VCS counterparts, may experience difficulties in maintaining a focus on values and mission when working with government. Faith-based organisations may also share frustrations over the short-term nature of some public policy programmes and funding regimes.

Resources: funding, leadership and support

Resources are fundamental to engagement in urban governance, whether through social action, partnership working and/or consultations. They may take various forms, including financial (for example, donations, fundraising income), human (for example, expertise, volunteers and leadership), physical (for example, buildings) and social capital (that is, access to networks of trust and reciprocity). Such resources can be found among faith communities and the wider VCS, although they are unevenly distributed. As with the VCS generally, income is unevenly spread across faith-based registered charities, with financial resources concentrated in a relatively small number of larger organisations (NCVO, 2006, 2007). Human and physical resource differentials also exist within and across faith-based organisations. Interviewees, for example, suggested that Christian and larger, more established faith groups tend to have greater access to paid workers and buildings than other faith communities. Similar resource differentials can also be found between larger more professionalised voluntary organisations and smaller more informal community sector organisations (Chapman, 2005). Such differences can affect organisational capacity, whether faith-based or secular, to engage in urban governance, with smaller and less well-resourced groups experiencing greater difficulties, especially where heavy reliance is placed on a few volunteers with the time, knowledge and skills to engage (Chapman and Lowndes, 2008). As Finneron (2007, p 41) suggests, the main barriers to effective participation for faith-based organisations are similar to those experienced by the wider VCS, including 'a lack of capacity to respond to the torrent of demands and a need to develop the requisite expertise and skills'.

While there are commonalities, there is also potential for distinctiveness. Interviewees, for example, pointed to the support, inspiration and energy that faith-based organisations and individuals can derive from their faith and the wider faith community in relation to 'living out' their values. According to one interviewee:

> 'What they [faith-based organisations] have that secular organisations don't have are priests, kind of teachers, who are key figures, who are authoritative exponents of the culture. So, you know, there's an explicit mission or message from those people to anybody who's involved in the group about the culture, about the values, about the basis of it, which you won't find in many secular groups except in the early days of those which have charismatic founders.' (Academic and former VCS employee)

Similarly, a bishop of the Pentecostal Church remarked that: living in the faith community 're-energises me and reminds me of why I'm doing this because we all probably forget because of the pressures'.

As for distinctive challenges, there is a perception among faith communities that they are discriminated against in the allocation of public funding due to their religious affiliation. Interviewees linked this to lack of understanding or acceptance that funding would be used for non-religious activities, and/or concerns among funders of proselytisation, or that certain sections of the community, for example women, young people, gays or people with no faith affiliation, would be marginalised or excluded (see also Reith, 2003). According to a trustee of a Jain temple, 'there is no recognition in terms of any funding availability because they treat us as a religious group and not a "community"'. Another interviewee reflected on the issue in the following terms:

> 'If somebody is actually undertaking a cultural activity, there's usually funding available. If it's a faith activity, there isn't. But if you mix the two, it often can limit your opportunities for accessing funding and achieving the objectives you want to achieve.' (Employee of a VCS organisation)

This suggests that faith-permeated organisations are unlikely to qualify for public funding and that a clear distinction needs to be made between 'religious' and social' purposes when applying for public funds. Yet, this can sometimes be problematic when faith and action are closely connected (Farnell et al, 2003). As Sider and Unruh's (2004) typology suggests, religious and secular purposes and characteristics are mixed in various ways across organisational and project aspects. Questions also remain as to what is, or is not, appropriate where faith and public funds are involved and what exactly counts as proselytisation. Does starting citizenship classes with a prayer or placing bibles on a table at a luncheon club for people to take if they wish count as proselytisation? Such distinctions map onto the religious content aspect of Sider and Unruh's typology. Faith-background organisations, for example, are seen to run programmes with no explicit religious content, but may make religious materials or resources available to beneficiaries who seek them out. This differs from faith-permeated organisations, where beneficiaries are expected to participate in religious activities and discussions of faith. These distinctions may be useful in drawing up guidelines to better assist bodies administering public funding to faith-based organisations, as recommended in the report of the Commission on Integration and Cohesion (2007).

Other barriers to accessing public funds by faith communities include lack of awareness of funding opportunities, ethical concerns concerning income sources associated with gambling (for example, lottery funding) and a tendency to look to their own communities for support. Research in North West England (NWRDA, 2003) indicates that faith communities are largely self-financing, with 27% of survey respondents indicating that they received public funding compared with 73% who had not (see also Lukka et al, 2003). Howarth (2007) suggests that the financial independence of many congregations and faith institutions helps provide a degree of stability and security compared with voluntary sector organisations that depend more heavily on public funding. Farnell et al (2003), on the other hand, point out that internally derived funds within faith communities are often scarce. An employee from a VCS organisation who was interviewed also expressed concerns that many faith-based organisations may 'be left behind' or not able to compete on a level playing field with other VCS organisations in relation to government policy agendas on commissioning and procurement of service delivery. More specifically, faith-based organisations are not viewed as being in an ideal position to tender for service provision contracts and are seen to lack capacity and/or awareness of current policy changes.

Representation: who, how and for whom?

Both faith and secular VCS organisations take part in lobbying activities and participate in policy-related consultations undertaken by public partnerships or statutory bodies at the national, regional and local levels. Individuals from these organisations may also sit on public partnerships as advisers or as 'representatives' acting on behalf of faith community, third sector and/or wider interests. In doing so, faith- and non-faith-based organisations alike contribute by widening representation; highlighting issues of client and community needs; promoting social justice; and providing specialist knowledge, expertise and access to local networks (NCVO, nd). As one faith representative of a mental health trust partnership stated:

> 'I really do passionately believe in equality, equity and justice. I believe that everybody is equal through my Christian faith … when I read my board papers, as I am about to do for a board meeting next Wednesday, I read it through those lenses and I am very concerned to note … whether there are clear discrepancies in the level of satisfaction [with service delivery] as you go from one group to another.' (Bishop within the Pentecostal Church)

Faith-based and secular VCS organisations also experience similar partnership-related tensions and challenges. These include difficulties in representing diverse needs and interests, securing policy influence, establishing appropriate systems of interest representation and accountability, and maintaining their independence. As a report from the Office of the Deputy Prime Minister (ODPM, 2006) remarks, a Local Strategic Partnership board may have only one or two places available for religious representation, which calls into question how such representatives should be selected and what mechanisms of communication and accountability should be established in relation to the wider religious constituency. One interviewee also commented:

> 'It's like within the VCS, we can represent a range of views but we cannot have one representative view for the whole of the sector because that would be unrealistic ... faith leaders may not reflect the views of the entire congregation or even a very significant part of that congregation.' (Employee of a VCS organisation)

Yet, as the same interviewee added, there is often a perception among the VCS that statutory partners and government expect or would like a single VCS view or voice (see also Taylor et al, 2004). Mechanisms for communication and accountability also vary in their extent, nature and effectiveness regardless of faith, as well as between faith-based organisations (see NCVO, nd; Gaventa, 2004; Chapman, 2005). In the case of faith 'representatives', partnership-related activities and agendas may be formally communicated and discussed among faith leaders, members of inter-faith forums and, in some cases, with faith or other communities via emails, websites or newsletters. Alternatively, feedback and discussion may 'not happen at all' (member of the Salvation Army). Finally, many organisations, whether faith-based or otherwise, also experience capacity and resource limitations affecting their ability to engage in consultations and influence decision making. As an NCVO (nd, p 25) report specifies, 'it is not uncommon for voluntary sector organisations to feel their involvement in partnerships has been tokenistic'.

While faith-based and secular VCS organisations have much in common, there is also potential for difference. Some faith-based organisations may, for example, be better placed to represent particular stakeholder interests, especially those associated with religious beliefs or norms and/or groups that are not 'reached' or who do not trust other statutory and voluntary sector organisations. According to the Neighbourhood Renewal Unit (NRU, 2004, p 1), some places of worship may be the only local organisation able to reflect the views of particular ethnic groups within a given locality, although Escott and Logan (2006) warn against the dangers of confusing faith and ethnicity, which they suggest undervalues the role of faith and marginalises the distinctive contribution of faith communities. Faith-based organisations may also have a distinctive role in highlighting the practical contribution of faith communities to urban governance and in working alongside statutory authorities to help reduce the isolation of some faith communities and counter trends towards religious extremism (see Escott and Logan, 2006; Finneron, 2007).

Faith-based organisations may also experience particular tensions and/or challenges. One interviewee, an academic and former employee within the VCS, suggested that issues of representativeness could be stronger for some faith communities, especially where representatives are leaders 'anointed by God' rather than elected by their constituents. Such 'faith' leaders are perceived to be more difficult to move or challenge. Another interviewee, from the Salvation Army, suggested that representation of women and young people might also be a challenge for some faith communities, although difficulties of this nature are also experienced in partnerships more generally, especially in relation to young people (Chapman, 2005). Finally, although new spaces have emerged for formal participation and representation at the partnership table, such opportunities appear less prevalent for 'faith representatives' than for the VCS more generally. According to Berkeley et al (2006, p 3), 'the only form of local public partnership that has really endorsed the concept of "faith representatives" being there to represent the constituency of local faith communities has been LSPs [Local Strategic Partnerships]'. On the other hand, opportunities exist for VCS participation and representation on Local Strategic Partnerships and other partnerships relating to primary care trusts, children's trusts, Connexions and educational improvement (see ODPM, 2005). Having said this, the nature of faith and VCS representation is complex; 'faith representation' may be subsumed within the VCS more generally and some 'people of faith' on partnerships may become 'de facto' faith representatives (Berkeley et al, 2006).

Conclusion

This chapter contributes to the limited evidence base concerning the relative contribution and experiences of faith-based and secular VCS engagement in British urban governance. Drawing on primary and secondary research, it has explored whether the contribution and experiences of faith-based organisations can be considered similar to or distinctive from that of the more secular VCS, and if so, on what basis and in what ways. The findings suggest that there are many similarities between the two groups, in terms of both processes and outcomes of engagement. These include:

- tendencies towards a value-driven motivation based on values such as justice, equity and solidarity;
- the types and uneven distribution of resources; and
- involvement in activities such as social action, service delivery, fundraising, consultations, partnership working and campaigning.

Both groups also face similar challenges and tensions that can, in some cases, hinder their ability to engage and contribute to effective performance and/or democratic outcomes. These include:

- value or mission drift;
- limited and uneven capacity; and
- challenges associated with acting as a representative on partnership bodies.

These similarities suggest that there is significant potential for faith-based and secular VCS organisations to support and learn valuable lessons from one another.

While there are many similarities, there are also potential differences, associated with:

- the underlying basis of values, beliefs and motivations;
- the types of needs addressed;
- the nature of leadership and wider community support; and
- interest representation.

Some, although not all, faith-based organisations may have a distinctive role in addressing spiritual, religious or other needs and in representing or engaging people with an active faith identity or people who would not trust or approach other organisations. A distinctive role is also evident for faith-based organisations in working alongside statutory partners in reducing the isolation of some faith communities and countering trends towards religious extremism. Furthermore, faith-based organisations may experience distinctive challenges or tensions when engaging in urban governance. These include:

- a lack of understanding of faith group beliefs, motivations and language by policy makers and practitioners;
- possible funding discrimination; and
- issues surrounding proselytisation and public funding.

It is important that these differences are recognised within the policy domain as they have implications for improved engagement with faith communities, together with arguments both for and against their involvement in the public realm.

Questions around distinctiveness are also relevant to debates on whether faith-based organisations can or should be considered part of the third sector, and whether this is desirable or appropriate from a faith-group or policy perspective. Commonalities in urban governance contributions and experiences suggest some logic in locating faith-based organisations within the third sector. However, this can also mask diversity and distinctiveness, which is fundamentally important to some groups and within certain policy contexts.

Together, the findings suggest that faith-based organisations have much to contribute to urban governance, although notable exceptions and limitations exist. In many ways their contribution and experiences mirror that of the wider VCS, whereas in others, it is distinctive. Unsurprisingly, the nature and degree of the 'faith dimension' lies at the heart of what distinguishes faith-based and wider VCS engagement. As Sider and Unruh's (2004) typology reminds us, this manifests itself in many different ways. Diversity within the faith and wider VCS sectors means that there are no clear-cut or universal distinguishing features between faith-based and wider VCS organisations beyond their link to a faith tradition. Differences are likely to be context-specific, suggesting a need for further research that both demonstrates and reflects this.

Notes

[1] The National Council for Voluntary Organisations is a voluntary and community sector umbrella organisation that supports third sector organisations in England and campaigns on their behalf.

[2] 2001 Census data: Office of National Statistics Crown Copyright Reserved (Nomis, 22/02/08).

References

Baker, C. and Skinner, H. (2005) *Telling the stories: How churches are contributing to social capital*, Manchester: William Temple Foundation.

Baker, C. and Skinner, H. (2006) *Faith in action: The dynamic connection between spiritual and religious capital*, Manchester: William Temple Foundation.

Berkeley, N., Barnes, S., Dann, B., Stockley, N. and Finneran, D. (2006) *Faithful representation: Faith representatives on Local Public Partnerships: Summary, key findings and recommendations*, London: Church Urban Fund.

Bishop, A. and Chorley, S. (nd) *Belief and behaviour through community projects: An investigation into the distinctive qualities that individual faith groups bring to community development work*, London: Faithworks.

Chapman, R. (2005) 'Third sector and empowerment in a multi-level polity', PhD thesis, University of Sheffield.

Chapman, R. and Lowndes, V. (2008) 'Faith in governance? The potential and pitfalls of involving faith groups in urban governance', *Planning Practice and Research*, vol 23, no 1, pp 57-77.

Commission on Integration and Cohesion (2007) *Our shared future*, London: Commission on Integration and Cohesion.

CULF (Commission on Urban Life and Faith) (2006) *Faithful cities: A call for celebration, vision and justice*, London: Church Housing Publishing/Methodist Publishing House.

DCLG (Department of Communities and Local Government) (2007a) *Third sector strategy for communities and local government: Discussion paper*, London: DCLG.

DCLG (2007b) *Improving opportunity, strengthening society: Two years on – A progress report on the government's strategy for race equality and community cohesion*, London: DCLG.

Edaugh, H.R., Chafetz, J.S. and Pipes, P. (2005) 'Funding good works: funding sources of faith-based social service coalitions', *Nonprofit and Voluntary Sector Quarterly*, vol 34, no 4, pp 448-72.

Escott, P. and Logan, P. (2006) *Faith in LSPs? The experience of faith community representatives on Local Strategic Partnerships*, London: Churches Regional Network.

Farnell, R., Furbey, R., Shams Al-Haqq, S., Macey, M. and Smith, G. (2003) *'Faith' in urban regeneration? Engaging faith communities in urban regeneration*, Bristol: The Policy Press.

Farnell, R., Hopkinson, J., Jarvis, D., Martineau, J. and Ricketts Hein, J. (2006) *Faith in rural communities: Contributions of social capital to community vibrancy*, Coventry: ACORA Publishing.

Finneron, D. (2007) 'Local governance, representation and faith-based organisations', in V. Jochum, B. Pratten and K. Wilding (eds) *Faith and voluntary action: An overview of current evidence and debates*, London: NCVO, pp 39-48.

Furbey, R. (2007) 'Faith, social capital and social cohesion', in V. Jochum, B. Pratten and K. Wilding (eds) *Faith and voluntary action: An overview of current evidence and debates*, London: NCVO, pp 34-9.

Furbey, R., Dinham, A., Farnell, R., Finneron, D. and Wilkinson, G. (2006) *Faith as social capital: Connecting or dividing?*, Bristol: The Policy Press.

Gaventa, J. (2004) *Representation, community leadership and participation: Citizen involvement in neighbourhood renewal and local governance*, Paper prepared for the Neighbourhood Renewal Unit, ODPM, Brighton: Institute of Development Studies.

Geddes, M., Davies, J. and Fuller, C. (2007) 'Evaluating Local Strategic Partnerships', *Local Government Studies*, vol 33, no 1, pp 97-116.

Grieve, J., Jochum, V., Pratten, B. and Steel, C. (2007) *Faith in the community: The contribution of faith-based organisations to rural voluntary action*, London: NCVO.

Halfpenny, P. and Reid, M. (2002) 'Research on the voluntary sector: an overview', *Policy & Politics*, vol 30, no 4, pp 533-50.

HM Treasury (2004) *Exploring the role of the third sector in public service delivery and reform: A discussion document*, London: HM Treasury.

HM Treasury and Cabinet Office (2007) *The future role of the third sector in social and economic regeneration: Final report*, London: HM Treasury and Cabinet Office.

Howarth, C. (2007) 'Faith-based organisations within civil society', in V. Jochum, B. Pratten and K. Wilding (eds) *Faith and voluntary action: An overview of current evidence and debates*, London: NCVO, pp 25-8.

Kearns, K., Park, C. and Yankoski, L. (2005) 'Comparing faith-based and secular community service corporations in Pittsburgh and Allegheny Country, Pennsylvania', *Nonprofit and Voluntary Sector Quarterly*, vol 34, no 2, pp 206-31.

Kendall, J. and Anheier, H.K. (1999) 'The third sector and the European Union policy process: an initial evaluation', *Journal of European Public Policy*, vol 6, no 2, pp 283-307.

Lowndes, V. and Chapman, R. (2005) *Faith, hope and clarity: Developing a model of faith group involvement in civil renewal: Main report*, Leicester: De Montfort University.

Lowndes, V. and Chapman, R. (2007) 'Faith, hope and clarity: faith groups and civil renewal, in T. Brannan, P. John and G. Stoker (eds) *Re-energizing citizenship: Strategies for civil renewal*, Basingstoke: Palgrave Macmillan, pp 163-84.

Lukka, P. and Locke, M. with Sorteri-Proctor, A. (2003) *Faith and voluntary action: Community, values and resources*, London: Institute for Volunteering Research.

Murphy, J. (2007a) *Press release: A greater role for faith based groups in UK welfare*, London: Department for Work and Pensions Media Centre.

Murphy, J. (2007b) *Seminar in partnership with Employment Focus 19th February 2007: What role for faith based groups in today's welfare state*, London: Department for Work and Pensions Media Centre.

NCVO (National Council for Voluntary Organisations) (nd) *A little bit of give and take: Voluntary sector accountability within cross-sectoral partnerships*, London: NCVO.

NCVO (2006) *The UK voluntary sector almanac 2006: The state of the sector*, London: NCVO.

NCVO (2007) *Faith and voluntary action: An overview of current evidence and debates*, London: NCVO.

NRU (Neighbourhood Renewal Unit) (2004) *Involving faith communities*, London: NRU.

NWRDA (Northwest Regional Development Agency) (2003) *Faith in England's Northwest: The contribution made by faith communities to civil society in the region*, Warrington: NWRDA.

ODPM (Office of the Deputy Prime Minister) (2005) *Local Strategic Partnerships: Shaping their future: A consultation paper*, London: ODPM.

ODPM (2006) *Review of the evidence base on faith communities*, London: ODPM.

Reith, T. (2003) *Releasing the resources of the faith sector: A Faithworks report*, London: Faithworks.

SCVO (Scottish Council for Voluntary Organisations) (2007) *Defining voluntary organisations*, Edinburgh: SCVO, Available at: www.scvo.org.uk/

Sider, R. and Unruh, H. (2004) 'Typology of religious characteristics of social service and educational organisations and programs', *Nonprofit and Voluntary Sector Quarterly*, vol 33, no 1, pp 109-34.

Taylor, M. (2004) 'The welfare mix in the United Kingdom', in A. Evers and J.L. Laville (eds) *The third sector in Europe*, Cheltenham: Edward Elgar, pp 122-43.

Taylor, M. and Warburton, D. (2003) 'Legitimacy and the role of UK third sector organisations in the policy process', *Voluntas: International Journal of Voluntary and Nonprofit Organisations*, vol 14, no 3, pp 330-2.

Taylor, M., Craig, G., Monro, S., Parkes, T., Warburton, D. and Wilkinson, M. (2004) 'A sea change or a swamp? New spaces for voluntary sector engagement in governance in the UK', *Institute of Development Studies Bulletin*, vol 35, no 2, pp 67-75.

Wright, S. and Dalenius, T. (nd) 'Life views': The report from a grassroots interfaith listening project*, Leicester: Leicester Council of Faiths.

TWELVE

Conclusions

Adam Dinham, Robert Furbey and Vivien Lowndes

Introduction

The preceding chapters have explored *controversies* that attend faith involvement in a liberal public realm; *policies* that provide its parameters, both endorsing a religious presence and sometimes circumscribing it; and *practices* of 'public faith' in various settings and sectors. This concluding chapter explores key themes emerging from the earlier contributions.

Must faith be 'other'?

The central question remains as to whether 'faith' is legitimate as a public category at all. 'Strong' secularists argue for the exclusion of religion from the public realm and its confinement to private life. A model of progressive secularisation informs this position, in which the Western liberal Enlightenment steadily marginalises religious institutions as historical curiosities, without social resonance, purpose or legitimacy. Thus, both 'religion' and religiousness become increasingly 'other'.

The concept of the 'other' is an expression of the colonialism associated with the Enlightenment, a process that identifies cultural 'essences' and works with binary opposites (Sandercock, 2003; Baker, 2007). Associated particularly with forms of ethnic categorisation, 'otherness' and the process of 'othering' can occur across other strong binary divides, such as that established by many religious and secular positions. It is this latter construction that is problematised here.

Yet, as Dinham and Lowndes observed in Chapter One, debates on secularisation are far from resolved. Even in Western Europe, religious faith finds significant, persistent and diverse expression (Davie, 1994; Norris and Inglehart, 2006). At the same time, the rise of religious fundamentalism certainly presents a perplexing and frightening 'other'. Gray (2007, p xvii) crystallises this development in arresting terms:

'Whereas Enlightenment thinkers believed religion would in future wither away or become politically marginal, at the start of the twenty-first century religion is at the heart of politics and war'.

Against this 'othering', a great weight of public religious expression is embedded both within society and in the psychosocial self. Some of this is subconscious – a sort of 'deep structure' that quietly informs the public realm. Where it is conscious it is not typically constructed as dramatically and violently 'other'. In Chapter Eleven, Chapman identified religious participation as a longstanding and continuing motivation for diverse forms of social service and political engagement. O'Neill's Canadian data in Chapter Seven suggested that the many who now practise a personal spirituality, not necessarily related to a major religious tradition and institution, are active in public life. This is reflected in UK research, including the locality-based qualitative work of Woodhead and Heelas (2005) and the nationwide statistical data of the Home Office Citizenship Survey (Home Office, 2005). Diverse and emerging expressions of faith, some articulated as clear beliefs on which to act and others present as inchoate instincts for a 'spiritual' dimension, serve to question a binary model of a straightforwardly secular majority of 'us' and a diminishing religious 'other'. Increasingly, we encounter many 'others' who derive identities from personal and institutional sources, both secular and religious.

Nevertheless, such considerations do not prevent the drawing of strong lines. Some boundaries are inter-religious or intra-religious, sustained by people of faith who focus on differences between themselves and the 'other' traditions around them. This is nowhere truer than for Muslims whose generalised and widespread 'othering' was observed by Cheesman and Khanum in Chapter Three. For them, Islam is subject to a process of 'othering' similar to that experienced by Catholics in Reformation Europe and repeatedly by Jews across the diaspora. This is compounded in government policy on the 'prevention of violent extremism' (PVE), which focuses exclusively on fundamentalist Islam (DCLG, 2007). While perhaps justified at the national and international level, the failure of PVE discourse (and funding) to cover the very real threats to community cohesion presented by far-Right activity at the local level (Goodwin, 2007) has served to compound the 'othering' of British Muslims. At the same time, the groundswell of inter-faith and multi-faith engagement reported on by Weller in Chapter Four suggests that this 'othering' is under the microscope for many people of faith, who seek points of commonality and mutuality rather than deepening a chasm of misunderstanding.

Several of the contributions to this book focus on another kind of difference – the division between religious and non-religious convictions. Dawkins (2003) draws on the distinction of Paul Geisert and Mynga Futrell between people of faith and those who are 'bright', that is, with a worldview 'free of supernatural and mystical elements'. Dawkins makes binary opponents of 'brights' and 'faith-heads'. He regards the latter as being infected by a deluding 'virus', strongly 'other' to scientific rationality. In Chapter Two Furbey argued that this stark distinction between scientific rationality and religious irrationality is misconceived. Ultimately, religious belief and non-belief constitute different metaphysical positions. But 'religion' is immensely varied, reflecting cultural diversity and historical change. If there are clear examples of religious traditions, past and present, which are obscurantist and at odds with science and rationality, there is also abundant evidence for the intertwining of science and religion.

Within science, too, there are differences. Science operates with self-imposed epistemological limitations, which have yielded huge advances in understanding. However, many scientists regard logical positivism as offering an unduly narrow definition of rationality. In those contexts where testable *experimental* data are not available, scientists and non-scientists, religious and atheist alike, apply reason through reflection on *experiential* data, informed by a wider cultural context. Central to culture are metaphor and myth, which also play a fundamental role in science. These constructions are often shared across science and religion, discouraging an image of science and religion as separate worlds, each experienced as irredeemably 'other'. Rather, there has been considerable mutual enrichment and also shared weakness. Both are evident in the close connections between the Protestant Reformation and the Western Enlightenment.

In Chapter Eleven Chapman presented a less philosophical, more empirically grounded, challenge to the 'otherness' of faith by exploring the extent of difference and similarity between faith organisations and secular organisations within the voluntary and community sector (VCS) in the UK. She found that many members of faith-based organisations share the same values as those prized by members of secular VCS organisations – justice, equity and solidarity being most frequently cited. Empirically, the boundaries between faith and non-faith organisations are often permeable and ill-defined. Many faith and secular organisations have similar ranges of activity: services, fundraising, advocacy and campaigning. In relation to government and local partnerships, both sets of actors are liable to the same conflicting experiences of exhilaration and frustration, similar concerns of 'mission creep', and ongoing dilemmas of 'incorporation' and 'representation' (see Chapman and Lowndes, 2008). Like VCS bodies, there are also large discrepancies of power and capacity among faith organisations of different religions and different denominations (Chapman and Lowndes, 2008).

Chapman noted that faith organisations may also vary from the wider VCS in important respects. They may disqualify themselves from certain spheres of activity or influence by their internal governance and equality procedures. More positively, they often have a strong record of working with highly marginalised groups (including homeless people, alcoholics and vulnerable families) and with people who may be reluctant to approach the state (including those in minority communities who encounter language or cultural barriers, or the fear or reality of racism). Faith organisations also tend to have strong local identifications and the capacity to develop a long-term and holistic approach to community service and social action (see Dinham and Lowndes, 2008). There is also a long tradition of faith-based (or faith-led) critical campaigning and self-organisation in pursuit of social justice – whether through international campaigns like Drop the Debt and Make Poverty History, or the local mobilisations of coalitions like London Citizens and Birmingham Citizens on issues of low pay, housing or immigration.[1] Elsewhere, Furbey (2006) has contrasted such 'troublesome' forms of faith action with the 'cuddlesome' faith engagement of government-sponsored partnerships and consultations.

It is possible, too, that faith organisations serve to emphasise elements of human-being in the public realm that are generally downplayed. Like other civil society organisations, faith groups may on occasion be susceptible to a vain and competitive entrepreneurialism in their efforts to expand their public profile and projects. But, in general, faith communities tend to focus their public activity not on the targets and outputs that have been criticised for commodifying human experience, but on the experience itself. Faiths can remind the public realm of the purpose for which it was created, namely the collective well-being of humankind. But, just as faith may revalorise the humanity of the public realm, so the functional and mechanical dimensions of that realm – the Weberian bureaucracy that makes it work – can in turn commodify faiths. In emphasising the 'value' of 'things', most frequently in terms of 'capitals' (Porritt, 2005) – economic, physical, cultural, social and moral – faiths could lose their distinctiveness to these overarching logics. Commodification may compromise the prophetic role (and vision of a better future) that sustains the critical voice of faith in the public realm (Bretherton, 2008).

A particular point of difference may also derive from the language of faith organisations and communities, a matter explored further below. It is an issue raised by Chapman but also by Baker in his study of church-based social action in inner-city Manchester (Chapter Six). Although Baker underlined the obstacles, frustrations and dangers of the 'blurred encounters' between faith and secular partners, he rejected a counsel of despair. The blurring of boundaries is a 'creative process' that promises 'a better quality of discourse and political deliberation'. Thus, philosophical reflection, empirical exploration and local experience do not invite the spectre of an implacable public battle between extreme 'others'. Reality seems more messy, more contingent and more hopeful.

Indeed, faith engagement may be considered a critical case in understanding the wider social process in which boundaries are being renegotiated between the state and civil society and between the public, private and personal spheres (Newman, 2005; Bevir and Rhodes, 2006). Faith narratives challenge the assumptions of a 'domain of rational deliberation that can be clearly marked from the passions and pleasures of the personal' (Newman, 2007, p 31). Faith engagement challenges dominant assumptions about what constitutes 'good governance' in the public realm. Perhaps trust is as important as accountability? Perhaps claims of social justice can trump those of due process? And perhaps public policy can take account of joined-up people as well as seeking 'joined-up government'?

Narrative dissonance within the public realm can have positive outcomes. The encounter between faith actors and those more normally associated with public policy and governance may yet prove productive in the fashioning of what Newman (2007) calls a new 'public imaginary' and Rhodes (1997) a 'new governing code'. As Jurgen Habermas (2007) notes: 'religions still bear a valuable semantic potential for inspiring other people beyond the limits of the particular community of faith'.

The inclusion of faith actors can support modes of deliberation and contestation that, although unfamiliar, are helpful. Indeed, their very *strangeness* provokes a broader process of questioning among public actors.

This is not just about securing tolerance and respect for different positions (Cantle, 2005); nor even about an aspiration to 'agonistic' or 'aversive' forms of deliberation, which do not presume consensus but seek to channel and confront disagreement (Mouffe, 2000; Norval, 2008). The key contribution is in valorising a passionate, 'affective' perspective that, at its best, is rooted in wisdom, tradition and culture but also looks forward to the realisation of new human and social potentialities. Such resources are not measurable: targets do not capture them or value the role they play. Yet they have the capacity to resonate with those who are alienated from politics in an era of managerialism, spin and celebrity, and the collapse of ideological certainties. Faith engagement is potentially part of a wider civil society movement to 're-inscribe the public domain with values associated with the private and personal spheres' (Newman, 2007, p 33), although some faith actors may consider counterparts within, for example, feminist and gay movements to be unlikely co-conspirators!

Ultimately, the 'othering' of faith may be a red herring. People of faith *are* everywhere in the public realm – as citizens, volunteers, public servants, elected members and organisational representatives. Whether they are there because of, or in spite of, their faithfulness, their presence suggests that the boundaries between private faith and its public performance may be less clear cut than is often supposed.

Challenging a 'neutral' public realm

Robert Furbey argued in Chapter Two that a straightforwardly 'neutral' public realm is a chimera. In fact, public life is always defined and shaped by the power of partisan dominant groups. Classical liberalism, with its Christian inheritance, has been the bearer of Enlightenment ideas. As MacIntyre (1988, p 145) argues, claims to 'neutrality' are open to challenge:

> The starting points of liberal theorising are never neutral between conceptions of human good; they are always liberal starting points ... liberal theory is best understood, not at all as an attempt to find a rationality independent of tradition, but as itself an articulation of an historically developed and developing set of social institutions and forms of activity, that is, as the voice of a tradition.

If there is no theoretically neutral, or pre-theoretical, ground from which adjudication between competing positions can be made, then classical liberalism should not be regarded as the defining basis of a 'neutral public realm'. Rather, it is 'in the mix' as one (albeit very influential) voice. This voice can vary in tone, just as can a 'religious' voice. Secular liberalism is a strong source of measured public deliberation; but, liberalism can itself also be illiberal, not least through the vehicle of the nation state that has often served to abstract away human particularity by imposing narrow universalising blueprints of a good human life (as in the vigorous and oppressive normativity of malehood and heterosexuality). In this light, faith can be seen as a particular arena for highlighting how public space is made up of the partialities of all of its actors, not just the religious ones. The presence of faith casts light on the illusion of neutrality and the inevitability of the blurring between the public and the private. Accused of preposterous partiality, public faith may actually have the capacity to illuminate the partiality of all things.

Indeed, until the late 20th century, the homogenising capacity of the modern territorial state and the related belief in secularising modernity gave a degree of plausibility to the idea of a neutral public realm. The expected journey from the ludicrous myths of faith towards the revealing truths of science has run somewhat out of steam. Both scientific rationalism and the spiritual instinct have travelled on concurrently, if not in unison.

The related effects of globalisation, growing social and cultural pluralism and critiques of modernity have combined to challenge not only the idea of 'neutrality' but also the image of *a* single public realm. In the 21st century the nation state is less sovereign, civil society is more complex, and public discourse and politics operate in more dispersed arenas, at different spatial scales and through a wider range of media. Jurgen Habermas (2007) refers to the existence of 'multiple modernities'. Janet Newman (2005) talks not about 'the public' but many 'publics', while Bevir and Rhodes (2006) point to the phenomenon of 'decentred governance' that both facilitates and reflects this complexity.

Such phenomena are well illustrated in Chapter Eight by Gale and O'Toole's case study of the Muslim Justice Movement in Birmingham, UK. The authors found ample evidence for a strongly differentiated public realm and, indeed, for the existence of multiple public realms. They charted the 'highly glocalised political sensibility' that motivated members to engage both with global Islam and local neighbourhood and college-based politics, collaborating with both Muslim and non-Muslim groups and causes, and using new information and communication technologies. Faith was clearly influential in shaping political activism and a broader understanding of 'the political'. While they showed awareness and willingness to engage in mainstream representative politics, the young men in the Muslim Justice Movement also operated in 'alternative public spheres' and employed both 'universalistic' and Muslim conceptions of justice.

Weller's assessment of inter-faith activity in the UK in Chapter Four also underlined the growing diversity of the public realm, identifying a 'new religious landscape', pluralised and 'post-Christendom'. Government invitations to faith communities to engage in partnership working have themselves added to the diversity and complexity of the public realm, prompting the consolidation and further development of arenas for debate and deliberation across faith and faith–secular boundaries. This is reflected in Farnell's analysis of partnership working in urban regeneration (Chapter Ten), and in Chapman's observations about the similarities between faith organisations and the VCS (Chapter Eleven).

The burgeoning of inter-faith networks and activities is in part a response to government overtures. But it is also a response by religious communities to their own experiences and a new awareness of each other in settings of growing religious pluralism. Government, or public policy, has not *caused* faith engagement in the public realm, nor does it simply incorporate faith actors. New, more participative, governance strategies have opened up spaces in which faiths (and others) can engage in new ways and with new people, approaches and perspectives. It is not simply a matter of the public realm 'scooping up' what is already there; a new political subjectivity among faith communities is also taking shape in response to the new opportunities. Faith actors' own agency is as significant as the provision of new deliberative spaces by public policy. In Weller's words, faith communities are engaged in 'parallel worked alternatives' through which are developing 'creative models' to address relations between faiths, society and the state.

Diversity versus neutrality – faith, plurality and conversation

If faith cannot be 'othered' in a series of neat binary oppositions between rational and irrational, scientific and mythological, neutral and prejudiced, public and private, then how does its connectedness to the public realm play out? It must do so within two meta-contexts. First, there is increasing religious diversity that demands the negotiation of values, theologies, motivations and, for that matter, resources in public space. How willing are faiths to engage in these negotiations? Do they have the organisational and leadership capacity to make significant interventions? Second, there is a concurrent rise in the politics of identity over ideology and the celebration of personhood over statehood. This focuses on the subjective experiences of people rather than the material aspirations of social classes or interest groups. Faith actors, like everybody else, must negotiate their role within multiple emergent public realms. How can they contribute to a plural politics? Are they ready for the civilised dialogue it entails, or are they actually more comfortable with the 'conversation-stopping certainties' referred to by Furbey in Chapter Two?

In Chapter Six, Baker argued that faiths often find it hard to enter into dialogue, at least with non-faith partners, without the conversation ending in miscommunication and confusion. He suggested that faith actors often self-censor, accepting the assumption of neutrality in the public realm and adopting secular vocabularies that serve to obscure their authentic contribution. For Baker, the problem is not that faiths and 'others' must find their common ground. Rather, it is one of 'literacy' – they do not yet share a language to make this effective.

Interestingly, some policy language has an increasingly 'religious' flavour. We hear about the government's aspirations to create 'flourishing communities', to enable an 'urban renaissance', and to nurture citizen 'well-being'.[2] Many dismiss such terminology as no more than spin and jargon. But it may actually reflect an 'affective' turn in British politics (Walker, 2008), which draws on, and could help sustain, critical and transformative discourses that are not afraid to embrace metaphor and metaphysics. It is interesting to note that scholarly studies of citizenship and civil society, notably Putnam's (2000) work on social capital, tend to adopt a 'paradise lost' form of argumentation that also looks forward to a redemptive transformation. Indeed, the 'official' promotion of citizen and community participation (by international organisations like the World Bank as well as national governments) has become something of a new governance theology (see Cooke and Kothari, 2001). While the language of Whitehall and town hall may still seem technicist in comparison with that of faith groups, the contemporary aspiration to more holistic ('joined-up') public policy and to 'community empowerment' (DCLG, 2008) must surely provide some openings for faith actors to articulate and valorise (extend even) their contributions to the wider public realm.

At the same time, Cheesman and Khanum (Chapter Three) argued that an overzealous liberalism is promoting freedoms that in the end inhibit real dialogue. They give the example of the state's passivity in relation to the ousting by radical clerics of the moderate leadership of the Finsbury Park mosque in North London. In failing to speak out, the authorities undermined the possibility that others might do so, since their stance allowed the conversation-stopping certainties of Abu Hamza's regime to take hold. This illustrates a familiar anxiety about the point at which liberalism should limit its own freedoms. Cheesman and Khanum argued that Islam is being 'othered' through a process of 'soft segregation of hearts and minds', which results in, and expresses, a compounding racism. Cantle (2007) has referred to this as a new phenomenon of 'faithism'.

Dialogue across these divides is surely a challenge. In their conversation in Chapter Five, Ahmed, Cantle and Hussain concluded that the challenge is one not only for faiths, but also for the entire multiculturalist settlement. The case of faiths is illuminating a wider unsettling of the public realm and the relationships within it. The question of how 'faiths and faiths' and 'faiths and others' get along is a question related to community cohesion more generally. Once again, it brings to the surface the deep-seated values inherent in the so-called neutral space of the public realm. The assumptions of multiculturalism are highly value laden. Far from being a rational-minded exercise in the evident truths of a post-religious realm, multicultural Britain is illuminated in highly partial terms, asserting values of tolerance, respect and diversity that are actually deeply contested. Multiculturalism, like faith, is just one of a whole range of epistemological and ontological outlooks in public space. In this way we are reminded of the partisanship of practically every social stance.

Indeed, the resonance of Modood's (2007) plea for 'moderate secularism' arises at least in part from the specificities of Britain's peculiar constitutional settlement. Britain has never been a strong secular state like France or, indeed, the US. While religious commitment features far less in the rhetoric of British than American politics, there is less anxiety about breaching the 'wall' between church and state (Towey, 2004, p 212). Although a far more secular society than the US, Britain has an established church with a constitutional role, including the presence of Bishops in the House of Lords. The historic permeability of the church/state boundary has made the inclusion of faith actors in governance (over and above service contracting) relatively more acceptable, even (ironically) where these actors come from non-Christian faiths. Indeed, a comparative European study has linked relatively high levels of 'state accommodation of Muslims' to the specific character of church–state relations in Britain (Fetzer and Soper, 2005, pp 146-7).

Such accommodation has gone alongside a policy thrust to define citizenship increasingly in terms of a common 'Britishness', for instance through the introduction of a citizenship test and a citizenship ceremony. But there are more subtle aspects of policy in relation to the production of citizens in other domains. Flint explored 'the inculcation of values' in his study of faith-based schools in Chapter

Nine. Some faith schools celebrate diversity and promote respect, tolerance, mutuality and commonality. This potentially forms the basis for more cohesion and less conflict – the institutionalisation of public dialogue within, between and beyond faiths. But values can also be aggressively single-faith, fervent and proselytising, rendering impotent the case for cohesion through education. Looking at whether faith schools institutionalise 'parallel lives' (Cantle, 2005), Flint concluded that the main boundary of separation effected by schools is actually around social class. The impact of faith as a public category can only be understood in relation to its intersection with other identities and social and economic cleavages.

In conclusion, we recognise that the notion of faith as a public category remains a source of great concern to many for whom religion is 'other'. The perceived threat to rationalism is paralleled by the fear of a public space being swamped by the religiously aggressive and doctrinaire, who aspire perhaps to a religiousness that will undermine liberalism, oppress women and minorities and result in intolerance and unpalatable 'certainties'. It is in fact precisely these concerns against which the so-called 'war on terror' is constructed. And yet this discourse manages to 'other' all religiousness, regardless of its thoughtfulness, historicity or humanity, asserting the chimera of public neutrality at one and the same time as demanding the rights and freedoms of liberalism.

In this concluding chapter, we have shown the limitations of attempts to 'other' faith on the usual grounds of rationalism versus superstition, science versus religion, private versus public and so on. These categories are no more neutral than the faith that they criticise. At the same time, the setting up of a range of separate epistemological domains, each with interior coherence but without connecting bridges, seems unsatisfactory too. It is particularly unsuited to a context of increasing plurality and the rise of public *realms*, which creates a demand for shared discourse across specific identities and interests. Clearly there are philosophical concerns and confusions about the relationship between the diverse values, ontologies and epistemologies of an ever-increasing range of 'publics'. But the authors in this collection are generally positive about the prospects for such bridging – both between faith groups and between faith and non-faith actors – on both empirical and philosophical grounds.

There are, however, many practical obstacles and challenges. Some of these relate to the ways in which different publics express themselves to one another. The question of 'faith literacy' is at the heart of the controversies, policies and practices of faith in the public realm. It is a necessary condition for conversation. Baker's 'blurred encounters' are a recipe for confusion in an already contested and overheated arena. Bringing into focus this blurredness is the beginning of a process that may generate greater complementarity and less competition between faithful and secular perspectives. Such literacy is a mutual endeavour, involving self-reflection and learning in order to understand better the values and practices of each other's domain. Taking issue with classic liberal premises, Habermas (2007) argues that:

> The citizens of a democratic community owe one another good reasons for their public political interventions.... This civic duty can be specified in such a tolerant way that contributions are permitted in a religious as well as in a secular language. They are not subject to constraints on the mode of expression in the political public sphere, but they rely on joint ventures of translation.

The acceptance of the 'other' is a key element in preparing for any conversation. At the same time, we have observed that the 'other' is less real than may be imagined. In fact, faith and non-faith actors have much more in common than is generally supposed. Public realms are already infused with religious ideas, populated with religious people, and full of spiritual hunger. The challenge lies in securing support and space for those 'joint ventures of translation' that can make possible creative and inclusive public conversations.

Notes

[1] For further information on these campaigns, see www.jubileedebtcampaign.org.uk; www.makepovertyhistory.org; www.londoncitizens.org.uk; and www.birminghamcitizens.org.uk

[2] See the Department of Communities and Local Government's website for details of these and other related policies: www.communities.gov.uk

References

Baker, C. (2007) *The hybrid church in the city: Third space thinking*, Aldershot: Ashgate.

Bevir, M. and Rhodes, R. (2006) *Governance stories*, Abingdon: Routledge.

Bretherton, L. (2008) 'The churches, broad-based community organising and pursuit of the common good', Paper presented to the ESRC Faith and Civil Society Seminar, Anglia Ruskin University, Cambridge, 26 February.

Cantle, T. (2005) *Community cohesion: A new framework for race and diversity*, Basingstoke: Palgrave.

Cantle, T. (2007) 'If faith is the new "race", is faithism the new racism?', Paper presented to the ESRC Faith and Civil Society Seminar, Anglia Ruskin University, Cambridge, January.

Chapman, R. and Lowndes, V. (2008) 'Faith in governance? The potential and pitfalls of involving faith groups in urban governance', *Planning Practice and Research*, vol 23, no 1, pp 57-75.

Cooke, B. and U. Kothari (eds) (2001) *Participation: The new tyranny?*, London: Zed Books.

Davie, G. (1994) *Religion in Britain since 1945*, Oxford: Blackwell.

Dawkins, R. (2003) 'The future looks bright', *The Guardian*, 21 June.

DCLG (Department of Communities and Local Government) (2007) *Preventing violent extremism: Pathfinder guidance*, London: DCLG.

DCLG (2008) *Communities in control: Real people, real power*, London: DCLG.

Dinham, A. and Lowndes, V. (2008) 'Religion, resources and representation: three narratives of faith engagement in British urban governance', *Urban Affairs Review*, vol 43, no 6, pp 817-45.

Fetzer, J. and Soper, C. (2005) *Muslims and the state in Britain, France, and Germany*, Cambridge: Cambridge University Press.

Furbey, R. (2006) 'Faith engagement: cuddlesome or troublesome?', Paper presented to the Faiths and Civil Society Seminar, Anglia Ruskin University, Cambridge, May.

Goodwin, M. (2007) 'The extreme Right in Britain: still an ugly duckling but for how long?', *Political Quarterly*, vol 78, no 2, pp 241-50.

Gray, J. (2007) *Enlightenment's wake: Politics and culture at the close of the modern age*, Routledge Classics edition, London: Routledge.

Habermas, J. (2007) 'Religion in the public sphere', Unpublished lecture, Available at: www.sandiego.edu/pdf/pdf_library/habermaslecture031105_c939cceb2ab087bdfc6df291ec0fc3fa.pdf

Home Office (2005) *Citizenship survey*, London: Home Office.

MacIntyre, A. (1988) *Whose justice? Which rationality?*, Notre Dame, IN: University of Notre Dame Press.

Modood, T. (2007) *Multiculturalism: A civic idea*, Cambridge: Polity Press.

Mouffe, C. (2000) *The democratic paradox*, London: Verso.

Newman, J. (ed) (2005) *Remaking governance*, London: Sage Publications.

Newman, J. (2007) 'Rethinking "the public" in troubled times', *Public Policy and Administration*, vol 22, no 1, pp 27–46.

Norris, P. and Inglehart, R. (2006) *Sacred and secular: Religion and politics worldwide*, Cambridge: Cambridge University Press.

Norval, A. (2008) *Aversive democracy: Inheritance and originality in the democratic tradition*, Cambridge: Cambridge University Press.

Porritt, J. (2005) *Capitalism as if the world matters*, London: Earthscan.

Putnam, R. (2000) *Bowling alone: The collapse and revival of American community*, New York: Simon and Shuster.

Rhodes, R. (1997) *Understanding governance*, Buckingham: Open University Press.

Sandercock, L. (2003) *Cosmopolis II: Mongrel cities in the 21st century*, London and New York: Continuum.

Towey, J. (2004) 'Faith and the public square', in E. Dionne, J. Bethke Elshtain and K. Drogosz (eds) *One electorate under God?*, Washington, DC: Brookings Institute.

Walker, D. (2008) 'Time to call off the engagement?', *The Guardian*, 21 May.

Woodhead, L. and Heelas, P. (2005) *The spiritual revolution: Why religion is giving way to spirituality,* Oxford, UK and Malden, MA: Blackwell.

Index